The Magical Tearoom on the Hill

Recipes, Tales and Adventures

Debra Murphy

From the sumit of Ben Nairnen, in the Arrochar Alps

Published in 2020 by Lawers Publishing

ISBN Paperback: 978-1-8382830-0-1
Hardback: 978-1-8382830-1-8
Ebook: 978-1-8382830-2-5

A CIP catalogue copy of this book can be found in the British Library.

Published with the help of Indie Authors World
www.indieauthorsworld.com

IndieAuthors
World

To Benjamin and Chloe

Contents

Key   12

Foreword   13

This is not just a recipe book. This is Mother Murphy's recipe book…   13

Naming the cakes and telling tales…   14

Making a dream come true   14

The growth of Mother Murphy   15

Ben Lomond – January 2013   16

Mother Murphy's begins with a storm   19

Cinder Toffee/Puff Candy   22

Scottish Vanilla Tablet   24

Helensburgh Highland Games and the kindness of strangers   26

Prime position at Stirling Farmer's Market   27

I think we should go to the Good Food Show   27

My dream comes true as Mother Murphy's Tearoom opens   28

What's all this gluten free stuff?   30

Tips, useful gadgets, and lessons learned   32

Now for some simple tips   35

Recipes   39

Jams, Jelly-Jams And Lemon Curd   41

Raspberry Jam   46

Strawberry Jam   48

Blackcurrant Jelly-Jam   50

Gooseberry Jelly-Jam   52

Redcurrant Jelly-Jam   54

Spiced Apple Jelly-Jam   56

Wild Berry Jelly-Jam   58

Finding an old pal   60

Michelle's Lemon Curd   62

Breakfast at the tearoom   64

It's not 3 o'clock yet!   65

Yvonne's French Toast (Eggy Bread)   67

Do your worst Mr M!   69

   The Posh Woman's Husband's Omelette   71

My amazing grandma   72

   Jade's Scotch Pancakes   74

Just get yourself an egg-poacher   77

   Poached Eggs   78

A border collie, deer, geese, and a buzzard   79

   Porridge And Blueberries   80

Lunch at the tearoom   **81**

Making a toddler eat her veg   81

   Andrina's Carrot And Coriander Soup   84

   Carrot And Sweet Potato Soup   86

   Chloe's Orange Pepper Soup   88

   Leek And Potato Soup   90

   Jim's Lentil Soup   92

   Split Pea Soup   94

   Home-Made Coleslaw   96

Waiting patiently for the titbits   98

   Susan's Home-Cooked Ham   100

Amy Johnson and the Victorian singer   102

   Elaine's Hummus   104

Baking at the tearoom   **106**

Developing our gluten and dairy free bread   106

   Mr M's Gluten Free Bread   110

   Banana Loaf   112

From high in the Derbyshire Peak District   114

   Annie's Gooseberry Jelly-Jam Bakewell Tart   116

Disqualified from the Great Murphy Bake-Off!   118

   Louise's Battenberg Cake   120

Oh no! Where has the track gone?   123

   Alasdair's Brussell Sprout Surprise   126

When there just has to be more than one version   129

   Nicola's Caramel Slice - Original   132

   Caramel Slice - Gluten Free   134

Caramel Slice – Gluten Free And Dairy Free 136

Is this one of your five-a-day? 138

 Bev's Carrot Cake 140

Completed homework gets you the cake 142

 Ellie's Apricot And Ginger Loaf 144

Posh folk in the tearoom 147

 Nicky's Cherry Loaf 148

Poetic licence without the crusts 150

 Anne's Fruit Tea Loaf 152

A Wee Poem **154**

Lycra-clad Murphys 157

Debra's Gluten Free Month – Monday, May 30th, 2016 157

 Laura's Chocolate Orange Cake 160

Courgettes in a cake! 162

 Craig's Coconut Cake 162

Yorkshire friendship hanging on a shaky nail 164

 Salena's Old-Fashioned Coffee Cake 166

The girl who would be Hannah 169

 Charlotte's Fab Slice 172

 Flapjacks 174

It's not a fly cemetery! 177

 Fruit Slice 180

The breeze blew around the open-topped car 182

 Myles' Grasmere Gingerbread 186

Two friends, laughter, chat, gossip, and cake 188

 Margaret's Lemon Drizzle Loaf 190

Surely not yellow food colouring! 191

 Evelyn's Lemon Meringue Pie 192

Watching them blossom 195

 Kirsty And Jade's Mint Chocolate Cake 196

The curse of Glen Lyon 198

 Shona's Candy Road 202

Building a snowman with Beatrix 205

 Russell's Rocky Road 208

Scones 211

Brian's Plain Wheat Scones 214

We've been waiting for a tearoom like you! 217

Tommi And Nanna's Cherry Wheat Scones 218

Fireman Friday 220

Fireman Friday's Sultana Wheat Scones 222

Is that thunder and lightning? 224

Old Jim's Treacle Wheat Scones 226

Rosemary's Plain Gluten Free Scones 228

Sultana Gluten Free Scones 230

Treacle Gluten Free Scones 232

Becoming 'The Magical Tearoom on the Hill' 234

Spice Girls' Apple Cake 236

But the ginger cake isn't gluten free! 239

Fiona's Stem Ginger Cake 240

Strawberry Heaven 242

Can thee park thi' parkin? 244

Debra's Yorkshire Parkin 246

Advent calendars and lots of vowels 248

Treasa's Polenta Cake 250

Plain and simple doesn't have to be boring 252

Traditional Victoria Sponge 254

Adapting the traditional Victoria sponge 255

Blackcurrant And Cinnamon Victoria Sponge 256

When fruit salad no longer cuts the mustard 258

Danielle's Viennese Whirls 260

Dressing up for cake 263

Dave's White Chocolate Fudge Cake 264

Covid-19 live chats 266

Karen's Chocolate Fudge Cake 268

Popeye, spinach, and a surprisingly good chocolate cake 270

Popeye's Surprisingly Good Chocolate Cake 272

Learning to be brave when ordering from a menu 275

Sticky Toffee Pudding 276

Sometimes you just want a biscuit   278

1 May, 2016 - first Sunday opening and Debra's gluten free month - Day 1   278

Creating our own digestive biscuits   278

A barking dog, a helicopter rescue, and lemon wannabes   281

Wannabe Digestive Biscuits   286

Love them or hate them   288

Neill's Bourbon Cream Biscuits   290

A man called Tom   292

Dashing Tom's Custard Creams   294

Is it a shortcake, German, or empire biscuit?   296

Lorraine's Empire Biscuits - Original Recipe   298

Kirsten's Empire Biscuits - Gluten-free Version   300

But I did them before the Great British Bake Off   302

Fig Rolls   304

A tale of misunderstanding   307

Ben's Gingerbread Men   310

Ginger Cream Biscuits   312

You need to learn to say please and thank you   314

Gina's Gingernuts   316

Licking the plate clean   317

Sasha's Lemon Cream Biscuits   318

Pocket-money comics   320

Jammie Dodgers   322

When Mother Murphy became Grandma   324

Minnie's Smiley Faces   328

My first published recipe   330

Nice Coconut Cream Biscuits   332

The humble oatcake   334

Sandra's Oatcakes   336

Strawberry Creams   338

Christmas baking at the tearoom   340

The deer destroyer   342

Teresa's Bailey's Mini Chocolate Yule Logs   344

Boozy Bakewell Tart   346

Soda Bread   348

Christmas truffles   350

Chloe's Christmas Truffles   352

Traditional Christmas cake   356

Traditional Christmas Cake   358

Royal Icing   361

When is a banana loaf not a banana loaf?   362

Wendy's Halfway There Loaf   364

Christmas Mincemeat   366

When Christmas mince pies were banned   368

Christmas Mince Pies   370

Some More Treats   372

Coconut Ice   372

Certainly not the cardboard variety!   375

Meringues   376

No Yorkshires on Christmas Day!   378

Yorkshire Puddings   380

Traditional afternoon tea   382

A new chapter for Mother Murphy's   386

Acknowledgements   388

About the Author   390

If baking is any labor at all, it's a labor of love. A love that gets passed from generation to generation.

Regina Brett (Journalist)

Key

Gluten Free   Dairy Free   Egg Free   Nut Free

Foreword

This is not just a recipe book. This is Mother Murphy's recipe book...

Let's start at the beginning... Why did I write this book? I love books: reading them, touching them, the covers, the paper, the smell, and of course, pictures, and I lose myself in the story, the history, the recipes, and the photos. My recipe books, from chefs and bakers far and wide, are well-thumbed and fill many shelves, but sometimes, especially when I started to cook and bake seriously, they were difficult to use, with much page-flicking needed to find the photo, the ingredients, and methods for different elements. If I wanted to make a lemon meringue pie, I wanted the photo, the ingredients, notes, and instructions to all be together, not have to go back and forth with floury fingers.

I wanted my book to be interesting, fun, moving, informative, and most importantly, easy to follow. It would tell the story of how Mother Murphy's Tearoom evolved, with a sprinkling of my life journey to show the hopes and dreams which were the essence of the Magical Tearoom on The Hill. I wanted my book to inspire others to follow their dreams just as I had.

I started writing; each day, another story or anecdote and a photo showed the inspiration for a recipe. Each recipe was logged, and customers would find me clicking away at my laptop and be a ready audience for the story behind the recipe. My Facebook posts and blog were my writing apprenticeship. I dipped my toes in the water. How would people react? The encouragement and positive feedback helped to develop this.

Are all the recipes in this book mine? Nowadays, wherever you look, you can find a recipe for almost anything. Over the years I've used recipes from other chefs and bakers, then adapted them, made them gluten and dairy free, added ingredients, tweaked a method, and made them into my own recipes. I hope you will do the same, and continue the evolution of my recipes and ideas to make them your own.

Naming the cakes and telling tales...

In the tearoom, many customers have their favourite cakes which they choose on every visit, if possible. To celebrate this passion, we named the cake or bake for them. I don't remember exactly how or why this started, but it became a great way of making our customers feel special and that's what I want our tearoom to do. Everybody deserves to feel special.

The Contents section lists the recipes twice! The first section tempts you with the titles of the tales and adventures – where you will see A Man Called Tom. The second part lists the recipes and customer name – where you will find Custard Creams (Dashing Tom's) – and yes, there is an explanation of how the cake got its name.

I've also included various walks and cycles, starting with me growing up in Halifax, West Yorkshire, and some of my adventures with Beatrix, our Border Collie. I share my unplanned heart attack on Ben Lawers, with a helicopter rescue, leaving poor Beatrix behind on the mountain, and then the tale of when Mother Murphy became Grandma – both heart-warming and heart-breaking.

All of these tales and snippets are part of the history of the tearoom, Mr M, me, and our lovely customers.

Go on, stick the kettle on, get yourself a slice of cake or a plate of biscuits, and enjoy the read. Even if you haven't been to Mother Murphy's Tearoom, you'll soon get to know me, Mr M, the Magical Tearoom on the Hill, and all the wonderful people in the tearoom family.

Making a dream come true

How on earth does a Yorkshire-born and bred girl find herself running a tearoom in Central Scotland?

Life started for me on the 18 October, 1965, in the upstairs bedroom of a stone-terraced house in Halifax, West Yorkshire. Being the second child, as was the norm at that time, I was born at home in front of an open coal fire. I do wonder if this is where my love of the open fire comes from. My mum often joked how she used to leave me in my crib in front of the lit fire with no fireguard.

My mother was of Irish descent, although she was born in Halifax. My maternal grandmother, Nora Walton, died when my mother was only a young girl, but my grandfather, Ernest Walton, was around for the early years of my life. Growing up, and indeed into my early adult life, I held onto the warm thought that I was Grandad Walton's favourite grandchild, as I was the one he chose to share his peppermints with.

This memory was cruelly shattered when my cousin Adrian scoffed at this idea, telling me that Grandad Walton also shared his peppermints with him! I still don't believe you, Ady!

My father was Scottish, born in Grangemouth, ironically just around the corner from Mother Murphy's Tearoom, but sadly he died a year or so before the tearoom opened. Dad had a traditional butcher's shop in the Halifax Borough Market, Ferguson's Butchers, and I can only wonder if he would be proud of his youngest daughter following in his footsteps, running her own business. I'll never know, but choose to believe he's looking down on me as proud as punch.

My Scottish paternal grandparents lived in Halifax for many years, and much of my childhood was spent with Grandma and Grandad Lammie. Grandma died when I was in my late thirties and I think of her

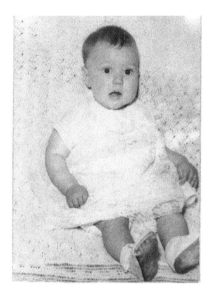

Six-month old Debra

every day. How I wish she could see the tearoom and share a cuppa with me. She'd be so proud of me making a new life for myself in Scotland. Grandma was my inspiration for the tearoom, always using a china cup, and living on dainty sandwiches and cake. I can't remember ever seeing her eat a full meal. However, she lived into her eighties and smoked heavily all her days. By my reckoning, as I've never smoked, I could live on tea and cakes to a very ripe old age!

My childhood was eventful and difficult, with things happening that would have, and still have, an effect on the way my life panned out. However, I am a survivor with two fabulous children beside me and, despite some ups and down, I finally learned to love myself. Once this had happened, the world just seemed to be a better place. I also met the man who turned out to be my soulmate. So here I am, a Yorkshire-born and bred lass, married to a Scotsman, and running a tearoom in Scotland.

The growth of Mother Murphy

To have my own tearoom had been a lifelong dream, but one that I never really believed would happen. For many years I worked in Learning and Development, and ended up running my own successful training company. Nevertheless, the tearoom dream didn't go away, and I made a foray into starting a home baking business, selling my cakes at farmers' markets, Highland Games, and fetes. My mind was working overtime – could we afford to run a baking business? Could we get the kitchen at home sorted? What about the training company? Would it work? Would people want to buy things from us?

Sometimes, though, life has a strange knack of making decisions for you or pushing you into making choices. A sudden illness and subsequent surgery gave me that nudge to follow my dreams. It may sound melodramatic, but I remember lying in the hospital bed after surgery, still not knowing what the outcome was going to be, and thinking to myself, If I'm going to die, I'm going to live my dream first.

Here's what happened…

Looking towards Ben Lomond from Rowardennnan

Ben Lomond – January 2013

2013 was a cold winter in Scotland, with a good amount of snow. One glorious Friday, I found myself at the Ardlui Hotel on the idyllic banks of Loch Lomond, enjoying a fabulous lunch in the restaurant looking out onto the snow-capped Ben Lomond. Excitement bubbled up inside me as I decided at the weekend I'd climb that particular Munro (the Munros are mountains in Scotland that are over 3,000ft/914m). Ben Lomond's the very first Munro I tackled a few years previously. I'd done lots of hiking in the Yorkshire Dales and the Lake District, but climbing a Munro for the first time is just something else.

As Jim was suffering with sore knees, and appreciating his dislike of wintry conditions, I decided I'd take myself off up the mountain alone – a bit of a Wainwright adventure. Jim's always telling me that I'm turning into Alfred Wainwright (a British fell walker, guidebook author, and illustrator) because I love to walk the hills alone, just as he did all those years ago. Not being a very experienced mountain climber, and always trying to reduce any danger to myself, a detour was taken on the way home to a well-known outdoor retailer on Buchanan Street in the centre of Glasgow, to explore the idea of purchasing my very first set of snow crampons. Me, buying crampons! I couldn't really believe it myself.

Sunday morning came, and a very early start was made. A flask of tea, plentiful sandwiches, chocolate-covered mint cake, several biscuits, and warm clothing, were all packed into my car along with my shiny new crampons, and off I went.

The sun had not yet had time to warm up the roads, and the drive along the single-track road from Balmaha to Rowardennan, along the banks of Loch Lomond, was very interesting indeed. The adrenalin was building up nicely by the time I (literally) slid my little Fiesta into the National Trust car park. Giving a huge, silent sigh of relief that I was still in one piece, I climbed gingerly out of the car, testing the icy ground to see if it was at all possible to stand up, giggling to myself at the thought of Jim's horror had he known what I was really up to!

The hike up Ben Lomond starts with a stroll through the forest, giving a gentle warm-up to the climb still to come. Not today, though, as the track was coated in a thick layer of solid ice. Would it even be possible to get out above the forest, never mind ascend the Ben?

Over the next hour or so, I struggled up the track. At least everyone else I saw was slipping and sliding in the same desperate manner, and I shared lots of light-hearted comments about the ice with fellow ice skaters (walkers).

Forgetting the ice, though, it was turning out to be a glorious winter's day. The sun was shining and the sky was clear blue, with not a cloud to be seen. I couldn't help but smile to myself, and leaving the icy path behind for the open hills, the going became much easier, with the most fantastic views. If anyone is suffering any sort of stress in their lives, take a winter walk up the hills and fells. Stress? What stress?

I climbed up the zig-zag path, helped along with a drink of water and chocolate-covered mint cake, with the air much warmer and the winter sunshine creating some wonderful colours. Reaching one of the many plateaus, it was easy to see that the ice had been replaced with snow. A lot of snow! The snow was just as treacherous as the ice earlier in the walk but, being very self-conscious, I kept my shiny new crampons in my rucksack. All sorts of thoughts were flashing through my head: Would I be able to put my crampons on? Had I bought the right sort? What would everyone think of me wearing crampons? After about twenty minutes of sliding about on the snow, and again starting to doubt whether I would reach the summit, I started to notice that all the walkers now passing me were not sliding about. Why would this be? Oh, yes, that's because they were not self-conscious about putting on their crampons!

At the next suitable rock, I sat myself down, gave myself a good talking to, and pulled my crampons from my rucksack. Before setting off from home I'd had enough foresight to take them out of the box, meaning I could almost hide the fact they were new.

Surprisingly easily, I stretched my crampons on over my boots and cautiously got to my feet. Immediately I felt a strange sense of confidence growing, with my boots now gripping the snow, and I was no longer taking one step forward and three backwards. Progress could now be made! I have to admit to feeling and acting a little like a child in the snow and ice. I was choosing to walk across sheet ice just because I could. Crampons, I have decided, are the best invention ever.

For the next couple of hours, I climbed steadily up the Ben, walking with a newfound confidence. At one point, I looked up and imagined I could see a group of firemen walking towards me in their full uniforms and helmets. I thought to myself that perhaps it was time for some more Kendal Mint Cake. However, the firemen were rapidly approaching me. As they reached my level, we had a bit of a chat about what they were doing coming down Ben Lomond in full uniform. They initially told me that somebody had reported a fire at the summit, but I didn't fall for that one! It turned out they were on a charity walk.

Reaching another plateau, I could now see my target summit. Usually, it would be a short hike up to the top, but today was a different matter. My new crampons had worked really well in ice and compact snow, but I was now walking in virgin snow, and with each step I sank up to my knees. It was hard going, but absolutely fabulous. Even though it was winter, the sun was beating down and making the most glorious colours in the snow. I'd often heard snow and ice described as crystal blue, without really understanding the saying, but today I saw it for myself. The snow was so pure and clean that it was literally glistening blue in front of my eyes. For the first time that day I felt a little disappointed that I didn't have Jim with me to share this sight, but realised he would have been suffering with the cold so much by this point that the colour of the snow would be far from his mind!

Eventually I managed to reach the summit – and what a view! Scotland has such a wonderful landscape, and the top of Ben Lomond provides you with a 360-degree view of the area. On a clear day like this, mountain after mountain can be admired. I dug out my foam mat from my rucksack and unpacked my lunch. There's nothing better than having a flask of tea and a home-made sandwich in the open air, looking out onto the vista. It was only a short stop, though, as the cold sets in quickly at such a height.

The descent was much easier, as I was able to walk in the footprints in the deep snow. The views going back down to Rowardennan are awesome. Once you're down the first steep section, the going is relatively easy and you can enjoy the amazing views. It seems that you have the whole of Scotland to look at and admire, with a final magnificent view of Loch Lomond and all its little islands panning out in front of you. In such calm, clear weather, the long walk back down the Ben takes on a sublime, peaceful experience.

I was going down the hill when I realised that, even with my fleece and outer jacket on and the straps of my rucksack, I could still feel a huge bulge in my lower abdomen. If I'm honest, I'd been aware of this growing lump for the last six months. Having joined Weight Watchers and lost two stone already, I guessed that I was now feeling something that had probably been there much longer. Perhaps now was the time to tell Jim about this lump and make an appointment at the doctor's.

I knew with all certainty that this wasn't an unplanned pregnancy, as at the age of twenty-five I'd had a full hysterectomy for different medical reasons, but kept hold of my ovaries. All different thoughts were going through my head now. If it was not a pregnancy, what could it be? I'd convinced myself many times over the last few months that I just needed a good old visit to the bathroom, but obviously that hadn't worked! The frightening fact remained: I had a huge lump in my lower abdomen and a building fear of what it might be.

It did take me a couple more weeks before I brought up the subject with Jim, who was horrified that he could now also feel the lump. A visit to the GP was made that week, and I was told there was indeed a mass in my stomach, probably the size of a small football, and that the chances were it was not very good news.

Fast forward a few months. The mass (or masses, to be precise) turned out to be ovarian cysts and, very fortunately for me, non-malignant. However, as the surgeon at the time was not too sure what he was looking at, he decided the best course of action whilst I was under the knife was to remove both my ovaries. Instant menopause for me then!

There was a time when I was quite unwell and unsure of the prognosis. As I mentioned earlier in the introduction, fearing the worst, I felt that it was now time to follow my dreams before it was too late. Anyone who has been in a similar fearful position will understand my mentality at that point. My all-time dream was to run my own tearoom, so I put plans in action to make sure that happened.

What would we call this new venture? As we were debating the name for the business, a Mother's Day card arrived, addressed to Mother Murphy. My son's cheeky comment became the name of our new business.

Mother Murphy's was here.

Mother Murphy's begins with a storm

The next year was a bit of a blur as I fought to get well. The changes were immense, both physically and psychologically, and never in my wildest dreams did I imagine that my life would be instantly changed by this operation and the removal of my ovaries. At my lowest point, simply walking from the front door to the end of the street to post a letter was a challenge. A few months later, and a good dose of HRT sorted by my consultant, life started to take some sort of shape again.

Part of the healing process was a fitness incentive which came in the shape of a ten-week-old Border Collie puppy we named Beatrix. This black and white bundle of fluff turned out to be my lifesaver in more ways than she'll ever know. She's grown up beside me, walked slowly with me as I recovered, snuggled up to me when I was weary, showered me in unconditional love, and became my best friend. We've had many an adventure together, including the time she pulled me down a snow-covered mountain to chase some skiers! Oh, and there's the time she barked for help when I had a heart attack up Ben Lawers. But that's a story for later.

The plan for the home baking business was still there, but how could it become reality? Our kitchen was tiny, with an oven so old that the dials had worn away, making it guesswork what temperature you were setting it to. There was no dishwasher and no work surfaces to do mass baking. Should we move? Where would we move to? With the idea of moving to a new house feeling just too stressful, the easy option seemed to be to have an extension built on to the kitchen. Yes, you can laugh! Moving to a new house would have been much less stressful; I know that now.

Architects, planners, council officials, and builders, all became regular visitors to our house and gradually the idea of a larger kitchen began to take shape. There were lots of mishaps, arguments, an immense amount of stress, and don't even get me started on the mess. At my lowest ebb, I recall hoovering dust from the bedroom walls.

Fast forward six months and the extension was growing, with a new kitchen beginning to appear from the dust. The builders agreed a completion date, so we organised an open day, 17th May, 2014, to launch Mother Murphy's Home Baking and Afternoon Teas in the garden, with an outdoor charity afternoon tea.

We passed the necessary food standards inspection on the new kitchen with flying colours, and we were ready. For the week leading up to the event, the sun had been shining brightly. And the rest of Scotland was still

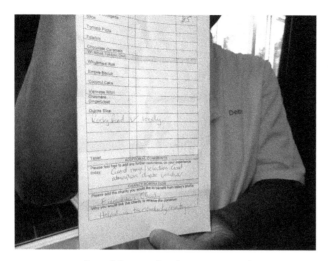
One of the completed comments card

basking in sunshine on May 17, but in Kirkintilloch the heavy clouds and strong wind told a different story. They say that the most stressful things in life are divorce and moving house. Well, I can tell you that this is nothing compared to putting up three new gazebos in full view of all your neighbours, in the howling wind and pouring rain. Manage it we did, though, and three gazebos were eventually up and secure, ready to fill with our lovely, freshly baked goods, and hopefully lots of people.

With terrific support from family, friends, and neighbours, we had a great afternoon despite the weather. Using a broom handle to push up the pools of rainwater collecting on the roof of the gazebos became a bit of a fun game for everyone to enjoy. We had a girl come along who was doing face painting for everyone, and I had a cupcake (what else!) painted on my face and Jim became a lion.

We asked people for charity donations and comments, instead of selling the cakes; our neighbour Ken suggested we donate to the Fire Fighters Charity. This made a perfect end to the day as another neighbour across the road was a fireman. My only regret from that day was that we were so nervous and stressed we totally forgot to take lots of photos!

The feedback was fabulous; our rocky road was called awesome that day, and we still make it to the same recipe today, because of that enthusiasm. You'll find the recipe for this later in the book.

Some of the delights, including our Awesome Rocky Road

Two other popular delights at this event were our home-made cinder toffee (puff candy) dipped in chocolate, and home-made tablet. As these treats became just as popular at all of our events and then in the tearoom, it's only fitting that the recipes for these slip in here. They're both quick and easy to make, so make a batch of them along with a fresh pot of tea, put your feet up, and continue to read about the making of Mother Murphy's Tearoom, the Magical Tearoom on the Hill.

*Cooking and baking is both physical
and mental therapy.*

Mary Berry

Cinder Toffee/Puff Candy

Makes a small tray

A word of warning. You're dealing with boiling sugar here. Don't be tempted to make a bigger batch in your pan at home, or once you add the bicarbonate of soda you'll have boiling sugar pouring over the top of your pan!

Once this has cooled, you can make this even more delightful if you break the cinder toffee into chunks and dip them in chocolate. Leave to set on parchment paper, and pop a few pieces into sweet bags for a lovely handmade gift.

Ingredients

1 teaspoon bicarbonate of soda

75g caster sugar

2 tablespoons golden syrup

Equipment

14" x 10" square baking tray

Method

1   Put the sugar and golden syrup in a large heavy-based pan and allow to melt slowly over a low heat, stirring gently to make sure all the sugar grains are melted.

2   Once melted, turn the heat up and allow to boil until the mixture changes colour and becomes a deep golden brown (not black!). This will only take a couple of minutes.

3   Take the pan off the heat and stir in the magical bicarbonate of soda. The mixture will explode into life like a volcano. Quickly mix to make sure all the bicarbonate of soda is blended, then pour the mixture immediately into a tray lined with parchment paper.

4   Leave to cool and set for about 15 minutes. The final cinder toffee will either be very crunchy or maybe a little chewy, depending on how hot you allowed the melting sugar to get.

5   If you want to make it extra indulgent by dipping in chocolate, put the chocolate in a bowl over a pan of gently simmering water on a low heat on the hob until the chocolate starts to melt. As the chocolate begins to melt, turn the heat off and allow the heat of the water to continue to melt the chocolate. Once nearly all the chocolate has melted, take the bowl off the hot water and allow the heat of the chocolate to melt the remaining chocolate.

6   Break the set cinder toffee into chunks and dip in the chocolate, then place on a piece of parchment paper to set.

7   Store in an airtight container, or pop into little sweet bags as gifts for friends.

Scottish Vanilla Tablet

Makes a small tray

When I first moved up to Scotland, I wasn't really sure what tablet was. Sometimes the commercial versions are a bit too sweet and grainy (a bit rich from somebody who loves Kendal Mint Cake, which is basically mint-flavoured sugar!), but home-made tablet is just so comforting.

Many recipes have you boiling the sugar mix on the hob for ages, but somebody once told me she made hers in the microwave, and that's how I do mine now. Our most popular flavour is vanilla, but over the years I've made many different flavours, including whisky, orange, cinnamon, ginger, and mint. My favourite, though, and the one that took everyone by surprise at our events, was liquorice. My mouth is watering now thinking about it.

As with the cinder toffee, you can cut this into small pieces and pop it into sweet bags to give as hand-made gifts to friends and family, marking the tablet into 9 x 9 small squares in the tin as it's setting. It's so sweet that you only need a small piece. We often placed a little piece of tablet alongside people's drinks in the tearoom, as a little extra treat for them. Of course, you can make your pieces any size you like.

Ingredients

397g tin condensed milk
450g caster sugar
50g unsalted butter, cut into small cubes
2 teaspoon vanilla extract or flavour of your choice

Equipment

1 x 8" square loose-bottomed baking tin

Method

1   Grease and line an 8" square baking tin with parchment paper.

2   Pop all the tablet ingredients, except for the flavouring, into the largest microwave bowl you have and stir well.

3   Cook on high in the microwave for 4 minutes. Remove the bowl from the microwave and stir well.

4   Return the bowl to the microwave and cook for a further 4 minutes on high, before taking back out of the microwave and stirring well.

5   Put the bowl back in the microwave and cook for a final 4 minutes on high.

6   Remove from the microwave, quickly add your flavour, and whisk for 3 minutes with a hand-held electric whisk until the mixture looks like it is starting to come away from the sides of the bowl.

7   Scrape the mixture into the prepared tin and smooth with a spatula.

8   Leave the tablet to cool for about 10 minutes before scoring into small squares with a sharp knife.

9   Allow to set completely in the tin before removing from the tin and cutting along the scored marks.

Helensburgh Highland Games and the kindness of strangers

On Monday morning came the dreaded phone call from Halifax to tell me that my dad was really ill. We set off immediately, but soon after leaving, another call told me he had died. It was a silent, long journey to Overgate Hospice at Elland, where I spent time with my dad telling him I loved him. My sister organised the funeral, some three weeks hence, so we returned to Scotland in the interim.

Just a little extra story here about getting ready for Dad's funeral during that three-week period. Walking up Sauchiehall Street, looking for a new outfit suitable to say goodbye to Dad in, I was drawn to the Doc Martin shop by a pair of shoes in the window. These shoes had lots of figures on them depicting heaven and hell, and I could imagine my dad rolling his eyes and saying, 'Eh, our lass, don't even think of wearing those.' Fifteen minutes later, out of the shop I came, armed with not only said shoes, but bright purple laces to add to them. Jim simply hugged me as I declared there would be no crying at the funeral, because looking down at my new risky shoes would make me smile. A few hours later we were back on the

Helensburgh Highland Games

train home, clutching new Doc Martins, a bright pink jacket, posh jeans, and a hint of a smile.

Anyway, it's during these times that you make decisions that are not always the best decisions – or maybe they are! We already had our first event organised for Mother Murphy's Home Baking and Afternoon Teas – the Helensburgh Highland Games on 24th May. I told myself that I was a tough cookie and doing the event would help get me through the next couple of weeks before the funeral. I baked until the house was full of wonderful smells, and cakes surrounded me. I was ok. Of course I was!

On the day of the Helensburgh Highland Games, there were weather warnings out for the West of Scotland, with high winds strong enough to cause disruption. I felt like the weather gods really were again laughing at me and putting me to the test. At least we only had one gazebo to put up, though! Arriving at the event early, we tried in vain to erect the gazebo without the frame breaking and the material splitting. I spent the next half hour sobbing on the wet ground, telling Jim that I couldn't do it, that I was a fool to think I could, and that this was the penalty for not sitting at home grieving like a normal daughter would.

That was when I realised how fabulous strangers can be. People seemed to come from all around and helped us to get the gazebo up and secured. To all those people that day, you don't know how important those few minutes of help were to me. Thank you.

How did the Helensburgh Highland Games go then? Well, the rain and gales threatened to blow down our gazebo many times during the day. Few people attended the games due to the weather warnings, but we learned a lot. We took way too much stock, but customers loved our cakes and bakes. The favourites were a new coconut cake, the now Awesome Rocky Road, and the strawberry jam. The policeman and policewoman sheltering under the gazebo, tasting and loving scones with lashings of home-made jam, even took jars of our jam home.

Prime position at Stirling Farmer's Market

Fast forward a few months, with the funeral behind me but never forgotten. I was devasted with the stress of the funeral and realising that Dad had really gone, but there was a strange incident a few weeks later. Working alone in the office of our training company, I suddenly felt that somebody was watching me. Looking up, I thought I could see Dad at the door, just smiling. I don't know much about the afterlife or spirits, but there was my dad just smiling at me. I felt he was telling me that he was ok and that I was going to be fine.

Jim and I were still working in our training company when we got our first cake and bake gig at Stirling Farmers' Market. This was a fabulous experience, as well as a leap up the learning curve. There was no gazebo to erect, as market stalls were ready for action, but this was of course still an outdoor market in Scotland. Often the weather got the better of the market, but we somehow managed to keep our stock protected. Jim was always cold, but our stall always seemed to have the perfect spot right outside Marks and Spencer's.

Over the months we attended Stirling Farmers' Market, we began to get customers looking for us, and especially our gluten and dairy free goodies. As usual, Awesome Rocky Road was popular, along with our home-made jams and Borrowdale Tea Loaves.

Our confidence was growing, but best of all, we were really beginning to enjoy ourselves.

I think we should go to the Good Food Show

Our confidence grew as we realised that people loved our products and how enjoyable the whole adventure had become. To showcase Mother Murphy's Home Baking and Afternoon Teas, we looked for other events, and one day I suggested to Mr M that we should have a stand at the Good Food Show Scotland. There was an instant look of shock, horror, and disbelief on his face, though he now claims it was his idea!

The Good Food Show Scotland is a three-day event, held at the Scottish Exhibition and Conference Centre (SECC) in Glasgow. The event is quite simply the ultimate experience for food lovers, where visitors can sample and buy food from many different cuisines, see the most helpful kitchen gadgets, and watch demonstrations by some of the UK's best loved celebrity chefs, cooking live and chatting. As an exhibitor it would offer us an opportunity to showcase our products to a huge new audience, with an anticipated 110,00 visitors to the show. It would be a massive opportunity, but equally a huge challenge for us.

Ben, my Mum, Anne, Debra, and Mr M

The first shock for us was the cost of being there. Despite having attended previous shows, our naïve selves thought it would be an opportunity for us to sell lots of produce. We didn't realise how many bigger companies would be alongside us.

For weeks before the three-day event (yes, three days!) I baked, baked, and then baked some more. The first day of the Good Food Show arrived and I could barely breathe, I was so anxious. I couldn't think, couldn't drink, and certainly couldn't eat any breakfast. Why was I doing this? I wondered. Fortunately, I had Jim and my mum to calm my nerves and tell me that everything was going to be fine. How they put up with my short fuse those few days before the event, I'm not quite sure, but I will be forever grateful – even if I didn't tell them at the time.

Day one of the Good Food Show was a bit of learning curve, to say the least. We set up the stall, rearranged it a few times, then waited. Very few people came and bought from our stall, but we had lots of people chatting to us, telling us how great the stall looked and asking where our Café was. At least by the end of day one, my nerves had settled and I was able to sleep that night.

Day two arrived. Team Murphy was ready to roll, with my son Benjamin and Anne, Jim's sister-in-law, joining us. With the five of us working on the stall, we were able to swap around and have breaks, look at the other stalls, and even visit some of the demonstrations. Ben was in his element and quickly started handing out free samples around the stall. There was much more interest in the stall once we were giving out freebies, I can tell you. We even had the fabulous Mary Berry and Paul Hollywood come to our stall that day. Ok, perhaps Mary Berry and Paul Hollywood walked past our stall that day!

Day three arrived and we were up with the larks again. We were a great team and all really enjoyed the final day. Ben loved the customer chats, handing round samples, and we were all excited by the interest there was in us extending our gluten free and dairy free range.

We'd done it, we certainly hadn't embarrassed ourselves, and we had learned a lot. We took way too much stock to sell, and needed more sample-sized produce. Though stressful at first, we had a lot of fun and it all cost a fortune. Most of all, though, I realised my dream was still to have my own tearoom where people could experience tea and cakes in a relaxed, cosy, and friendly atmosphere.

My dream comes true as Mother Murphy's Tearoom opens

Onwards and upwards! We spent the next few months looking at many different cafes and tearooms, good ones, bad ones, very bad ones, and terrible ones. I knew how my tearoom would look, but only the beautiful, very expensive Betty's in York came close to my ideal. My tearoom would be the place my Grandma would have liked to visit. We'd use only china teacups, because my lovely Grandma would only drink tea from her own china teacup. We'd use proper leaf tea and tea strainers, not teabags dunked in mugs. All our cakes would be hand-made by us. All ingredients would be sourced as locally as possible, and the best quality we could afford. As for the décor, it would be simple but would, of course, have to be shades of purple and white.

I was able to draw down on lovely memories I have growing up, chatting with my Grandma about her trips to different cafes. Every Saturday, Grandma and Grandad would take a bus trip out from Halifax and go to a different café for their lunch. I listened with interest to her tales of what she enjoyed, what she had to eat and drink, what she liked or hated, and why she wouldn't go back to certain cafes.

Debra and Mr M in their brand new tearoom

These chats gave me the vision for my tearoom. Grandma's pet hates were loud music, fake cream, and milk jugs carried inside the cups. Grandma would tut and shake her head, telling me about these things; she didn't want the music stopping her talking to Grandad (and listening to the other customer conversations, no doubt); didn't want a possibly dirty milk jug to stand inside her clean cup; and couldn't understand why it was so difficult to serve real fresh cream in the cakes.

We finally found a place for our tearoom – a little café in Falkirk. The perfect size for Jim and I to manage ourselves, with a bit of cleaning and decorating we could almost walk in and open straight away. We took the keys to our new place at the beginning of March 2015, and the open day was set for the first of

April. I know! Everyone said how silly it was opening on April Fools' Day, but since when did I do anything the sensible and easy way?

March flew by with us cleaning, decorating, ordering equipment, setting the menu, and generally getting into a bit of a flap. We scoured the charity shops for china crockery, and ordered individual three-tier cake stands for the afternoon teas. I wanted everyone to have their own three-tier stand because, in my opinion, nobody should have to share their afternoon tea. Despite the flurry of activity, I never once questioned whether we should be doing this. My dream was going to come true. I was going to open my own tearoom.

1st April, 2015 came, and the tearoom opened. Our perfect tearoom was gleaming. Purple and white, serving real leaf tea, proper coffee, with china crockery and, most importantly, all the cakes baked by us. I was bursting with pride. Bursting with pride for what I'd achieved, but bursting with pride and joy that I'd not done it alone but with my soulmate alongside me – Jim, who very quickly became known as the magnificent Mr M.

What's all this gluten free stuff?

In Mother Murphy's tearoom, just about all the menu can be prepared and served gluten and dairy free. Indeed, most of our cakes and bakes are gluten free and dairy free, with not a chocolate brownie in sight. It may then come as a surprise to some people to find out that neither myself of Mr M are coeliac nor gluten intolerant. So why, you may well ask, do we have such a large choice in gluten free and dairy free?

It all stems from the time when we were planning our home-baking business, never imagining for one minute that we would be able to open our very own tearoom. I'd try out different cakes and bakes on anyone and everyone I came into contact with, in both my work and home life, but noticed that some people always refused my cakes because they couldn't eat gluten. Gluten? What's this then? Coeliac Disease? Never heard of it!

In my naivety, I boldly told people that I'd make them a gluten free cake no problem. Well, I can tell you that my food waste bin was overflowing at times trying out this gluten free stuff. The cakes looked lovely, but fell apart when I tried to cut them. The crumbs were very tasty, though. I did lots of research, lots of trials, lots of sampling, but finally started to get cakes and bakes that tasted just as good as gluten versions – in some cases, even better.

By the time we'd opened up Mother Murphy's Tearoom, I'd realised that our range of cakes and bakes that were 'Delicious Without' were just as popular in the tearoom as they had been at the markets and Highland Games. I do believe that it was by good fortune I'd made 'Delicious Without' both gluten free and dairy free. It appears that although it's difficult for people to get good gluten free food in eating establishments, it's perhaps just as difficult to get good dairy free food.

Always keen to make sure we're doing the best we can in the tearoom, we decided to attend the Allergy Show at the SECC Glasgow in April 2016. My hope was that we'd be able to see what other people were doing; talk to people with different allergies; get some samples of good gluten free food; and get new ideas for the tearoom. What an eye-opener the Allergy Show was! The samples were mostly uninteresting and bland. After an hour, Mr M simply refused to taste any more samples, but then I heard someone praising the doughnuts. Always a sucker for a hot, sugar-coated doughnut, I was instantly drawn to the stall, and before I knew it I had a bag of these warm delights in my hands. Sampling didn't take long. I took one bite of the first one and promptly gave the rest of them away to somebody walking past. Even worse was a custard cream biscuit I tried.

Now, growing up in a not-so-wealthy Yorkshire household, the Family Favourite range of basic biscuits with bourbons, custard creams, and coconut creams, were really the only biscuits to be seen in our biscuit barrel. Basic as they might have been, I just loved custard creams – the look, the smell, and the way you could pull them apart and scrape the cream away with your teeth, the taste. Oh, the memories! These free samples of the custard creams at the Allergy Show were small, pale, and the worst tasting biscuit I've ever tried.

As we left the show, we pondered why everyone else seemed to find the samples delicious when we found them, frankly, terrible. Were we just too critical? There was one way for me to find out. I decided to live a strict coeliac regime for a month, to try to get an idea of how it feels to live a totally gluten free life, and find out whether our tearoom was really geared to deliver a great gluten free menu.

How difficult could it be, with a tearoom full of gluten free cakes and bread. The next two weeks were spent looking at all the foods at home and checking which things I'd have to change. Oh dear, this was not quite as simple as I'd thought! It's one thing to be able to say your cakes are gluten free, as I know exactly what ingredients I'm putting into them, but not quite so quick and easy in the outside world. I soon found out how long it takes to do the shopping when you have to look at the tiny ingredients lists of every single product you are thinking of popping into your mouth.

Sunday, 1st May, 2016 arrived. Time for elevenses in the tearoom. Actually, it's always tea and biscuit time for me! I know, I'll have a cup of tea and a digestive biscuit, I thought to myself. Oh no! Digestive biscuits were now off the menu for me. I looked across our wide array of cakes and bakes. Not a single biscuit for coeliacs. There was shortbread for those who could eat gluten, but nothing in our 'Delicious Without' range for anybody who simply wanted a little biscuit to go with their drink. New bake number one identified – gluten and dairy free digestive biscuits. With the Allergy Show still fresh in my mind, and particularly the custard cream memory, I also set about creating a custard cream to sit in our 'Delicious Without' range.

In November 2016, I felt very privileged and proud to be asked to be guest speaker at the Forth Valley Gluten Free Group. Of course, I took along some samples, including a small, bite-sized version of our new custard creams. People there couldn't get enough of them and, needless to say, there were none left at the end of day. I think it's fair to say that some people went home with their pockets full of them.

Another of my proudest moments was to have my Nice Coconut Cream biscuit recipe published in the October 2017 issue of the Gluten Free Magazine. These have to be one of my favourite biscuits and everyone loves them, with many not even realising they're gluten free and dairy free.

How do I decide which gluten free and dairy free options to offer? Not everyone wants or needs to eat a gluten free and dairy free diet, and there are some things – bread being the obvious one – that are just not palatable for many people (including those who have to eat it). We do have lovely home-made gluten free bread in the tearoom, but we couldn't replace our wheat bread with this for all our customers.

During my month as a coeliac, I realised that those living a gluten free and/or dairy free life accept poor quality food and choices, because very often there is only one thing on the menu for them to eat. This then leads to, dare I say, their tastes becoming accustomed to this poor quality food, and before long they become like the people at the Allergy Show, believing that things are great simply because it's the only thing they can eat.

We put every effort into making everything we serve the best we possibly can. When I'm converting a recipe to make it gluten free and dairy free, the finished product has to look and taste as good as the previous non gluten free/dairy free version. Simply having a cake that's gluten free for the sake of it isn't good enough for us. There's a lot of quality assurance and taste-testing in the tearoom, and customers love to give me their opinions, good or bad.

I believe that the best customers to test my gluten free/dairy free recipes are those who can eat gluten and dairy. If they can tell that it's gluten free and dairy free, and tell me it's not as good as the previous version, it doesn't get served and goes back to the testing (or discarded). There are some recipes, like our now famous pancakes, that are gluten free and dairy free and we only ever make that version. Everyone eats gluten free and dairy free pancakes, and everyone loves them. Cakes and bakes are almost all gluten free and dairy free.

There are, of course, some exceptions. Our Rocky Road will always be full of gluten and dairy. I've created an adaptation of this recipe in the form of our Candy Road, made using our Wannabe Digestive biscuits, home-made cinder toffee to replace the Maltesers, and some lovely gluten free and dairy free chocolate from Plamil foods. This will never replace our Rocky Road, but some customers prefer our Candy Road to Rocky Road. To prove this point, Candy Road has now become Shona's Candy Road, as she just loves this and prefers it to Rocky Road, even though she can have both gluten and dairy.

Never say never, though. One day we may find that we have bread that can be enjoyed by all, along with tasty gluten free black pudding. Then, and only then, we will think of having the tearoom 100% gluten free. This would be much easier for us working in the tearoom, as we wouldn't have to have separate working stations, separate griddles or utensils, and I wouldn't have to do the baking in a separate kitchen at home to avoid cross-contamination.

Tips, useful gadgets, and lessons learned

I've tried in this book not to use confusing or technical terms. I remember all too well my domestic science lessons being such a toil when we were just being taught the theory of cooking and baking. All those years ago, I just couldn't see the need for all the different information we were expected to learn and memorise. I just wanted to be told how to make something, about the different flavours, and to be warned about what not to do or what might go wrong. And I wanted this book to do this. You should be able to flick to any recipe and be guided how to make that recipe, without having to refer back to a detailed technical chapter. I haven't written things like, 'make using the creaming method', or 'make a genoise cake'. In each recipe, I've simply tried to advise you what to do at each stage.

Over the years I've seen adverts for amazing kitchen gadgets that I just had to have. My cupboards have bulged to bursting point with all these so-called must-have items, which often in reality never really lived up to the promise. Now I've a few gadgets in the kitchen that I wouldn't be without. Make sure that whenever possible you get things that can be used in the freezer, oven, dishwasher, and microwave.

I still have lots of the said amazing gadgets (some still in the boxes!), and one day I'll have a big clear-out. Perhaps that's for another book, though – 'Antique Gadgets from Mother Murphy's Cupboards'. In the words of Julie Andrews in the Sound of Music, here are a few of my favourite things.

Useful Gadgets

Baking Beans – Get yourself a large tub, or a couple of tubs, of ceramic baking beans. These are perfect when blind-baking pastry (baking pastry cases without the filling). Each ceramic bean conducts heat evenly, which helps to prevent air bubbles forming and your pastry base shrinking when baking without its filling. You can use them time and time again. Just remember that when they come out of the oven, they are hot. I empty mine into a big metal sieve to cool, before popping them back in their plastic tub ready for next time.

Baking Tins and Trays – Treat yourself to the best quality tins and trays you can afford. Ask for them as Christmas and birthday presents to build up your stock. Go for the heavy, non-stick type, and they should last you for years. Get yourself a selection of sizes and shapes, but again, don't go mad with your choice and buy a whole load of tins that you'll use for only one cake. My best buy has to be the tins for making Battenberg Cakes.

Baking Parchment – This is invaluable when baking. Don't go for greaseproof paper, as you still need to grease this. Parchment paper can be used to cover baking trays and baking tins, and nothing seems to stick to it. You can buy ready-cut parchment for the base of sandwich tins, deep tins, or loaf tins, which save a lot of time and effort. I always grease the tin before putting the parchment paper in, just to keep the paper in place when you're adding the mixture.

Cake Lifter – I have a large, square cake lifter. How I ever managed without this, I don't know. It's perfect for lifting cakes from the container to the serving plate without damaging them or having to use your fingers. Make sure you get one that is stainless-steel, that's easy to clean, and can go in the dishwasher.

Cake Tester – Metal cake testers are great and reusable. They take the guesswork out of knowing whether your cakes are baked or not. If you put the tester into the centre of the cake and it comes out clean, your cake is ready. If there is some mixture stuck to the cake tester, pop the cake back in the oven for a few more minutes before testing again. Another good use for the cake tester is to draw lines across the piped icing when creating the feather icing on the Bakewell Tarts.

Cooling Trays – Most cakes and bakes are better for cooling on a wire rack once you remove them from their baking tins. I have a three-tier wire rack system, which allows me to stand the wire racks on top of each other, taking up less space in the kitchen. They have folding legs for easy storage and can be popped in the dishwasher for easy cleaning, if necessary. I also use them when I'm drizzling icing or chocolate on cakes and biscuits (just put a tray underneath to catch the icing and chocolate that drizzles through the racks).

Cutters – Get yourself a good quality set of round cutters for scones, biscuits, and fondant icing. You can get some that are plain on one side and fancy on the other. There are sets you can buy that come in a box to keep them safe and tidy. It's also worth getting a few cutters for gingerbread men. How many cutters and what shapes you get is up to you – you'll not be short of choice, but you can quickly end up with cutters you bought simply for one biscuit and never use again. I also have something called an accordion cutter, which is great for cutting pastry, biscuits, and bakes into equal-sized portions, both before and after baking. This is ideal when cutting biscuits that need to match when you put them together, or just to get the pieces the same size for selling in the tearoom when you don't have a specific individual cutter.

Fish-Slice – this is great for transferring delicate pastries or biscuits to baking trays, ready for baking. It's also perfect for removing the baked goods from the baking trays and transferring them to cooling racks (avoiding breaking them and burning your fingers). It's great for cutting through the baked biscuits before they cool if they have spread in the oven and are touching. I suppose you could even use it for transferring fish from a baking tin, too!

Food Processor – Invaluable for blitzing and blending different mixtures. I use mine for blitzing biscuits ready for the traybakes, making pastry, blitzing nuts, and even use it for breaking up the peppermints for our mint chocolate fudge.

Free-Standing Mixer – Some people see these as a lazy option. I used to be one of those people who thought you could only make pastry using your hands, and a hand-held whisk was all you needed. I now know that a free-standing mixer is great for making gluten free pastries and biscuits. I use mine for beating dairy free frostings to make sure they are as light as a feather, and meringues can be whipped up in a couple of minutes. One of the best things I find with the free-standing mixer is you can have the mixer running slowly as you add more ingredients to the bowl – something you struggle to do if you're using a hand-held whisk.

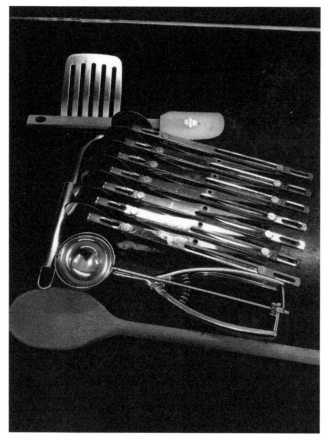

Clockwide from the bottom —
wooden spoon, ice cream scoop, fish-slice, spatula, accordion cutter

Ice Cream Scoops – I have two different sizes of scoops. I'm not sure I've ever used these to scoop ice cream, but I do use them all the time. They're great for spooning mixture into baking tins or muffin tins, making sure you get the same amount in each one, or for getting pancake mixture onto the griddle.

Oven Gloves – Make sure you have a couple of really good pairs of oven gloves. Don't go for fancy, frilly ones. Just make sure they are thick, long enough to cover all your hands and wrists, and can be washed in the washing machine. I have oven gloves for using when baking gluten free and separate ones for non-gluten free food. It would be a shame to go to all the trouble of avoiding cross-contamination when baking, only to spoil it with a rogue crumb touching your food from the oven gloves.

Pancake Maker – I like to use an electric griddle for making our pancakes. I can cook four pancakes at one time on my electric pancake maker. It's great for keeping the griddle at a constant temperature for a long period of time, and the pancakes don't stick.

Pastry Brush – Get yourself a good quality pastry brush. Use a silicone one to make sure you don't get bristles coming out of it onto the food. These are especially great for brushing milk onto your scones before baking, or brushing jam onto your marzipan for the Battenberg Cakes.

Piping Bags – I buy rolls of these from Lakeland and use them constantly. Get yourself a set of different piping nozzles and you're set for anything. Apart from the obvious piping of butter cream and icing, they're great for getting the mixture into the Battenberg Cake sections or mini-cake tins, and for piping Viennese Whirls. A good tip for filling the piping bags is to pop the bag into a jug as you fill it, and it will not tip over.

Spatula – This is probably my most essential kitchen tool. Get yourself a couple of good quality silicone ones that are heat resistant. They are perfect for stirring and for scraping out every last bit of mixture from pans and bowls.

Weighing Scales – I like to use digital scales, but the choice is yours. I also like to use scales where I can put my bowl/pan/tin directly onto the scale, rather than having a little container to weigh into.

Wooden spoons – You can never have too many wooden spoons. Large ones with extra-long handles are especially helpful when making jams, toffee, or caramel, when you're dealing with boiling mixtures that bubble and splash up as they cook.

Now for some simple tips

Baking Blind

When you're baking goodies such as Bakewell Tart, Lemon Meringue Pie, or quiches, you need to part-bake the pastry case first without the filling, which is known as blind baking. Blind baking is usually done because your

filling will either need to bake for a shorter time than your pastry, or won't be baked at all. Blind baking can also help to give a golden, crisp pastry and prevent the filling from making it go soggy.

First, line your uncooked pastry case with parchment paper. (I use a parchment paper cake tin lining for this, as it covers the base, holds the baking beans, and there's enough left to fold over to protect the pastry from over-cooking during the baking.) Fill the lined pastry case (about halfway up the sides) with some sort of weights. I like to use ceramic baking beans, but you could use dried lentils, beans, or rice. The beauty of ceramic baking beans is they can be used over and over again. Whatever you use as a weight, this stage is vital when baking blind or the raw pastry will puff up when baking and the sides may also collapse inwards.

There are lots of suggestions as to why this should be called blind baking. The one I feel inclined to believe is that pastry making was usually delegated to an under-chef who didn't know what the filling would be, so was 'blind-baking'.

I still smile at the time many years ago when I asked Mr M to make some Bakewell Tarts for the tearoom. I left him to this and reminded him to blind bake the cases. I returned home just as he was trying to pick each ceramic baking bean out of the cooked pastry, as he didn't realise he had to put parchment paper over the pastry first!

Making Gluten Free Pastry and Biscuits

Gluten free pastry and biscuit dough is a bit tricky to get the hang of, but it's not as difficult as you'd think. Just as with wheat-based versions, if you pop them in the fridge for half an hour before trying to roll them out, they'll be much easier to handle. Make sure you have a well-floured worktop. I don't find it necessary to roll out between cling-film, as some people advise. The beauty of gluten free pastry and biscuit dough is that there's no gluten to develop by over-working them.

If you roll out your pastry and it tears as you try to cover your pie tin with it, call it a few names, squash it up, and re-roll it. That will do the trick! It also means that you can re-roll biscuit dough to use up every last bit, as you won't ruin the biscuits by developing the gluten.

Pre-Heat Your Oven

Always pre-heat your oven whilst you are preparing your bakes. That way, your oven is at the correct temperature before you put your bakes in. Cakes and biscuits can be ruined if they are put in an oven that is too cold, because they need the hot temperature to bake correctly.

Room Temperature

Try to have all your ingredients at room temperature before using them. This helps to prevent eggs curdling when you beat them into your mixture. Take the eggs and butter/margarine out of the fridge half an hour or so before you want to use them.

Take Your Time and Enjoy

Baking should be done because you enjoy it. Take your time and relax. Spend time beating the fat and sugar together before adding the eggs, because it really does make a difference to how light the finished bake is. Take your time beating the ingredients for the butter icing and frosting, as again this gives you a lovely light finish.

Use the Right Ingredients for the Recipe

Always go for fresh, organic, and local ingredients, if you can source and afford them. A lemon is not just a lemon. Go for large, un-waxed lemons, and the same with oranges. Use unrefined sugars if possible, and as you become more familiar with baking, try different sugars, such as dark and light brown muscovado sugar. Use the right type of flour – self-raising flour is best if you need your bake to rise, where plain flour is best for biscuits and pastries. For gluten free baking especially, experiment with ingredients such as rice flour, polenta, and cornflour.

If you're using butter, use a good quality butter. When using dairy free versions, check they are suited to baking (with a minimum of 60-79% fat), as some makes contain too much water and will affect your bake. I like to stick to the same brands of ingredients if possible, as I know how they work and how they taste. It really does make a difference to your finished goodies.

Talk to other cooks and bakers about what they use. You'll soon have your own preferred ingredients once you've tried them a few times.

Weigh Out All Your Ingredients First

I like to prepare my ingredients by weighing them all out into bowls before I start mixing anything. That way, you can make sure you have all the ingredients you need before you start the process. I used to

weigh everything into one bowl, but so many times I tipped too much of one ingredient in, and then the mixture was ruined. It's also good to crack your eggs into a bowl first before adding them to your mixture, to make sure you don't get any eggshell into the mixture. Having all your ingredients weighed out into bowls also means you won't need to wonder if you remembered to put all the ingredients into the mixture, as they will all be in front of you and can see if you have one left over. It's a bit like DIY furniture; if you have a screw left over, you have a problem!

Recipes

Jams, Jelly-Jams And Lemon Curd

I know, I know! Most cookery books have jams at the end of their recipes. Well, as I said at the start, this is not just a recipe book; this is Mother Murphy's recipe book.

I wanted my book to take you on a trip around the tearoom, from the planning stage, watching Mother Murphy's grow, and then through the running of the tearoom. I pondered for a long while over what order to put the recipes and stories in. Should it be quite simply in alphabetical order, or should it be in categories like biscuits, cakes, and bread?

As you can see, I decided I'd start with our jams and see where the book went from there. Why? Well, just like bread, I believe that jam is a staple in our lives, and this is especially so in the tearoom. Where would you be at breakfast time without a lovely jam or curd to go on your toast? Where would you be at morning coffee time without jam for your scone? How could I produce our lovely cakes and bakes if I didn't have a selection of jams to use? Of course, we could buy some very good commercial jams, but for me, home-made jam it has to be, and I never once considered buying jam for the tearoom. We're proud to say that we have used only our home-made jams, jellies, and curds.

Let's take a closer look at jams and jellies. What's the difference between a jam and a jelly-jam? Well, they're both made from fruit boiled with sugar, the main difference being the form the finished fruit takes. In jelly-jams, only the juice of the fruit is used so there are no bits, which some people prefer. In jams, crushed or chopped fruit is used, and there are lumps of fruit. This also means that jams are usually less stiff than jelly-jams. Sometimes jams get called preserves, but I just call these runny jams! I remember with horror the only jam I could get my daughter Chloe to eat was the cheapest jam ever from the supermarket, with absolutely no pips or fruit pieces to be seen. I would even question if any real fruit had even been close to going into the jar! But that was all she would eat (along with white bread and crisps), meaning cheap jam it was on her butties for many years.

Once you've tried home-made jams or jellies, you'll find it almost impossible to eat shop-bought varieties. Home-made jams and jellies have a wonderful flavour, lovely texture, and great colour. OK, home-made may not have the extraordinary long shelf-life that shop-bought varieties seem to have, but in my experience, this doesn't present a problem at home or in the tearoom. I know that as soon as I've made a new batch of any type, customers can't get enough of it. I'm also pleased to report that Chloe now prefers my jams to the supermarket versions. Phew!

At the tearoom we try to have a good variety of jams and jelly-jams for customers to choose from. Strawberry and raspberry jams are always the favourites – with lumps of juicy fruit and wonderful flavours. When it comes to jelly-jams, though, you can't beat our wild berry jelly-jam made with rosehips, brambles (blackberries), wild raspberries, and bilberries (blaeberries).

For our jams and jellies, we always aim to use Scottish fruit from local pick-your-own farms or by foraging for hedgerow fruit. Our favourite place to get the sweetest, juiciest strawberries is from Brialand's Farm, a lovely pick-your-own fruit farm on the A84 between Stirling and Callander, alongside Blair Drummond

Safari Park. Every summer since we started Mother Murphy's, we have a day out, pick all the strawberries we need (sampling lots of them in the name of quality assurance, of course), then we treat ourselves to tea and cakes in the tearoom there. Well, it's hot, hard work picking strawberries! A little tip here is to remind those helping you with your strawberry picking to pull the hulls off the strawberries as they pick them, making your job of preparing the fruit for jam-making much easier back at home.

Other fruits (gooseberries, redcurrants, blackcurrants, and raspberries) we pick at Craigie's, a fruit farm near Kirkliston, not a million miles from Edinburgh Airport. This usually involves a couple of day trips, as some of the fruits ripen at different times. Again, after the hard work, we go into the cafe there for tea and cakes. Imagine, drinking tea and eating date slices, looking out to sea, watching all the planes coming and going, while we speculate on whether people are setting off on holiday or coming home.

Of course, living in the central belt of Scotland, there's an abundance of hedgerow fruit just waiting to be picked and made into goodies. It's such a shame that so much of this wild fruit goes to waste, as people don't seem to make time to pick the offerings that nature generously provides. Every year whilst walking our Collie dog, Beatrix, I marvel as the different seasons pass and we watch with interest how the various fruits are growing.

Once March comes along, the whole of nature seems to come to life. The raspberry bushes start to

grow fresh green shoots, then little white flowers. A little later, the bramble bushes come to life and the apple trees begin to blossom. As the summer develops, the rosehips go from buds to flowers to wonderful rosehips, bursting with juice and flavour. If we're lucky enough (and faster than the birds), we can also gather blaeberries (or bilberries, as I know them). Finally, as autumn arrives, apples start to ripen and fall from the trees – hence the phrase 'windfall fruit'. By the end of autumn, our freezer is usually full of fruit ready to be made into jams or jellies. Most fruits, with the exception of strawberries, freeze very well, allowing us to make jams and jellies throughout the year and keep the tearoom stocked. Then of course, there are the bilberries on the mountains of Scotland, especially Beinn Ghlas and Ben Lawers, but that's another story! (See A Barking Dog, A Helicopter Rescue, and Lemon Wannabes)

Before we move onto the recipes, though, a little word of warning. Don't be tempted to double up on the fruit when making batches of jams or jelly-jams, or the mixtures won't be able to boil sufficiently to give a good set, and you'll most certainly end up re-boiling your un-set jams, spoiling the texture, taste, and colour of the finished product. Trust me, I've tried this, and now only make small batches at a time, saving time (and frustration) in the long run, as there are now no re-boils in our kitchen. I've tried working with smaller quantities, but find that the mixture burns too easily and you can't get that fierce boil you need to encourage the jam or jelly-jam to set.

I still remember with cold sweats the first year we made gooseberry jelly-jam. We assumed that gooseberries would have ample pectin in them and had not, at that stage, discovered the benefits of using commercial pectin. The gooseberry jelly-jam came out a wonderful colour and tasted fabulous, but sadly, jelly-jam it was not. The first attempt came out like runny glue. We put this back to the boil and crossed our fingers. Again, there was no set. Third time lucky, we boiled the mixture again and managed to get a jelly of a fashion. It might not have been the perfect consistency for jelly-jam, but it tasted wonderful.

I remember putting this in as many different cakes and bakes as I could – Gooseberry Bakewell and Gooseberry Victoria Sponge, to name but a few. The customers loved it on their scones and, like with our home-made lemon-curd, some people were seen eating this straight from their little pots on the scone plates, with it not even getting as far as their scones.

After several years of having re-boils in our jams and jelly-jams, I was pleasantly surprised to discover that using a commercial liquid pectin provided me with a natural tool to ensure I could produce great jams and jelly-jams every time. Using Certo pectin means that your precious fruit requires less boiling, resulting in the jam or jelly keeping its flavour and colour by the simple addition of a boost of nature's very own gelling agent.

Of course, most jams and jelly-jams are naturally gluten free, so there's no need to worry about this in the tearoom. Some people put a knob of butter into their mixtures to disperse the froth that builds up during boiling. This does work, but then the jams and jellies are no longer dairy-free.

In one of one of Hugh Fearnley-Whittingstall's cookery books, he talks about how the froth is just air and you shouldn't waste time or the finished product by trying to get rid of it. I now just take some time gently stirring the finished jams and jellies, to let the mixture settle for the froth to naturally disperse before putting it into jars. That way, my jams and jelly-jams remain both gluten free and dairy-free, allowing even more people to enjoy them. If it's good enough for Mr Fearnley-Whittingstall, it's good enough for me.

Baking can be done with a few simple ingredients, so it's about simplicity and nostalgia - people are reminded of their childhood.

Paul Hollywood

Raspberry Jam

Makes about 7 x 225g jars

Sterilising Jam Jars – Jams and jelly-jams should be poured into warm sterilised jars, prepared so they are ready just about the same time as your jam. There are two simple ways to do this – a) putting the washed and drained jars and lids upside down in a cool oven (140°c) for 15 minutes; or b) putting them through a hot wash in the dishwasher.

Jam-Making Pan – I'd suggest investing in a stainless-steel preserving pan. These have a thick, heavy base for even heat distribution, and the wide, deep sides allow for a rapid boil without the jam mix burning or boiling over the sides of the pan.

Stir Gently – Throughout the jam making, stir occasionally, gently using a long-handled wooden spoon. Stirring too often and vigorously allows cold air to enter the pan and extends the boiling time, taking away some of the goodness and colour of your fruit.

Keeping Your Jam – Your jam is ready to eat once cold, but your sealed jams and jellies will keep for at least 12-18 months in a cool, dark place. Once opened, store in the fridge and use within a couple of weeks.

Ingredients

900 raspberries
1.25g granulated sugar
125ml pectin (I use Certo)
8 x 225g sterilised jam jars with lids

Method

1   Place the raspberries in your jam-making pan and roughly crush them with a potato masher.

2   Add the sugar, and heat gently on a low heat on the hob until all the sugar is dissolved and there are no sugar crystals remaining, stirring occasionally using a long-handled wooden spoon. This should take about 10-15 minutes.

3   While the sugar is melting, place a saucer in your freezer, ready to use for testing the setting of your jam.

4   Once the sugar has all dissolved, turn the heat up to high, bring the mixture to a good boil until it reaches 105.5°c on a sugar/jam thermometer, and boil for 4 minutes.

5   Remove from the heat, add the Certo, and stir well.

6   Wait a couple of minutes for the bubbles to settle. Take your saucer out of the freezer, and place a teaspoon of the jam mixture on the cold plate. Wait for a minute then, using your finger, push the jam gently and see if it wrinkles. (This is what's known as the wrinkle test). If it does, the jam is ready. If not, pop it back on the heat, bring back to 105.5°c, and boil for another minute before repeating the wrinkle test.

7   If you wish, carefully skim off the froth from the jam. Stirring gently will also disperse the froth. You could add a knob of butter, but this will stop your jam being dairy-free.

8   Pour into the sterilised jars, filling each jar to the brim. (This is where the saying jam-packed comes from.) Be very careful, as this mixture is extremely hot. Don't forget to use oven gloves when putting the lids on, as the glass jars will be hot, too.

9   Leave to cool overnight, then put a label on each jar and enjoy over the months to come.

Strawberry Jam

Makes about 8 x 225g jars

Sterilising Jam Jars – Jams and Jelly-Jams should be poured into warm sterilised jars, prepared so they are ready just about the same time as your jam. There are two simple ways to do this – a) putting the washed and drained jars and lids upside down in a cool oven (140°c) for 15 minutes; or b) putting them through a hot wash in the dishwasher.

Jam-Making Pan – I'd suggest investing in a stainless-steel preserving pan. These have a thick, heavy base for even heat distribution, and the wide, deep sides allow for a rapid boil without the jam mix burning or boiling over the sides of the pan.

Stir Gently – Throughout the jam-making, stir occasionally, gently using a long-handled wooden spoon. Stirring too often and vigorously allows cold air to enter the pan and extends the boiling time, taking away some of the goodness and colour of your fruit.

Keeping Your Jam – Your jam is ready to eat once cold, but your sealed jams and jellies will keep for at least 12-18 months in a cool, dark place. Once opened, store in the fridge and use within a couple of weeks.

Ingredients

> 1kg strawberries
> 3 tablespoons lemon juice
> 1.4 kg granulated sugar
> 125ml pectin (I use Certo)
> 8 x 225g sterilised jam jars and lids

Method

1   Cut out the hull (green bit) from the strawberries, using a sharp knife, put them in your jam-making pan, and roughly crush them with a potato masher.

2   Add the sugar and lemon juice, then heat gently on a low heat on the hob until all the sugar is dissolved and there are no sugar crystals remaining, stirring occasionally with a long-handled wooden spoon. This should take about 10-15 minutes.

3   While the sugar is melting, place a saucer in your freezer ready to use for testing the setting of your jam.

4   Once the sugar has all dissolved, turn the heat up to high, bring the mixture to a good boil until it reaches 105.5°c on a sugar/jam thermometer, and boil for 5 minutes.

5   Remove from the heat, add 125 ml of liquid pectin, and stir well with a long-handled wooden spoon.

6   Wait a couple of minutes for the bubbles to settle. Take your saucer out of the freezer and place a teaspoon of the jam mixture on the cold plate. Wait for a minute then, using your finger, push the jam gently and see if it wrinkles. (This is what's known as the wrinkle test.) If it does, the jam is ready. If not, pop it back on the heat, bring back to 105.5°c, and boil for another minute before repeating the wrinkle test.

7   If you wish, carefully skim off the froth from the jam. Stirring gently will also disperse the froth. You could add a knob of butter, but this will stop your jam being dairy-free.

8   Pour into the sterilised jars, filling each jar to the brim. (This is where the saying jam-packed comes from.) Be very careful, as this mixture is extremely hot. Don't forget to use oven gloves when putting the lids on, as the glass jars will be hot, too.

9   Leave to cool overnight, then put a label on each jar and enjoy over the months to come.

Blackcurrant Jelly-Jam

Makes about 8 x 225g jars

The colour of home-made blackcurrant jelly-jam is so rich and vibrant, with a taste that is simply divine! Don't limit this delight to your toast and scones, but try it with duck breast, cold meats, or on oatcakes with cheese.

Sterilising Jam Jars – Jams and jelly-jams should be poured into warm sterilised jars. There are two simple ways to do this – putting the washed and drained jars and lids upside down in a cool oven (140°c) for 15 minutes, or putting them through a hot wash in the dishwasher.

Jam-Making Pan – I'd suggest investing in a stainless-steel preserving pan. These have a thick, heavy base for even heat distribution, and the wide, deep sides allow for a rapid boil without the jam mix burning or boiling over the sides of the pan.

Stir Gently – Throughout the jam-making, stir occasionally, gently using a long-handled wooden spoon – too often and vigorously allows cold air to enter the pan and extends the boiling time, spoiling your lovely fruit.

Straining the Fruit – To get all the lovely juices from the cooked fruit, strain the pulp through a jelly bag or clean nylon sieve, held over a clean bowl. Make sure there the jelly bag is held high enough above the bowl catching the juice, so that the strained juice does not touch the jelly bag or sieve. You can get a stand to hold these.

Keeping Your Jam – Your jam is ready to eat once cold. Sealed jars will keep for at least 12-18 months in a cool, dark place, but once opened, store in the fridge and use within a couple of weeks.

Ingredients

Stage 1	Stage 2
900g blackcurrants	*Blackcurrant juice you have now made*
600ml cold water	*1360g granulated sugar for each 1130ml of blackcurrant juice*
	125ml pectin (I use Certo) for each 1130ml of blackcurrant juice
	8 x 225g sterilised jam jars and lids

Method

Stage 1

1   Put the blackcurrants in a large jelly pan with the water. No need to top and tail them, or worry if any stalks are remaining. Bring to the boil and simmer for 10-15 minutes until soft.

2   Empty the blackcurrants with all the juice into a muslin jelly bag over a large bowl, and leave overnight for the juice to strain through. Don't be tempted to rush this stage or force the juice through the fruit, as this will result in a dull jelly-jam. You want a clear, bright jelly-jam, so take your time with this stage.

Stage 2

1   Place 1130ml of the strained blackcurrant juice into your jam pan with 1360g of granulated sugar, and allow the sugar to melt slowly on the hob over a very low heat until there are no sugar crystals remaining, stirring occasionally with a long-handled wooden spoon. This should take about 10-15 minutes.

2   While the sugar is melting, place a saucer in your freezer, ready to use for testing the setting of your jelly.

3   Once the sugar has all dissolved, turn the heat up to high, bring the mixture to a good boil until it reaches 105.5°c on a sugar/jam thermometer, and boil for 2 minutes.

4   Stir in 125ml of Certo liquid pectin, bring the mixture back up to 105.5°c, then keep boiling for 30 seconds.

5   Take the pan off the heat. Wait a couple of minutes for the bubbles to settle. Take the saucer out of the freezer and place a teaspoon of the jelly mixture on the cold plate. Wait for a minute then, using your finger, push the jelly gently and see if it wrinkles. If it does, the jelly is ready. (This is what is known as the wrinkle test.) If not, pop it back on the heat, bring the jelly back to 105.5°c, and boil for another minute before repeating the wrinkle test.

6   If you wish, carefully skim off the froth from the jelly. Stirring gently will also disperse the froth. You could add a knob of butter, but this will stop your jelly being dairy-free.

7   Pour the jelly through a sterilised strainer again into a sterilised jug, then pour into the sterilised jars, filling each jar to the brim. (This is where the saying jam-packed comes from.) Be very careful, as this mixture is extremely hot. Don't forget to use oven gloves when putting the lids on, as the glass jars will be hot, too.

8   Leave to cool overnight, then put a label on each jar and enjoy over the months to come.

Gooseberry Jelly-Jam

Makes 8 x 225g jars

'Because life is too short to top and tail gooseberries.' Like our other jellies, don't limit this to your toast. Try it with cooked meats, oatcakes with cream cheese, digestive biscuits, or in toasted ham sandwiches.

Sterilising Jam Jars – Jams and jelly-jams should be poured into warm sterilised jars. There are two simple ways to do this – putting the washed and drained jars and lids upside down in a cool oven (140°c) for 15 minutes, or putting them through a hot wash in the dishwasher.

Jam-Making Pan – I'd suggest investing in a stainless-steel preserving pan. These have a thick, heavy base for even heat distribution, and the wide, deep sides allow for a rapid boil without the jam mix burning or boiling over the sides of the pan.

Stir Gently – Throughout the jam-making, stir occasionally, gently using a long-handled wooden spoon – too often and vigorously allows cold air to enter the pan and extends the boiling time, spoiling your lovely fruit.

Straining the Fruit – To get all the lovely juices from the cooked fruit, strain the pulp through a jelly bag or clean nylon sieve held over a clean bowl. Make sure the jelly bag is held high enough above the bowl catching the juice, so that the strained juice does not touch the jelly bag or sieve. You can get a stand to hold these.

Keeping Your Jam – Your jam is ready to eat once cold. Sealed jars will keep for at least 12-18 months in a cool, dark place, but once opened, store in the fridge and use within a couple of weeks.

Ingredients

Stage 1	Stage 2
454g gooseberries	*Gooseberry juice you have now made*
60ml cold water	*1360g granulated sugar for each 1130ml of gooseberry juice*
	125ml pectin (I use Certo) for each 1130ml of gooseberry juice
	8 x 225g sterilised jam jars and lids

Method

Stage 1

1   *Put the gooseberries in a large jelly pan with the water. No need to top and tail them. Bring to the boil, and simmer for 10-15 minutes until the fruit is soft and mushy. You will find it helpful to mash the fruit with a potato masher as they start to soften.*

2   *Put the gooseberries and all the juice into a muslin jelly bag over a large bowl. and leave overnight for the juice to strain through. Don't be tempted to rush this stage or force the juice through the fruit, as this will result in a dull jelly-jam. You want a clear, bright jelly-jam, so take your time with this stage.*

Stage 2

1   *Place the strained gooseberry juice (make this up to 1130 ml with cold water if you don't have enough) into a jam-making pan with 1360g of granulated sugar, and allow the sugar to melt slowly on the hob over a very low heat, stirring gently.*

2   *While the sugar is melting, place a saucer in your freezer, ready to use for testing the setting of your jelly.*

3   *Once the sugar has all dissolved, turn the heat up to high and bring the mixture to a good boil until it reaches 105.5°c on a sugar/jam thermometer.*

4   *Add 125ml of Certo liquid pectin and bring the mixture back up to 105.5°c, then keep boiling for 2 minutes.*

5   *Take the pan off the heat. Wait a couple of minutes for the bubbles to settle. Take the saucer out of the freezer, and place a teaspoon of the jelly mixture on the cold plate. Wait for a minute then, using your finger, push the jelly gently and see if it wrinkles. If it does, the jelly is ready. (This is what is known as the wrinkle test.) If not, pop the jelly back on the heat, bring back to 105.5°c, and boil for another minute before repeating the wrinkle test.*

6   *If you wish, carefully skim off the froth from the jelly. Stirring gently will also disperse the froth. You could add a knob of butter, but this will stop your jelly being dairy-free.*

7   *Pour the jelly through a sterilised strainer again into a sterilised jug, then pour into the sterilised jars, filling each jar to the brim. (This is where the saying jam-packed comes from.) Be very careful, as this mixture is extremely hot. Don't forget to use oven gloves when putting the jar tops on, as the glass jars will be hot, too.*

8   *Leave to cool overnight, then put a label on each jar and enjoy.*

Redcurrant Jelly-Jam

Makes 8 x 225g jars

Wait until you see the colour of this jelly-jam! Like the other jelly-jams, don't limit this delight to your toast and scones, but try it with cold meats or on oatcakes with cheese.

Sterilising Jam Jars – Jams and jelly-jams should be poured into warm sterilised jars. There are two simple ways to do this – putting the washed and drained jars and lids upside down in a cool oven (140°c) for 15 minutes, or putting them through a hot wash in the dishwasher.

Jam-Making Pan – I'd suggest investing in a stainless-steel preserving pan. These have a thick, heavy base for even heat distribution, and the wide, deep sides allow for a rapid boil without the jam mix burning or boiling over the sides of the pan.

Stir Gently – Throughout the jam-making, stir occasionally, gently using a long-handled wooden spoon – too often and vigorously allows cold air to enter the pan and extends the boiling time, spoiling your lovely fruit.

Straining the Fruit – To get all the lovely juices from the cooked fruit, strain the pulp through a jelly bag or clean nylon sieve held over a clean bowl. Make sure the jelly bag is held high enough above the bowl catching the juice, so that the strained juice does not touch the jelly bag or sieve. You can get a stand to hold these.

Keeping Your Jam – Your jam is ready to eat once cold. Sealed jars will keep for at least 12-18 months in a cool, dark place, but once opened, store in the fridge and use within a couple of weeks.

Ingredients

Stage 1	Stage 2
1.8kg redcurrants	*Redcurrant juice you have now made*
290ml cold water	*1.4kg granulated sugar for each 1130ml of redcurrant juice*
	125ml pectin (I use Certo) for each 1130ml of redcurrant juice
	8 x 225g sterilised jam jars and lids

Method

Stage 1

1   *Put the redcurrants in a large jelly pan with the water. No need to top and tail them, or worry about any stalks remaining. Bring to the boil and simmer for 10-15 minutes until soft.*

2   *Empty the redcurrants and all the juice into a muslin bag over a large bowl, and leave overnight for the juice to strain through. Don't be tempted to rush this stage or force the juice through the fruit, as this will result in a dull jelly-jam. You want a clear, bright jelly-jam, so take your time with this stage.*

Stage 2

1   *Place strained redcurrant juice (make this up to 1130 ml with cold water if you don't have enough) into a large jam-making pan. Add the granulated sugar, and allow the sugar to melt slowly on the hob over a very low heat, stirring gently.*

2   *While the sugar is melting, place a saucer in your freezer, ready to use for testing the setting of your jelly.*

3   *Once the sugar has all dissolved, turn the heat up to high, bring the mixture to a good rolling boil until it reaches 105°c on a sugar/jam thermometer, and boil for 2 minutes.*

4   *Add 125ml of Certo liquid pectin and bring back to a good boil up to 105°c, then keep boiling for a further minute.*

5   *Take the pan off the heat. Wait a couple of minutes for the bubbles to settle. Take the saucer out of the freezer and place a teaspoon of the jelly mixture on the cold plate. Wait for a minute then, using your finger, push the jelly gently and see if it wrinkles. If it does, the jelly is ready. (This is what is known as the wrinkle test.) If not, pop it back on the heat, bring back to 105°c, and boil for another minute before repeating the wrinkle test.*

6   *If you wish, carefully skim off the froth from the jelly. Stirring gently will also disperse the froth. You could add a knob of butter, but this will stop your jelly being dairy-free.*

7   *Pour the jelly through a sterilised strainer again into a sterilised jug, then pour into the sterilised jars, filling each jar to the brim. (This is where the saying jam-packed comes from.) Be very careful, as this mixture is extremely hot. Don't forget to use oven gloves when putting the jar tops on, as the glass jars will be hot, too.*

8   *Leave to cool overnight, then put a label on each jar and enjoy over the coming months.*

Spiced Apple Jelly-Jam

Makes 5 x 225g jars

A great recipe for using windfall apples for amazing jelly-jam to go with so many things, including cheese and oatcakes, but it's also lovely with cooked meats, especially roast pork. No need to peel and core the ingredients, just roughly chop them.

Sterilising Jam Jars – Jams and jelly-jams should be poured into warm sterilised jars. There are two simple ways to do this – putting the washed and drained jars and lids upside down in a cool oven (140°c) for 15 minutes, or putting them through a hot wash in the dishwasher.

Jam-Making Pan – I'd suggest investing in a stainless-steel preserving pan. These have a thick, heavy base for even heat distribution, and the wide, deep sides allow for a rapid boil without the jam mix burning or boiling over the sides of the pan.

Stir Gently – Throughout the jam-making, stir occasionally, gently using a long-handled wooden spoon – too often and vigorously allows cold air to enter the pan and extends the boiling time, spoiling your lovely fruit.

Straining the Fruit – To get all the lovely juices from the cooked fruit, strain the pulp through a jelly bag or clean nylon sieve held over a clean bowl. Make sure the jelly bag is held high enough above the bowl catching the juice, so that the strained juice does not touch the jelly bag or sieve. You can get a stand to hold these.

Keeping Your Jam – Your jam is ready to eat once cold. Sealed jars will keep for at least 12-18 months in a cool, dark place, but once opened, store in the fridge and use within a couple of weeks.

Ingredients

Stage 1	Stage 2
900g apples, roughly chopped	Apple juice you have just made
2 large un-waxed lemons, roughly chopped	450g granulated sugar for each 575ml apple juice
50g fresh root ginger, roughly chopped	125ml pectin (I use Certo) for each 575ml apple juice
1 cinnamon stick	
About 10 whole cloves	

Method

Stage 1

1   Put the apples, lemons, ginger, cinnamon, cloves, and 1.7 litres of water in a large jam-making pan. Bring to the boil, then reduce the heat and simmer until the apples are very soft.

2   Empty the mixture and all the juice into a muslin jelly bag over a large bowl, and leave overnight for the juice to strain through. Don't be tempted to rush this stage or force the juice through the fruit, as this will result in a dull jelly-jam. You want a clear, bright jelly-jam, so take your time.

Stage 2

1   Place strained apple juice (make this up to 575ml with cold water if you don't have enough) into a large jam-making pan. Add the granulated sugar, and allow the sugar to melt slowly on the hob over a very low heat, stirring gently.

2   While the sugar is melting, place a saucer in your freezer, ready to use for testing the setting of your jelly.

3   Once the sugar has all dissolved, turn the heat up to high, bring the mixture to a good rolling boil until it reaches 105°c on a sugar/jam thermometer, and boil for 2 minutes.

4   Add 125ml of Certo liquid pectin and bring back to a good boil up to 105°c, then keep boiling for a further minute.

5   Take the pan off the heat. Wait a couple of minutes for the bubbles to settle. Take the saucer out of the freezer and place a teaspoon of the jelly mixture on the cold plate. Wait for a minute then, using your finger, push the jelly gently and see if it wrinkles. If it does, the jelly is ready. (This is what is known as the wrinkle test.) If not, pop it back on the heat, bring back to 105°c, and boil for another minute before repeating the wrinkle test.

6   If you wish, carefully skim off the froth from the jelly. Stirring gently will also disperse the froth. You could add a knob of butter, but this will stop your jelly being dairy-free.

7   Pour the jelly through a sterilised strainer again into a sterilised jug, and pour into the sterilised jars, filling each jar to the brim. (This is where the saying jam-packed comes from.) Be very careful, as this mixture is extremely hot. Don't forget to use oven gloves when putting the jar tops on, as the glass jars will be hot, too.

8   Leave to cool overnight, then put a label on each jar and enjoy over the coming months.

Wild Berry Jelly-Jam

Makes 8 x 225g jars

Between July and October, nature provides us with an abundance of different berries – wild raspberries, brambles, bilberries, and rosehips. I use this wild berry jelly on toast, on digestive biscuits with cream cheese (try it!), in cakes and bakes, and in cheese and ham toasted sandwiches.

Sterilising Jam Jars – Jams and jelly-jams should be poured into warm sterilised jars. There are two simple ways to do this – putting the washed and drained jars and lids upside down in a cool oven (140°c) for 15 minutes, or putting them through a hot wash in the dishwasher.

Jam-Making Pan – I'd suggest investing in a stainless-steel preserving pan. These have a thick, heavy base for even heat distribution, and the wide, deep sides allow for a rapid boil without the jam mix burning or boiling over the sides of the pan.

Stir Gently – Throughout the jam-making, stir occasionally, gently using a long-handled wooden spoon – too often and vigorously allows cold air to enter the pan and extends the boiling time, spoiling your lovely fruit.

Straining the Fruit – To get all the lovely juices from the cooked fruit, strain the pulp through a jelly bag or clean nylon sieve held over a clean bowl. Make sure the jelly bag is held high enough above the bowl catching the juice, so that the strained juice does not touch the jelly bag or sieve. You can get a stand to hold these.

Keeping Your Jam – Your jam is ready to eat once cold. Sealed jars will keep for at least 12-18 months in a cool, dark place, but once opened, store in the fridge and use within a couple of weeks.

Ingredients

Stage 1

1.4 kg wild berries (I use mainly brambles but add in some wild raspberries, rosehips, and bilberries, if I can get my hands on any)

150 ml cold water

Stage 2

1.5 kg granulated sugar for each 1130ml of your wild berry juice

250ml pectin (I use Certo) for each 1130 ml of your wild berry juice

Juice of 1 lemon

8 x 225g sterilised jam jars and lids

Method

Stage 1

1 Put the wild berries in a large jelly pan with the water. No need to top and tail any of the fruit, but if you are using rosehips, cut these in half. Bring to the boil and simmer for 10-15 minutes until soft.

2 Empty the wild berries and all the juice into a muslin bag over a large bowl, and leave overnight for the juice to strain through. Don't be tempted to rush this stage or force the juice through the fruit, as this will result in a dull jelly-jam. You want a clear, bright jelly-jam, so take your time with this.

Stage 2

1 Place the strained juice (make up to 1130ml with cold water if you don't have enough) into a large jam-making pan with the sugar and lemon juice. Allow the sugar to melt slowly on the hob over a very low heat, stirring gently.

2 While the sugar is melting, place a saucer in your freezer, ready to use for testing the setting of your jelly.

3 Once the sugar has all dissolved, turn the heat up to high, bring the mixture to a good boil until it reaches 105.5oc on a sugar/jam thermometer.

4 Add the Certo and bring back to 105.5oc, then keep boiling for a further minute.

5 Take the pan off the heat. Wait a couple of minutes for the bubbles to settle. Take your saucer out of the freezer and place a teaspoon of the jelly mixture on the cold plate. Wait for a minute then, using your finger, push the jelly gently and see if it wrinkles. If it does, the jelly is ready. (This is what is known as the wrinkle test.) If not, pop the jelly back on the heat, bring back to 105.5oc, and boil for another minute before repeating the wrinkle test.

6 If you wish, carefully skim off the froth from the jelly. Stirring gently will also disperse the froth. You could add a knob of butter, but this will stop your jelly being dairy-free.

7 Pour the jelly through a sterilised strainer again into a sterilised jug and pour into the sterilised jars, filling each jar to the brim. (This is where the saying jam-packed comes from.) Be very careful, as this mixture is extremely hot. Don't forget to use oven gloves when putting the jar tops on, as the glass jars will be hot, too.

8 Leave to cool overnight, then put a label on each jar and enjoy over the coming months.

Finding an old pal

By around 2002, my working life was starting to change. I was now the training manager of a social care company and travelling throughout Scotland and Northern Ireland. Can you imagine it, getting paid to travel around Scotland to work in places like Fort William, Skye, and Stornoway? It really was like a dream come true for me. On a monthly basis I had to drive through Glencoe to get to my work and was just blown away by the scenery. I vividly remember struggling to deliver a training course in Fort William, because all I could see from the window was the amazing sight of magnificent Ben Nevis, with its zig-zag path going up the side of it. Many of my future adventures in the amazing Scottish hills and mountains were planned during these working travels.

It was whilst working for this company that I got to know a lady called Michelle, who just has to be one of the loveliest people I've had the pleasure to call my friend. Sometimes people come into your life and your life is just all the better because of it. Michelle was always smiling, always positive, and had a wicked sense of humour. However, as often happens, our lives went in different directions as our jobs changed and I moved around the country.

Through the power of Facebook, though, after not seeing or hearing from the lovely Michelle for over ten years, she popped back into my life. Where was she? Living just around the corner from the tearoom! It just goes to show that people are destined to be in your lives and you in theirs.

Now, when Michelle found out that not only was our tearoom round the corner from her house but that we had home-made lemon curd, it didn't take her long to visit. I still have this image of Michelle running along Thornhill Road, pushing people out of the way to get to the tearoom. Was it because she wanted to meet up with me again, or was it because she wanted the lemon curd? I know which one I choose to think is the case, and therefore it seemed right that our lemon curd should become Michelle's Lemon Curd.

Shop-bought lemon curd doesn't compare in the slightest to home-made lemon curd. Since making my first batch of lemon-curd, I've never bought a jar from the supermarket again. The only drawback of the home-made variety is that you can't keep it as long as a jar of jam, and it really needs to be kept in the fridge – although this never seems to be a problem for me!

Once you've tried this, I can guarantee that you'll find yourself going through all your recipe books looking for different goodies to put this treat into. Don't just stick to putting it on toast – although hot toast with home-made lemon curd is just a fabulous treat at any time. In the tearoom, I put this in our Victoria Sponges, fill muffins with it, use it to sandwich the Battenberg Cakes, and serve it with scones. One of our customer favourites, though, is when I use this in our Bakewell Tarts. Of course, ours is gluten free and dairy free, allowing more people to enjoy it.

I usually put out a lemon curd warning on Facebook, telling everyone I've made some, and the jars I have for sale disappear in a day or so. Of course, I always put one aside for Michelle.

Michelle has now set up her own company, Lifeline – Mind Body Soul – providing alternative and holistic services. If you have any aches or pains, you should try her KCR treatment. I have, and it's amazing!

As Michelle started to follow us on Facebook and be a visitor in the tearoom, she entered our competition to name our take-away afternoon teas. She won it with her suggestion of 'Posh Picnic'. So, if you come along to the tearoom and get one of our Posh Picnics, think of Michelle running back home along Thornhill Road, giggling, with her pockets full of jars of our home-made lemon curd.

Michelle and Debra

Michelle's Lemon Curd

Makes about 5 x 225g jars

Those people who say they don't like lemon curd have probably never tasted home-made lemon curd. It doesn't last for months or years like the commercial versions you can buy, but in my experience, home-made lemon curd never gets chance to last that long!

Try home-made lemon curd on hot toast, toasted crumpets, between two slices of thick bread, on scones, on digestive biscuits, inside cakes, inside cupcakes, or quite simply eaten straight from the jar.

Make sure you use un-waxed lemons, and buy the most expensive, biggest lemons you can. Don't be tempted to just use bottled lemon juice, as this doesn't give the amazing lemon flavour and smell you want. Oh… and take your time. Have yourself something to read between each zap in the microwave, and you'll not be tempted to rush.

Sterilising Jam Jars – Lemon curd should be poured into cold sterilised jars. There are two simple ways to do this – putting the washed and drained jars and lids upside down in a cool oven (140°c) for 15 minutes, or putting them through a hot wash in the dishwasher.

Keeping Your Lemon Curd – Your lemon curd is ready to eat once cold. Sealed jars will keep six weeks, stored in the fridge. Once opened, store in the fridge and use within seven days.

Ingredients

  200g stork block (or butter if you don't need this to be dairy-free)
  700g caster sugar
  Grated zest of 5 un-waxed lemons
  5-7 un-waxed lemons, depending on their size – you will need 300ml lemon juice
  5 free range eggs, lightly beaten
  5 x 225g sterilised jam jars and lids

Method

1   *Put the stork, sugar, lemon zest, and lemon juice in a large microwavable bowl on full power for two minutes. Stir and put in again for two minutes at a time until the stork and sugar have dissolved.*

2   *Add the beaten eggs and continue to cook in two-minute bursts, stirring each time. As the mixture starts to thicken, reduce the bursts to one minute. Do this until the mixture is thick enough to coat the back of a spoon. Be patient with this stage.*

3   *Strain the mixture through a sieve into a large wide jug to remove the lemon zest, any pips, and any cooked egg bits.*

4   *Pour the lemon curd into cooled sterilised jars and seal with a lid.*

5   *Once cooled, label and store in the fridge.*

6   *This will keep for six weeks unopened in the fridge. Once opened, though, use within seven days.*

Breakfast at the tearoom

Breakfast is referred to as the most important meal of the day, but in my younger days mine was often something containing chocolate. Growing up in Halifax, the home of Rowntree Mackintosh (now Nestlé) where my mum worked, I thought it was normal for homes to be filled with white bags of unwrapped, mis-shaped chocolate bars and sweets.

To add to this, one of my aunties worked at the other large employer in Halifax, United Biscuits (McVities), supplying us with equally mis-shaped biscuits. How I survived childhood without losing my teeth or becoming diabetic is still a mystery!

I've always enjoyed walking and having time to myself. Sometimes, when the world seemed heavy around me with no-one and nowhere to turn to, walking alone helped, especially if surrounded by lovely scenery and views – and the local area of Northowram and the Shibden Valley was perfect for this.

In my early teens I had a morning paper round and was up with the larks to deliver papers around the local country lanes. Yes, all you young readers, news used to be printed on paper to be delivered through letterboxes by hard-working youngsters earning pocket money.

Debra as a young cyclst

Being high in the Pennines, winters were often very snowy and the roads blocked for what seemed weeks with un-cleared snow (in reality, this was probably just for a few days). Of course, there were not as many cars then, so not as many people had the need to shift tonnes of snow.

Trudging round my morning paper route one severe winter, I had to walk in the footsteps of the local postman because the snow was so deep. Thinking back to this, I'm warmed by the actions of this unknown postman who was probably keeping a sneaky eye on this sad, often weeping young lass, laden down with heavy newspapers in the heavy snow, and lacking any other sustenance other than two unwrapped toffee crisps.

My secondary education was at a girls' grammar school with only about 350 pupils, about three miles and two bus journeys away from my house. I've always been a terrible traveller, prone to a bit of travel sickness (and still am), so I hated those bus journeys. To add to the travel sickness, the buses seemed full of schoolchildren who were all friends with each other, but I was trying to escape the noise and laughter because I didn't know how to join in with them. I often heard people saying what a loner I was and in a world of my own, when in reality I was just a young girl needing somebody to sit with me, stay a while, and hear my thoughts.

Once my little sister started school, it was my job to walk her to the local infant school before heading off to my grammar school. Sometimes my bus journey, even though it took me through the lovely Shibden Valley, was more than I could bear. Even knowing that I'd be late for morning registration and suffer the wrath of Mrs Arnold, my form teacher and French teacher, I'd often choose to 'miss' the bus and walk. Of course, more biscuits and sweets helped the journey. This was probably my only bit of planned naughtiness throughout my whole life!

As cycling became a serious hobby of mine, the contents of breakfast took on much more importance, and I'm pleased to say that the whole of my childhood wasn't spent having toffee crisps to start the day. The photo below is me as a 13-year-old in the early years of my cycling. Look at the old-fashioned shoes and toe clips! If you look closely, you can probably see a toffee crisp in my back pocket!

In the tearoom, we're conscious that mealtimes are very different for everyone. Sometimes when you're having dinner, others are just having breakfast or are even already on their tea. (Remembering, of course, that in Yorkshire we have breakfast, dinner, tea, and supper!) We made a conscious decision when opening the tearoom to ensure that if somebody wanted a breakfast roll in the afternoon, they could have one . Our motto is 'It's never too late for breakfast', though they do need to get into the tearoom before 3pm when hot food finishes – a rule that has been known to be broken when presented with a sad face or a hungry-looking worker.

It's not 3 o'clock yet!

Bear with me here. It's not my intention to suggest that people don't know how to make French Toast or that it's a difficult recipe. There is a book entitled, If Nobody Speaks of Remarkable Things, but in the kitchen, a similar saying could be made: 'If nobody speaks of the simple things.' What could seem like a very simple thing for one person could be daunting for another. For that reason, French Toast is included in my book.

In the tearoom, French Toast wasn't originally on the menu. One day, a customer came in feeling a bit under the weather and couldn't decide what to have. A few suggestions were made, and somehow eggy bread came into the conversation. Well, you know how it is. Once one person sees and smells something, they then order it, tell somebody else about it, and before you know it, it's become a staple item on the menu.

Yvonne

And it's here that I have a confession to make. I'm not very good at making French Toast. In truth, I'm rubbish at making French Toast. Mr M is the French Toast master. I did make it one day and the customer looked sadly at it and said, 'Oh!' Say no more! That's my whole point of adding this into the book. I can bake the fiddliest cakes and biscuits, but sometimes a simple thing can beat me and I'm not ashamed admit it.

We now serve French Toast in the tearoom just as it comes or with crispy bacon, but also get some strange requests. We've made French Toast topped with poached egg, served with sugar, with maple syrup, and even black pudding. However you want yours is the best way for us to serve it to you.

Why Yvonne's French toast, you might ask. Well, the tearoom had been open for about a year when Yvonne made her first visit to Mother Murphy's, quiet as a mouse and hardly speaking to anyone at all. We chatted, and then each time she came in, we got to know her a little more. Over time, Yvonne's confidence grew and her cheeky personality started to show through. It wasn't long before she became a regular in the tearoom, and she is now part of the Mother Murphy's Tearoom family.

One of her favourite things to do was to arrive at the tearoom on a Sunday afternoon at around 2.45pm (we stop serving hot food at 3pm) and order French Toast with crispy bacon. We always have a joke that she's too late for hot food – but she always manages to get her way!

We don't mind, though, and one day we'll have her French Toast ready for her as she arrives.

Yvonne's French Toast (Eggy Bread)

Serves 1 - Can be made gf/df

I'm pleased to say that I've now progressed to making French Toast in the tearoom. Margaret (of Margaret's Lemon Drizzle) has this most Thursdays, and even gives her thumbs-up to my French Toast now.

Ingredients

Two slices of white bread (gf if preferred)
2 free range eggs
A large dash of milk (dairy-free milk if preferred)
Knob of butter (dairy-free if preferred)

Method

1   *Melt a knob of butter in a small non-stick frying pan.*

2   *Break the two eggs into a small bowl, add a dash of milk, and whisk with a fork.*

3   *Slice the two pieces of bread in half.*

4   *Dip each piece of bread in the egg mixture to coat both sides thoroughly.*

5   *Put all four pieces of egg-soaked bread into the hot frying pan on a medium heat.*

6   *Once golden brown, turn the bread over and cook the other side until golden brown.*

7   *Serve immediately.*

Margret giving the thumbs up to my French Toast

Simple ingredients prepared in a simple way - that's the best way to take your everyday cooking to a higher level.

Jose Andres

Do your worst Mr M!

Just like poached eggs and French Toast, omelettes are one of those things that can be easy to make once you know how. Did you know that many food establishments buy in ready-made omelettes! That's right; along with ready-made fried eggs, scrambled eggs, and poached eggs. Next time you go to a buffet breakfast somewhere, make sure your eggs haven't been lying under the heat lamp for hours.

As with French Toast, omelettes were not originally on our menu in the tearoom, but just sort of crept their way onto it. I'm not the best at making omelettes and get in a bit of a panic if Mr M isn't in the tearoom to make them. I have to admit that it's not the first time I've told customers they can have anything off the menu except for French Toast and omelettes when I've been there alone. Some customers come along to the tearoom especially for Mr M's omelettes, but sadly, I've not yet heard anyone saying they've travelled across the country to sample one of my omelettes!

Judith, Brian and Nicky

One customer who does come for Mr M's omelettes is the lovely Brian, who travels all the way from Dunfermline. Brian and his wife, Nicky, first came to the tearoom in search of safe gluten free food for Nicky. I think they called in for a cup of tea and piece of cake, but stayed all day. Since then, they've become regulars, and are now certainly a big part of our tearoom family. Many a very enjoyable afternoon has been spent chatting away to Brian and Nicky. They may not live in Falkirk, but they are certainly known by lots of our regular local customers now. Our tearoom is just that sort of place, where strangers very quickly become friends.

Brian and Nicky are full of fun and certainly up for a good get-together and singsong if the opportunity arises, and have probably been to more live gigs than most people can ever hope to. Whenever possible, they've attended our Afternoon Tea for 16 events. I think the one that sticks out in my mind the most is the Old-Fashioned/Victorian Afternoon Tea. People attending that day turned up in some absolutely fantastic costumes. We had a Victorian singer, a couple of Victorian barmaids, and a Victorian swimmer. I was a Victorian waitress and Mr M ended up being part of a Laurel and Hardy double act with Dashing Tom. We even had a Suffragette and a girl from Poldark.

Then Brian and Nicky turned up in all their finery. Nicky was certainly a posh lady, with an equally dapper husband at her side. They introduced themselves to the party as a Posh Lady and her Husband. So, they are now fondly known as 'the posh folk' at the tearoom.

When Brian sits down at the table, you know he's desperate for a good latte and a plate of wholesome food. It's not the first time he's said to Mr M to just put him something together. Very often, this ends up being an omelette. On one occasion, Mr M asked Brian what he'd like in his omelette and Brian said, 'Do your worst, Mr M.' Well, Mr M didn't disappoint him.

I chuckled to myself in the kitchen as I watched Mr M thinking about what he could put in this ultimate dish. The finished omelette was absolutely jam-packed, with bacon, sausage, peppers, onion, cheese, and black pudding. All this was served with a lovely caramel latte and two slices of hot buttered toast. Brian's face was a picture when he saw it. Not a morsel was left, mind you.

Therefore, it only seemed fitting that our omelettes should become the Posh Woman's Husband's Omelettes.

At the afternoon tea, some people brought along jokes and stories to tell. Here's Brian's joke:

Q) What's the difference between a kangaroo and a kangaroot?
A) A kangaroo lives in Australia, and a kangaroot is a Geordie stuck in a lift.

The Posh Woman's Husband's Omelette

Serves 1 person

Ingredients

2 free range eggs
Splash of milk
Your choice of filling such as:
- *Chopped peppers*
- *Sliced tomato*
- *Sliced onion*
- *Grated cheese*
- *Grilled bacon*
- *Cooked ham*

Method

1. *Break the eggs into a small bowl.*
2. *Add two splashes of milk and whisk gently with a fork to blend.*
3. *Put a small knob of butter in an omelette pan, and heat on a medium on the hob until the butter has melted and coated the bottom of the pan.*
4. *Pour the egg mixture into the pan and allow to cook until the egg is no longer liquid.*
5. *Add the filling of your choice at this point, covering just half of the omelette.*
6. *Using a spatula, lift the edge of the omelette to check if it's cooked. If it's lightly browned, fold the omelette over on itself.*
7. *Cook for a further minute or two to your choice.*
8. *Carefully slide the omelette from the pan onto a serving plate.*
9. *Serve with two slices of hot buttered toast.*

My amazing grandma

Grandma Lammie was just my favourite person. She was Scottish through and through, but had lived in Halifax all my life. I recall fondly how she liked to shop in the little Tesco store in Halifax, as there she could get her favourite Scottish Plain loaf. I remember the waxy feel of the wrapper with its design that stood out from the rest of the loaves on the shelf.

She was also partial to the Scotch Pancakes she could buy there, and her afternoon treat was to have a pancake with butter and jam, along with a cup of tea – in her china cup, of course. By the time I'd started to visit Scotland on a regular basis, before moving up here, my beloved Grandma was already very ill. One of the requests she made was for me to bring her back a proper macaroon bar. On my next visit, I did just that, and I still remember Grandma's face as she nibbled at the macaroon bar. Naturally, she wanted me to share in this delight, which I happily did, and we had a very pleasant time chatting about Scotland. Sadly, there were not very many more memories to be shared with Grandma after that. I, of course, never had the heart to tell Grandma that I didn't like the macaroon bar!

It's with pride that one of the most surprising successes we've had in the tearoom has to be our pancakes. This recipe is an adaptation of a few recipes I have found over the years, but it's now been changed to be both gluten free and dairy free.

The most popular request for these is to be served with crispy bacon and maple syrup. Some customers even ask for crispy bacon, maple syrup, and banana. Personally, just a good dollop of home-made jam or lemon curd does it for me. I am my Grandma!

I always try to make sure that if we are serving a gluten free and dairy free product, then it must be as good as a wheat and dairy version. And these lovely pancakes certainly fall into that category.

I remember one customer coming in with his family and asking for pancakes, adding, 'But don't give me the gluten free rubbish.' I advised him that we only serve gluten free ones, and that if he didn't like them I wouldn't charge him for them and we'd make him something else. The plate was almost licked clean, and he then had the nerve to ask for the recipe as he left the tearoom!

Grandma and Grandad Lammie

Jade

One of the benefits of getting new customers in the tearoom is that they then tell the rest of their family and friends about us. I'm pleased to say that this happened with the Isdale family. First Beverley came in, who brought along her dad, Dashing Tom, who then brought in his son, Allan, who then brought his daughter Jade.

If ever there was somebody that looked forward to her visits to the tearoom it's this little girl who is always well mannered, pleasant, and always, always with a lovely, beaming smile. It has to be pancakes for Jade at each visit, with some butter and a potato scone. She always tells us that Mother Murphy's is her favourite tearoom, and we always tell Jade that she's our favourite customer.

Jade's Scotch Pancakes

Makes about 35 pancakes

Ingredients

Pancake Flour Mixture
320g rice flour

240g cornflour

100g ground almonds

2 teaspoons xanthan gum

For the Pancakes
520g of the Pancake Flour Mixture

100g caster sugar

1 teaspoon salt

4 teaspoons gluten free baking powder

2 teaspoons bicarbonate of soda

1000ml almond milk

4 free range eggs, lightly beaten

160g stork margarine block melted

Method

Making the Pancake Flour Mixture

1   Place all the ingredients for the Pancake Flour Mixture in a large bowl and mix well. Store in an airtight container until you need it.

Making the Pancakes

1   Put the almond milk and eggs in the free-standing mixer or large bowl, and beat lightly until well blended.

2   Add the melted stork to the milk mixture and beat until well blended.

3   In another bowl, mix 520g of your Pancake Flour Mixture with the sugar, salt, baking powder, and bicarbonate of soda.

4   With the mixer on a slow speed, add the dry ingredients to the egg mixture, one tablespoon at a time, until it has all been added.

5   Once all the flour mixture has been added, turn the mixer up to medium speed and whisk until you have a smooth batter with no lumps. Remember to turn the mixer off and use a spatula to scrape the bottom of the bowl to make sure there are no lumps at the bottom.

6   Heat the griddle pan over a medium heat, or use a pancake maker.

7   Using a small ice cream scoop, pour a dollop of batter on the hot griddle to make a pancake. I can cook 4 pancakes at one time on my electric pancake maker. Cook until bubbles form on the surface of the batter, then flip the pancake and cook until golden brown.

8   Repeat with the remaining mixture.

9   Serve warm with your choice of topping.

10 If you are not eating them straight away, as you take the pancakes off the griddle, place them on a clean tea towel to cool. Once cold, these freeze perfectly and just need re-heating on the griddle for a minute or two.

11 Get yourself 3 warm pancakes straight from the griddle, though, and spread them with a great helping of chocolate Nutella spread, and think of Jade enjoying her favourite treat.

I think cookery shows have become so sophisticated, and everyone's so marvellous at it, but there are people like me who aren't into the cooking malarkey, who still don't know how to boil an egg for three minutes.

Anton Du Beke

Just get yourself an egg-poacher

For the same reason that French Toast has been included in this book, the humble poached egg has also been added. If you look hard enough, you can find lots of different hints and tips on poaching eggs from the top chefs, such as add vinegar to the pan and whisk before adding the eggs; crack the eggs into cling-film… If you ask me, the easiest way to get perfect poached eggs is to buy a 4-hole egg poacher. The poached eggs come out perfect every time, with cooked whites and just runny yolks.

Personally, I can cope with eating an egg that's a little overdone, but can't stomach a poached egg with the white still slimy. Once you get used to your pan and your hob, you'll quickly learn how long your eggs take to be just right for you.

In the tearoom, we serve poached eggs by themselves, on toast, on gluten free toast, on pancakes, in a roll, and have even served them on French Toast. I like mine on a couple pieces of toasted and buttered home-made soda bread. However you like to eat yours is perfect.

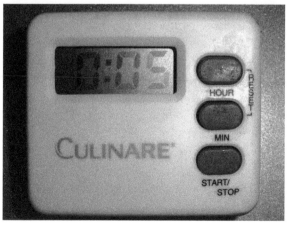

Poached Eggs

Serves 1

Ingredients

    2 Scottish free-range eggs

    Knob of butter (dairy free if preferred)

Method

1   *Put enough water in the egg poaching pan to fill to about a third full, and bring to the boil. Don't put too much water in or the water will boil up over the eggs as they poach.*

2   *Coat the egg holders with butter or oil of your choice.*

3   *Once the water is boiling, break an egg into each of the holders.*

4   *Put the lid on the pan and set your timer or watch for 5 minutes.*

5   *Whilst the eggs are poaching, put your toast on.*

6   *Once the timer bleeps, take the eggs off the heat.*

7   *If the whites of the eggs look firm, the eggs will be cooked. Carefully tip your eggs out onto your hot buttered toast. If the eggs seem stuck to the holder, use a palette knife to gently ease them out.*

8   *Enjoy.*

A border collie, deer, geese, and a buzzard

The alarm goes off every morning at 6am, waking me up with a heart-stopping noise. A quick jump in the shower then I'm off out of the door with Beatrix, our Border Collie dog. I walk the same route for roughly six months of the year, heading off down a single-track road, along a bridle path, and finally the canal towpath – a walk of about 35-40 minutes, though it's too dark in the winter months in Scotland to do this walk at 6am.

Beatrix our Border Collie

Sometimes I have the pleasure of observing the deer, seeing the geese fly in formation, watching the buzzard fly overhead, or simply having a heart-to-heart with Beatrix. Those of you with dogs will fully understand how I can have deep and meaningful conversations with my Border collie. Those of you who've never had a dog will probably now be thinking that I'm straight out of Alice in Wonderland.

Do I mind getting up early in all weathers? Not at all. I could be watching the early sunrise, seeing the fog lifting, feeling the rain on my face but, no matter what the weather, I always enjoy those 40 minutes of peace and a sense of freedom.

By the time I'm heading back home, I'm always looking forward to my breakfast, which will be just ready for serving when I return. The benefit of undertaking the morning walk is that Mr M is on porridge duty. Slow-cooked porridge with warm blueberries – yummy! I'm quite ashamed to admit that Mr M puts warm mashed banana in his porridge. Never, ever, in my porridge, though!

Growing up, I couldn't face eating porridge, after being given some prepared by my Scottish Grandad who made it with water and salt! Fortunately, many years later I watched a programme following the World Porridge Making Contest, when the winner was making his porridge and adding warmed fruit to it, and I've been hooked on porridge ever since. I really do now feel something is missing from my day if

Two deer following us

I've not started it with a bowl of warm porridge – even in the summer months. If I can sit out in the garden eating my porridge, all the better… even if it does mean sitting with my coat and hat on.

Porridge is served in the tearoom and prepared in the same way as we do at home. There's no rushing the process in the microwave or using the horrendous instant oat pots. We only use certified gluten free oats in the tearoom, so everyone has gluten free porridge (but not everyone realises this).

Porridge And Blueberries

Serves 1 person

Ingredients

30g Scots gluten free porridge oats
250ml milk (I use skimmed)
A good handful of fresh blueberries

Method

1   *Put the oats and milk in a pan, and put on the lowest heat you can on your hob. Allow to cook slowly, barely bubbling.*

2   *Stir occasionally to prevent it sticking to the bottom of the pan. The oats will soak up the milk, and the porridge is ready when it is the consistency you prefer. I like mine when it is still a little bit runny, but others like to be able to stand the spoon it. However you like it is perfect!*

3   *Whilst the porridge is cooking, put the fruit in a small pan and warm gently on the hob, or pop it in the microwave for 30 seconds.*

4   *Put the porridge into your favourite dish, top with the warm fruit, and enjoy. Cooking the oats slowly seems to bring out the sweetness in them, but you can add sugar or honey if you choose.*

Lunch at the tearoom

Mother Murphy's Tearoom has a simple menu, not because we're not capable of cooking fancy, exotic foods, but because we set out to be a traditional tearoom with simple food that people recognise and remember. Our customers look for things they know – sandwiches with fillings they recognise and, of course, cakes they remember from their childhood and growing up.

The other reason is to allow us to cook everything ourselves fresh to order. There is no hot holding of food or pre-preparing of sandwiches. We have a sign on our board that says, 'Everything is cooked to order and there may be a short wait for your yummy food. Thank you for your patience.' We very rarely get complaints from people having to wait for their food, as we're the type of tearoom where everyone talks to each other. The wait for food is just a chance to chat, gossip, sneak in a bit of crochet or crafting, and browse through our small hand-made gift and card selection.

When I'm out in restaurants, cafes, and tearooms, I'm often amazed at their huge menu. Either these places employ a whole army of chefs and bakers, or they buy in their foods pre-prepared. Yes, there really are places that buy in pre-cooked omelettes and even pre-cooked fried eggs. Who would have thought you could even buy (or want to buy) pre-cooked fried eggs!

As I said in the introduction to Breakfast at the Tearoom, we serve all food from our menu all day, but stop offering hot food at 3pm. Everyone is different and has different tastes, needs, and lifestyles. So, if you'd like to pick from our breakfast menu at 2pm in the tearoom, that's fine by us. I'm a bit the same, and often you'll catch me having a bowl of porridge in the afternoon.

Making a toddler eat her veg

It still amazes me how much soup is loved by the lovely people in Scotland especially, it would seem, if the soup should happen to be lentil. Mr M is no exception, and if given the chance, I'm sure he'd happily eat soup for his breakfast.

When the tearoom first opened, we tried lots of different recipes and types of soups, but being just a small tearoom, we couldn't justify having more than one soup a day. As we were catering for those with coeliac disease, we had to ensure that our one soup was totally gluten free, right down to the stock we used. This ruled out minestrone or even Scotch broth – thankfully, I say. Who even likes pearl barley?! We also had to ensure that it was dairy free to fit in with our 'Delicious Without' range (gluten free and dairy free).

This meant that there could be no cheese or cream added to the soups. Mind you, if you ask me, I don't think cheese or cream should go anywhere near soup!

Then, of course, we wanted to ensure we could provide a nice home-made soup for anyone who is vegetarian – pea soup was ok, but no pea and ham soup. We did worry about having to limit our soup choices in the tearoom, but need not have stressed at all as we quickly found out that whilst a few customers would like the fancy varieties, the majority of our customers just wanted lentil soup.

In saying that, I've added a few of our different soups into this section, including my favourite Orange Pepper soup which I started making when my daughter, Chloe, was only about two years old. Chloe was a sickly child and incredibly fussy with her food. Worried she would starve to death or have some major deficiencies, as she seemed to live on lightly toasted white bread, I saw this soup in a magazine and was immediately taken by its bright orange colour. A totally blended, smooth, bright orange soup; could I make this and fool my little one into eating something healthy without her knowing it? I set about making the soup – sweet orange peppers, carrots, potatoes, onion, and garlic, along with some lovely home-made white bread rolls. Teatime came and Chloe climbed up onto her seat and I could almost sense that she was preparing to toss aside her food as usual. I put a small bowl of the soup in front of her with a small roll. No fuss, no questions, no tantrums. Before I knew it, Chloe was asking for more! Whenever I'm going to see Chloe now, she still asks me if I'm making her orange pepper soup.

Now, if I had my own way, all soups would be completely blended. That way I wouldn't know what strange and weird vegetables are hidden in them. However, like I keep saying, you can't please everyone all of the time. Some customers like a blended soup, some a chunky soup. To blend or not to blend, the choice is yours.

Of course, once we had invested in a gigantic blender for Mr M to use in the tearoom, he was always happy to produce a blended soup. No more messing with the food processor. Boys and their toys!

Our soup recipes make a giant pot of soup – adjust the quantities to suit your own needs, but they do freeze well. You can pop them into soup freezer pouches or small containers, perfect to pull out of the freezer for a quick ready-made meal.

Mr M. blitzing the soup

Only the pure in heart can make a good soup.

Ludwig Van Beethoven

Andrina's Carrot And Coriander Soup

Andrina

This recipe makes a big pot of soup. Adjust the quantities accordingly if you want to make a smaller pot, but it does freeze well.

If you're going to be making a lot of soups, it's worth investing in a large stainless-steel soup pot. These pans have deep sides, a fitted lid, can hold lots of soup, and have a special base to help the pot heat up quickly and evenly. They can be washed in the dishwasher and are suitable for all heat sources. For smaller amounts, use your largest, deepest pan with a lid.

Andrina is one of our earliest customers. Arriving at the tearoom on her first visit, she sat herself in a corner eating a piece of Coffee Cake. A few days later she came back and started to chat, then quickly became one of our regulars, enjoying the laughter, chat, and safety of the quiet tearoom. Andrina has tried lots of different crafts, but if truth be known, she is happiest sitting with a bowl of soup, a bacon sandwich, latte, and choosing which cake to have with her second latte.

One of Andrina's favourite soups was the carrot and coriander soup. This is a refreshing soup – not quite as thick and filling as our carrot and sweet potato, but equally good.

Ingredients

  1 tablespoon olive oil
  4 onions, peeled and sliced
  4lb carrots, topped, tailed, peeled, and sliced
  6 potatoes, peeled and chopped
  3 teaspoons ground coriander
  4.5 litres of cold water mixed with 125g Knorr Vegetable Bouillon paste
  Large bunch of fresh coriander, roughly chopped
  Salt and freshly ground black pepper to taste

Method

1. *Heat the oil in a large pan. Add the onions and carrots and cook for 3-4 minutes until they start to soften.*

2. *Stir in the ground coriander, season to taste and cook for a further minute.*

3. *Add the chopped potatoes and stock and bring to the boil.*

4. *Simmer until the vegetables are tender.*

5. *Allow to cool for a few minutes and blend until smooth.*

6. *If freezing, pour into freezer containers and freeze once cooled.*

Carrot And Sweet Potato Soup

This recipe makes a big pot of soup. Adjust the quantities accordingly if you want to make a smaller pot, but it does freeze well.

If you're going to be making a lot of soups, it's worth investing in a large stainless-steel soup pot. These pans have deep sides, a fitted lid, can hold lots of soup, and have a special base to help the pot heat up quickly and evenly. They can be washed in the dishwasher and are suitable for all heat sources. For smaller amounts, use your largest, deepest pan with a lid.

I was never a sweet potato fan but, made into a soup, this is almost as comforting as Chloe's Orange Pepper Soup. Who would have thought I'd find myself enjoying vegetables! I did insist that Mr M made this into a fully blended soup for me, though.

Ingredients

1 tablespoon olive oil

3 onions, peeled and chopped

6 tablespoons fresh root ginger, chopped

9 large carrots, topped, tailed, peeled, and chopped

3 large sweet potatoes, peeled, and chopped

4.5 litres of cold water mixed with 125g Knorr Vegetable Bouillon paste

6 garlic cloves, peeled and chopped

Salt and black pepper to taste

Method

1   *Heat the oil and lightly fry the onions in olive oil for about 10 minutes or until soft.*

2   *Add the ginger and garlic and cook for 1 minute.*

3   *Add the carrots and sweet potato and cook for two minutes, stirring.*

4   *Add the water and stock paste and bring to the boil.*

5   *Lower the heat, add the seasoning, and simmer until the vegetables are tender.*

6   *Allow to cool for a few minutes and blend until smooth.*

7   *If freezing, pour into freezer containers and freeze once cooled.*

Whatever I'm doing, I'm in that moment and I'm doing it. The rest of the world's lost. If I'm cooking some food or making soup, I want it to be lovely. If not, what's the point of doing it?

Sade (Singer and Musician)

Chloe's Orange Pepper Soup

This recipe makes a big pot of soup. Adjust the quantities accordingly if you want to make a smaller pot, but it does freeze well.

If you're going to be making a lot of soups, it's worth investing in a large stainless-steel soup pot. These pans have deep sides, a fitted lid, can hold lots of soup, and have a special base to help the pot heat up quickly and evenly. They can be washed in the dishwasher and are suitable for all heat sources. For smaller amounts, use your largest, deepest pan with a lid.

As mentioned in the introduction to soups, I started making this soup when my daughter, Chloe, was only about two years old. If, like I was, you're struggling to get children to eat their vegetables, try some of this. With its bright orange colour and totally blended, they'll not even know what they are eating. Chloe would still have me make this for her every time I see her, though she loves to make it herself now for her own family.

Ingredients

1 tablespoon olive oil

1 onion, peeled and chopped

6 cloves of garlic, peeled and chopped

8 orange peppers, deseeded and chopped

9 large carrots, topped, tailed, peeled, and chopped

9 large potatoes, peeled and chopped

4.5 litres of cold water mixed with 125g Knorr Vegetable Bouillon paste

Salt and black pepper to taste

Method

1. *Heat the oil and lightly fry the onion, garlic and peppers for about 10 minutes or until soft.*

2. *Add the carrots and potato and cook for two minutes, stirring.*

3. *Add the water and stock paste and bring to the boil.*

4. *Lower the heat, add the seasoning and simmer until the vegetables are tender.*

5. *Allow to cool for a few minutes and blend until smooth.*

6. *If freezing, pour into freezer containers and freeze once cooled.*

Leek And Potato Soup

This recipe makes a big pot of soup. Adjust the quantities accordingly if you want to make a smaller pot, but it does freeze well.

If you're going to be making a lot of soups, it's worth investing in a large stainless-steel soup pot. These pans have deep sides, a fitted lid, can hold lots of soup, and have a special base to help the pot heat up quickly and evenly. They can be washed in the dishwasher and are suitable for all heat sources. For smaller amounts, use your largest, deepest pan with a lid.

In my time up in Scotland, I've been surprised to find the different traditions that take place at funeral teas. I was first introduced to Leek and Potato Soup at one said funeral, and was really not quite sure how I was going to eat it. Already trying to mop up my tears, I was also trying to hide the fact that I couldn't face eating the bowl of soup in front of me with its gigantic pieces of leek floating around. So, I simply swirled my spoon around a few times, wiped my mouth with the napkin, and looked apologetically at the other people who were tucking into their soup with obvious pleasure. By the time the steak pie arrived, I was ready to tuck into that, though! And there was me thinking that you just got curled-up sandwiches and sausage rolls at a funeral tea.

In the tearoom, when we started to make our different soups, I managed to persuade Mr M to make his soup with smaller pieces of leek. It was still not a blended soup, but I could actually enjoy this with more manageable chunks of leek.

Ingredients

1 tablespoon olive oil

8 leeks, washed and sliced

6 medium potatoes, peeled and chopped into large chunks

6 medium carrots, topped, tailed, peeled, and grated

4.5 litres of cold water mixed with 125g Knorr Vegetable Bouillon paste

2 bay leaves

Salt and ground pepper to taste

2 handfuls of fresh parsley, chopped

Method

1 *Slice and lightly fry the leeks in the olive oil for about 10 minutes or until soft.*

2 *Add the water, stock paste, potatoes, grated carrot, and bay leaves.*

3 *Bring to boil then turn down the heat and simmer for about 45 minutes to an hour until soft.*

4 *Season to taste and remove the bay leaves.*

5 *Add the chopped parsley.*

6 *If freezing, pour into freezer containers and freeze once cooled.*

Jim's Lentil Soup

This recipe makes a big pot of soup. Adjust the quantities accordingly if you want to make a smaller pot, but it does freeze well.

If you're going to be making a lot of soups, it's worth investing in a large stainless-steel soup pot. These pans have deep sides, a fitted lid, can hold lots of soup, and have a special base to help the pot heat up quickly and evenly. They can be washed in the dishwasher and are suitable for all heat sources. For smaller amounts, use your largest, deepest pan with a lid.

Of all the different soups we made in the tearoom, Jim's Lentil Soup was by far the most popular. Some people would go without soup, if lentil wasn't on the menu that day. Mind you, they never saw the disaster we had one day when Mr M dropped a whole, opened, giant bag of lentils in the kitchen. It felt like we were picking up lentils for months afterwards, but I've not tasted a lentil soup anywhere to match Mr M's.

Ingredients

1 tablespoons olive oil
1lb leeks, washed and sliced
3lb carrots, topped, tailed, peeled, and grated
4.5 litres cold water mixed with 125g Knorr Vegetable Bouillon paste
1lb red lentils, washed.
Salt and freshly ground black pepper to taste

Method

1   *Slice the leeks, grate the carrots, and lightly fry in the olive oil for about 10 minutes or until soft.*

2   *Add the water and stock paste and bring to the boil*

3   *Add the lentils and gently bring back to the boil.*

4   *Simmer for around 45 minutes to 1 hour, stirring regularly to prevent the lentils from sticking to the bottom of the pan.*

5   *Season to taste*

6   *If freezing, pour into freezer containers and freeze once cooled.*

Jim enjoying the fruits of his labour

Split Pea Soup

This recipe makes a big pot of soup. Adjust the quantities accordingly if you want to make a smaller pot, but it does freeze well.

If you're going to be making a lot of soups, it's worth investing in a large stainless-steel soup pot. These pans have deep sides, a fitted lid, can hold lots of soup, and have a special base to help the pot heat up quickly and evenly. They can be washed in the dishwasher and are suitable for all heat sources. For smaller amounts, use your largest, deepest pan with a lid.

I was a little unsure about us making this in the tearoom. My experience of pea soup had always been pea and ham, and I can almost taste the salt just thinking about it! As we were making our soups suitable for vegetarians, the ham had to go – so ours became simply split pea. I persuaded Mr M to have this as one of his totally blended soups and, together with the addition of the cumin, he changed this unassuming soup from being bland and salty to a lovely, smooth, velvety, slightly spicy, comforting and warming soup.

Gus and Denise are two of our lovely customers who just make you smile talking to them, as they are both full of mischief, with a great sense of humour. Gus often manages to sneak in solo visits to the tearoom, and I enjoy an hour or so chatting to him about my exploits on the hills, or listening to him recalling his walking and climbing days in the Lake District and Scottish mountains.

The Split Pea Soup was one of their favourite choices, followed of course by a cake or two and some Earl Grey Tea or a Cappuccino.

Denise and Gus

Ingredients

1 x 16oz bag of dried split peas

1 tablespoon olive oil

1 teaspoon salt

2 onions, peeled and chopped

4 carrots, topped, tailed, peeled, and chopped

4 celery sticks, chopped

3 medium potatoes, peeled and chopped

1 teaspoon ground cumin

4.5 litres cold water mixed with 125g Knorr Vegetable Bouillon paste

Salt and black pepper to taste

2 bay leaves

Method

1. *Soak the split peas overnight in cold water.*

2. *Heat the oil and sauté the onions and cook for about 10 minutes or until soft.*

3. *Add the celery, carrots, potatoes, cumin, pepper, ¼ litre of water, and cook for another 5 minutes.*

4. *Add the drained split peas, remaining water, stock paste, and bay leaves.*

5. *Bring to a boil then simmer for around 60-90 minutes until the peas have softened, stirring to make sure the soup does not stick to the bottom of the pan.*

6. *Remove the bay leaves and blend the soup.*

7. *Season with salt and pepper as required.*

8. *If freezing, pour into freezer containers and freeze once cooled.*

Home-Made Coleslaw

Makes a large bowl

Coleslaw! I can just hear everyone saying, 'Does she think we are so stupid that we don't know how to make this?!' In my defence, when I wanted to make some coleslaw for the first time, I had to go hunting on the internet and searching my recipe books for a simple recipe. It's the same old thing, really – what might seem like a simple thing for some people to do can be difficult for somebody else until they've been shown how to make it.

'When I rule the world, cabbage will be banned,' I told everyone when I wrote my very serious manifesto for Mother Murphy for Prime Minister, but was promptly reminded by our customers that we wouldn't then be able to serve our wonderful home-made coleslaw. My manifesto was quickly amended to banning cooked cabbage!

I believe it's the simplicity that makes our coleslaw so lovely. I'd never made coleslaw before we opened the tearoom, but had tasted lots of different ones when eating out. Some were ok, but most of them were not to my liking and tasted quite bitter. There were also some that had strange and unknown ingredients hiding in them, only to be discovered once you had popped a forkful into your mouth.

We debated whether we should make our own coleslaw or buy in a ready-made version. As we were trying to have the menu at the tearoom made by ourselves, as much as possible, we started to make our own. We opted to go for minimal ingredients, but using the best quality mayonnaise we could. Using the lovely Hellman's mayonnaise, we were able to ensure that the coleslaw would be still both gluten free and dairy free.

Our coleslaw recipe is very simple, easy to make, and our customers just love it. This recipe makes a huge bowl, but just adapt the ingredients for your needs. We serve a small dish of our coleslaw with all our meals and sandwiches. Another popular choice is to have our coleslaw on a jacket potato with cheese. How will you enjoy yours?

Ingredients

> 1 small white or red cabbage
>
> ½ red onion
>
> 2 carrots, topped, tailed, peeled, and grated
>
> 1 teaspoon fine sea salt
>
> 1 pinch of ground black pepper
>
> 3 large dollops of Hellman's Real mayonnaise

Method

1   *Remove the outer leaves of the cabbage. Cut the cabbage in half and remove the hard-centre piece. Chop the remaining leaves as finely as possible. Wash and drain the chopped cabbage and place in a large bowl.*

2   *Peel and chop the half onion, again as finely as possible. Place the chopped onion in the bowl with the chopped cabbage.*

3   *Add the grated carrot to the chopped cabbage, onion, and salt and pepper, and mix well.*

4   *Add the mayonnaise and mix until all the vegetables are coated in the mayo. Add more mayo if you think it is too dry. Enjoy.*

Waiting patiently for the titbits

Many years ago, I was a young wife with little experience of how to cook (except for my cookery lessons at school) and had no cookery books. I had no idea about different spices, herbs, and flavours really, but was amazed at the spice shelves in the supermarkets, especially the ones by Schwartz. And I was in awe at the different names and colours in the lovely jars. During one big shop (as we say in Yorkshire), I saw some leaflets advertising cookery books by Schwartz and couldn't resist ordering them.

When they arrived through the post, I thought that all my Christmases had come at once. Five cookery books, all mine! It was in the Christmas book that I saw a recipe for cooked ham. Who even knew you got ham in such big pieces? I was used to the wafer-thin ham you bought in packets at the supermarket. I still have these books and refer to them regularly. Thank you, Schwartz.

Very quickly, this recipe became a favourite of mine, and I couldn't believe that I could cook something so wonderful. Over the years I've continued to make a version of this for different occasions, and eventually had my own signature dish for Christmas Eve – Honey Roast Ham served with home-made soda bread, home-made relish, Jim's roast potatoes, and Heinz baked beans. My mouth's watering now just thinking of it.

Susan

This lovely ham was something that I only made at Christmas and it really was our festive treat. However, we now have this ham every week, because it's one of the customer favourites in the tearoom (though Mr M now cooks the ham). It's soaked in water overnight, bubbles away most of the following day on the hob, and gets finished off in the oven. Customers love being in the tearoom when this is going on, because there are always little bits that fall off the joint to be tasted by willing testers. Mind you, sometimes Mr M has to be persuaded to share these bits, as he likes to take them home for Beatrix, our Collie.

I did wonder if seeing this every single day would spoil the ham for me, but no. I could still eat it every day. My favourite meal is still the ham with roast potatoes and baked beans.

This ham is lovely warm in a roast dinner, but is equally good served cold as in my Christmas Eve Ham. We serve this in the tearoom in sandwiches, in toasties, on jacket potatoes, or just in a salad.

We like to think that we've made our tearoom accessible to all, and that those who need to find us will do just that. Sometimes there are special people who give others a helping hand to reach the tearoom, and Susan is one of those people. One morning Susan, in her supporting care role, brought along one of the people she supports on a day-to-day basis. Initially, Susan was in the tearoom purely in a caring role. But the caring role lasted for the first visit.

After finding the tearoom, Susan realised that not only was it the perfect environment for one of her lovely ladies, but also a place she enjoyed spending time in herself. Now we're lucky enough to have Susan in the tearoom every week. She continues to support the individual, but has also encouraged her to come along to the tearoom unsupported. Susan now has somewhere safe to bring the lady she is supporting, but also has a place she herself feels comfortable and at ease in. I can tell you that if any of my family or friends required support, I would hope that the care came from somebody just like Susan.

Every week when Susan comes in, she has the same thing – a ham sandwich with all the trimmings. However, this has to be Mr M's special home-cooked ham, and with the salad inside the sandwich not as a side salad. Oh, and there mustn't be any cucumber or pickle anywhere near Susan's lunch.

It's very often a Friday when Mr M cooks the ham, so Susan sits very patiently in anticipation of sampling the ham straight out of the oven. Of course, as she loves Mr M's home-cooked ham so much, it just had to be named Susan's Home-Cooked Ham.

Susan's Home-Cooked Ham

Makes a lot of ham!

Ingredients

1 ham joint
Handful of whole cloves
2-3 tablespoons demerara sugar mixed with
enough runny honey to make a paste

Mr M adding the cloves to the roast ham

Method

1. *Remove all the packaging from the ham joint. Make a note of how much your joint weighs. Put the joint in your largest pan, cover with cold water and put the lid on the pan. Leave overnight. This will help to get rid of some of the salt to stop the finished ham being too salty.*

2. *The following day, empty out the water from the pan, re-fill with clean water, and put the pan on the large ring on your hob. Put the lid on the pan, bring the water to the boil and then turn down to simmer. This will need to bubble away for 20 minutes for each pound your joint weighs.*

3. *In the last 20 minutes of cooking, pre-heat your oven to 200°c.*

4. *Remove the pan from the heat and carefully empty the water. Take the joint from the pan and place it in a large roasting tin. The outer layer of fat on the joint should now just peel away easily and can be discarded.*

5. *Make diagonal cuts along the outside of the joint with a sharp knife, and put a whole clove in each of the crosses.*

6. *Spread the sugar paste over the joint, being careful not to knock out the cloves.*

7. *Put the ham into the pre-heated oven and cook for about 20 minutes or until the outside is crispy and darkened. You may wish to keep checking and spooning the sugar juice back over the joint as it cooks.*

8. *Remove the ham from the oven and place on a rack ready to serve or to cool ready to freeze.*

9. *As the cooked joints freeze very well, you could cook a large joint, cut it into smaller joints and freeze any that you are not going to use in the next day or so.*

Amy Johnson and the Victorian singer

At the tearoom, our aim is to provide a menu where gluten free and dairy free choices are the norm and not the exception. If, by doing that, we can also provide choices for vegetarians and vegans, then even better. I'm constantly trying to make sure we have different choices in the tearoom, and was looking for something to add to the sandwich fillings for our afternoon teas for vegetarians to have other than cheese and egg. At one of our Afternoon Teas for 16, I made home-made hummus and it went down a treat.

Debra and Elaine

Hummus is a savoury dish made from chickpeas blended with tahini, lemon juice, and garlic. I've served this in sandwiches, but it's also fabulous with toast, or with home-made oatcakes and salad. You can add garlic to your hummus, but in the tearoom we leave this out, as we now know not everyone can tolerate garlic. A sprinkle of paprika looks very pretty when serving, but again can be omitted if wished.

In the introduction to the book, I mentioned that we like to give customer names to our goodies, according to whichever one is their favourite. Sometimes there are customers who would really just eat any cake that's there (providing it was gluten free, of course). Elaine is one of those people. Every visit to the tearoom starts with Elaine looking at the selection of cakes and deciding which one to try. There is no favourite for Elaine. I think cakes in general are her favourite.

Elaine first came into the tearoom in November 2015, a few months after we opened the tearoom. We now know it was the anniversary of her husband's birthday, and he had recently died. Obviously, on that day we didn't know any of this. Elaine came in with her four daughters and we just got on like a house on fire. She told us later that when they left that day, they all said it was just like going to their Auntie's house.

It wasn't long before Elaine was one of our regular customers, and she is now well and truly a friend and a tearoom family member. Over the few years the tearoom has been opened, Elaine has joined us for tea and cakes, chats, craft, discussions, and yes, a few tears.

Somehow, Elaine and I managed to find ourselves singing together at our Afternoon Tea events. Never in my wildest dreams (or nightmares) did I ever imagine I'd be singing in front of other people. But I can tell you, the practice evenings we had, together with Mr M, were just as much fun for us as the actual events. We laughed, we giggled, and we were scolded by Mr M for not being able to play the tambourine and sing at the same time.

If you look at the videos on Mother Murphy's Facebook page, you'll be able to see us singing our hearts out. Of course, I was the backing singer and Elaine was the real singer, with Mr M on guitar.

As Elaine really would eat any cake in the tearoom, it was too difficult to choose a cake to name after her, so I felt it only appropriate she gets her name alongside the hummus. After all, it was Elaine for whom I first made this.

Elaine's Hummus

Makes a large bowl

Ingredients

200g tinned chickpeas

2 tablespoons lemon juice

1 teaspoon ground cumin

Pinch of fine sea salt

1 tablespoon tahini

4 tablespoons cold water

2 tablespoons extra virgin olive oil

Sprinkle of paprika to serve

Method

1   Drain the tinned chickpeas.

2   Put all the ingredients in a food processor and blitz until smooth.

3   Add more lemon juice, cumin, and salt to taste.

4   Sprinkle with ground paprika to serve.

If you eat a cake whole, technically you've really only had one slice!

Debra Murphy

Baking at the tearoom

We all know we should be trying to live our lives without sugar and fat, don't we? And eating cake every day and all day long won't give you a healthy diet. But what would life be without a treat? There is nothing better than sitting down with a steaming pot of tea, china crockery, and a slice of something home-made. Throw in a couple of friends, mix with a good dollop of laughter and a sprinkling of gossip, and you have the perfect treat.

At the tearoom, all our cakes are home-made. They may not be the perfect shape or absolutely equal portions, but trust me, home-made cakes and bakes are a world away from the artificial flavours of commercially-bought ones.

I love how you can put simple ingredients together and produce wonderful goodies to be enjoyed by yourself, your family, your friends or, in my case, by our lovely customers. Watch somebody's face when they taste a home-made cake; you can see them relax into their seat, the smiles start, the chatting begins, and the slice of cake has become an event to be remembered.

In the tearoom we always use china cups and saucers for our tea, using leaf tea, and we use teapots (that don't spill) with tea strainers. Cakes and bakes are served on a small china plate with an old-fashioned cake fork or butter knife and, of course, a napkin. Trust me, it's the little things that make all the difference. Go on, try it and you'll find that you enjoy your food a little more, you'll relax a little more, and friends will linger a little longer.

Developing our gluten and dairy free bread

Bread: who doesn't love a slice of home-made bread spread with lashings of home-made jam or lemon curd?

When my children were growing up, Saturday mornings were spent making enough bread for the week and freezing it. We'd then have some home-made bread rolls and soup for lunch before heading out for the afternoon.

If we're to believe what the history books tell us, bread originated in Egypt, where the first grinding stone, or quern, was invented around 8000bce. The un-leven bread produced then would be much like the chapatis and tortillas we have now. Eventually, leavened bread (where a rising agent such as yeast is added to produce fermentation and cause the dough to rise) became a symbol of Egyptian culture. It's thought that the first leavened bread was most likely to be the result of some floating yeast landing in a bowl of thick gruel. How do historians even know such things!

Later, in medieval times, along came trencher bread. These were flat, old loaves of bread that were cut in half and used as plates during feasts. It's believed that after the diners were finished with the food, the used trenchers were given to the poor. Later, these were made from wood and often had writing on the back of them, which was thought to encourage conversations once the food had been eaten.

Following my research into bread, at the tearoom we set about making some trenchers in our craft sessions. We didn't make these out of bread, but took some cork mats, added a bit of decoupage on them, and these were used to stand hot teapots on the tables. We had great fun with this, with the crafters even adding their own sayings to their trenchers. Unfortunately, the tablecloths still bear the evidence that I was allowed to use glue!

Bread over the years has changed and we now have the most amazing choices of loaves: sliced, unsliced, white, wholemeal, seeded, sweet, spicy, rolls, wraps, chapatis, and tortillas. Of course, there is heavy processing of bread now to meet the daily demand for this, with loaves now manufactured to last more than a day or so in the supermarkets.

In 1961, the British Baking Industries Research Association in Chorleywood, Hertfordshire, developed the Chorleywood Bread Process (CBP) – a method of producing bread with greater volume and lightness that was also labour efficient and low cost. Let's not go into the real ins and outs of the merits of this process, except to say that making your own bread, whether gluten or gluten free, has got to be better than the bread produced using this process! There is also the debate about whether it's this processing method that's increased the gluten content in the bread we eat today.

I have to admit to not being a big bread eater nowadays, but we do need a good bread to serve to our customers. It's not practical for us to make home-made bread for all our customers, as we'd be constantly bread making and have no time for cake-making or talking to our lovely customers. And while we've tried to buy in different brands of gluten free bread, we haven't really found one that we're totally happy to serve. Actually, we've found some that we'd be ashamed to serve in the tearoom!

So, with the taste of these often disgusting gluten free breads still in our mouths, Mr M set about having a go at making some of his own and, after a few trials, disasters, and lots of food waste, he now makes an exceedingly good loaf of gluten free and dairy free bread. All the customers love this bread, not just those needing or choosing a gluten free diet.

Mr M is very protective of his bread, though, and we joke that customers will need to come along to the tearoom with a prescription from their GP before he'll serve it to them. He has a fear of somebody coming and needing (no pun intended) his bread and finding that he's given it away to all the other customers.

Now, as often happens when you get a husband and wife working together, we have little 'discussions', and one of these little chats was about him making the bread. The result of the discussion was him saying to me, 'You could always have a go at making the bread.' Anyone that knows me will recognise that this is just fighting talk to me. Let's just say that in the tearoom you'll often get Mr M's lovely gluten free bread, but you're now just as likely to get Debra's gluten free bread. I've challenged the customers to tell us which they prefer, but they've all declared that they are equally as good as each other. Very diplomatic customers!

If you read all the cookery books from the famous people such as Paul Hollywood, Mary Berry, and Jamie Oliver, you'll pick up lots of amazing tips and hints for bread making. Indeed, I've used many of their recipes over the years and produced some wonderful bread, enjoying the process of kneading, proving, re-kneading, and finally baking the dough. Sharing home-made bread with others, and watching their faces as they enjoy it, is truly one of the best things about baking.

Then there's gluten free bread making. For this to work, you first need to forget everything you've ever learned about bread making and getting that lovely soft dough that can be kneaded and re-kneaded. Instead, imagine making something that looks a little bit like smooth porridge, and you'll start to get the picture of how gluten free dough appears. There are, however, less stages in gluten free bread, as there is no kneading (you can't knead runny porridge). And once you've made the dough, you simply leave it to rise then bake it.

I still don't think (I may be wrong, and am happy to be corrected) that any gluten free bread will ever match soft, fluffy bread made with gluten. The gluten is, of course, the viscoelastic protein found in grains such as wheat, barley, and rye. This simply means that it is viscous (it binds together) and elastic (it stretches). This is the stuff that makes wheat bread so lovely, and is probably one of the things that most people who can't eat gluten miss the most.

Sometimes I believe you have to accept that something will not be the same, just like vegetarian sausages will never be sausages. But you can still work at it and you can produce something that is tasty, enjoyable, and 100% better than the manufactured gluten free versions. I'm very happy to serve our gluten free bread, and our customers obviously enjoying it is high praise indeed.

I'd like to add here that since starting this book, the gluten free bread available in most supermarkets has vastly improved. Warburton's now do a great tiger loaf. There's also a whole range of bread from the Promise Bread Company, and we get some fantastic brioche rolls from one of our food suppliers. I hope that the quality of commercially produced gluten free and dairy free products will continue to improve, but meanwhile there will always be small places like Mother Murphy's who strive to make great home-made gluten free and dairy free products without mass production.

Baking is how you start kids at cooking in the kitchen. It's fun whether it's baking bread or cookies. With baking, you have to be exact when it comes to ingredients.

Sandra Lee

Mr M's Gluten Free Bread

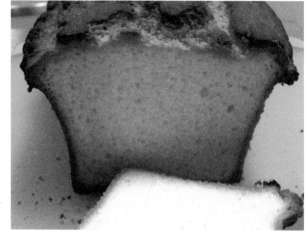

Makes two 2lb loaves

I use a free-standing mixer when making this bread, and it really does help to be able to have the mixer running when gradually adding the water and then the flour. I'm sure you'd be able to use a hand-held whisk, too, but it would just be a little fiddly.

The loaves are sliced once they're completely cold and then frozen, ready for slices to be taken out as and when required in the tearoom. Don't be tempted to try and slice the loaves when they're even slightly warm. Believe me! I've tried this, with disastrous results.

In all honesty, our bread recipe is devised from the recipe that you can find on the back of a packet of Dove's Farm Free From bread flour, but we've been more specific in which oil, sugar, and vinegar to use, and the method we have settled on.

Ingredients

4 free range egg whites
12 tablespoons olive oil
2 teaspoons cider vinegar
4 tablespoons caster sugar
2 teaspoons salt
900ml tepid water
1kg gluten free white bread flour (I use Dove's)
4 teaspoons easy bake yeast (I use Allinson's)
2 x 2lb loaf tins

Method

1. Preheat oven to 220°c/200°c fan oven.

2. Put the egg whites, sugar, salt, vinegar, water, and 6 tablespoons of the oil into a free-standing mixer (or use an electric whisk) and, using the balloon whisk attachment, whisk until frothy.

3. With the mixer running on a slow speed, add the water slowly and continue to whisk until well blended and frothy.

4. Put the flour and yeast into a bowl and mix until well blended.

5. Change the attachment on the free-standing mixer to the dough hook and, again with the mixer running slowly, add the flour and yeast mix one tablespoon at a time until it has all been added.

Mary loving Mr M's Gluten Free Bread.

6. Turn the mixer up to high and beat until you have a smooth batter with no bits. Remember to stop the mixer and use a spatula to scrape down the side of the bowl to get all the flour well mixed. Turn the mixer back on and beat again until every bit of flour is blended into the mix.

7. Take the bowl off the mixer and add the remaining 6 tablespoons of oil, folding in with a spatula until just blended. You should have a mixture something similar to runny, smooth porridge.

8. Pour the mixture into the loaf tins, dividing equally between the two. (You could weigh them to make sure they are identical if you wish.) Gently smooth the top with a spatula.

9. Put the loaf tins into a plastic bag and tie the ends of the bag to keep the air in. Try and get the bag to stand higher than the edges of the loaf tins.

10. Leave until the dough has risen to the top of the loaf tins. This will take anywhere from 50 minutes to 2 hours, depending on the temperature of your kitchen. I usually pop the oven on at this point, ready for the loaves to go in when they have risen.

11. Carefully remove the plastic bags and bake the loaves for 50 minutes.

12. Remove from the loaf tins and leave to cool on a wire rack.

13. Once cooled, slice and then put into a freezer bag and freeze. You can then take out slices as you need them.

Banana Loaf

Makes two 2lb loaves

We all do it, don't we? There's a bunch of bananas on the table that we keep telling ourselves we're going to eat, but before you know it, they're turning black and getting ready to run off the table. There's really only one thing to do here – make yourself a lovely, moist, sweet banana loaf. You could even convince yourself it's one of your five a day!

Serve this sliced just as it comes, or with butter and some extra honey. It's rather splendid with hot custard, too.

Ingredients

For the Loaf

500g peeled ripe bananas

500g soft brown sugar

5 free range eggs

200g stork block melted

500g gluten free self-raising flour (I use Dove's)

¾ teaspoon of xanthan gum

For the Honey Topping

2 tablespoons honey

2 tablespoons Demerara sugar

Equipment

2 x 2lb loaf tins, greased and line with parchment paper

Method

For the Loaf

1 Preheat oven to 160°c/140°c fan oven.

2 Line two 2lb loaf tins with parchment paper (I use a parchment paper liner).

3 Put the bananas and sugar in a free-standing mixer (or use an electric whisk) and mix for a couple of minutes until blended. There's no need to mash the bananas first if they are ripe, as they just blend in the mixer.

4 Add the eggs to the banana mix and beat on medium speed until well blended and light.

5 Melt the stork block in the microwave and pour into the banana mix slowly, with the mixer running on a slow setting.

6 Mix the flour and xanthan gum together, then add to the banana mix and beat for a couple of minutes until well blended.

7 Pour the mixture into the prepared loaf tins and bake in the pre-heated oven for 60 minutes or until a cake tester comes out clean.

8 Remove from the oven and leave to rest for 5 minutes.

For the Honey Topping

9 Brush the top of the loaves with the honey and sprinkle with the Demerara sugar.

10 Put back into the oven for 5 minutes.

11 Remove from the oven and allow to cool in the tins.

From high in the Derbyshire Peak District

Growing up in Yorkshire, there was never a great deal of money going around, and any biscuits or cakes that appeared were always a treat. One of my favourites was a Mr Kipling's Bakewell Tart. These were an expensive treat and not something we saw in our house on a regular basis. Now, though, you can buy these very cheaply at the supermarket, and it's reported that Mr Kipling's factory makes thousands of them each day. I may not be in that league, but each one made at Mother Murphy's is individually made by me!

The Bakewell Tart we love, with that crisp pastry, almond frangipane filling, sweet icing topping, and finished with that wonderful feather icing, is believed to have originated in the picturesque town of Bakewell in the Derbyshire Peak District. Of course, this is not to be mistaken for the Bakewell Pudding, rumoured to have been made by mistake away back in 1820. Bakewell Pudding has a flaky pastry base with a layer of jam, topped with a filling made of egg and almond paste. Those who love Bakewell Puddings will pour scorn over the Bakewell Tart, and vice versa. You'll note there is no Bakewell Pudding in my book!

Anyway, I just had to have this sweet treat in our tearoom, and was over the moon to find that my Bakewell Tart quickly became one of our customer favourites. My next dilemma was whether it would be possible to make this gluten free and dairy free yet still remind me of my childhood treat, and more importantly, would our customers still love it?

My first few attempts at making the gluten free and dairy free pastry resulted in something close to cement, but following a lot of research and taste-testing, I finally managed to make a great pastry using polenta.

With the filling and icing being naturally gluten free and dairy free, I just needed to ensure the chocolate for the feather icing was the same.. Of course, now that I've sourced the amazing chocolate from Plamil Foods, this is not a problem.

Our Bakewell Tarts are now always gluten free and dairy free and, yes, our customers still love them. My niece, Annie, says that our Bakewell Tart is just simply the best thing she has ever tasted, especially when I put our home-made gooseberry jelly-jam in it. Praise indeed, when Annie needs neither gluten free nor dairy free goodies. As it was down to Annie's mum and dad, Paula and Danny, that I was introduced all those years ago to Mr M, our Bakewell Tart just has to be Annie's Bakewell Tart.

Bakewell Tarts in the tearoom are always popular and we just change the fillings to have something a little different – from our Boozy Bakewell with gluten free and dairy free Christmas mincemeat, through to gooseberry jelly-jam, strawberry or raspberry jam, and lemon curd.

Danny, Brendan, Paula, Daniel and Annie

Whatever you fancy for the base of yours is up to you. As long as you keep the crisp pastry and the almond filling, you'll not go far wrong. Home-made jam or lemon curd makes all the difference for this treat.

Serve this with a good helping of hot, steaming custard and you have just turned a teatime delight into heaven!

Annie's Gooseberry Jelly-Jam Bakewell Tart

Makes a 9" round tart or twelve mini tarts

Ingredients

For the Pastry Base:
100g stork block
50g caster sugar
1 free range egg, lightly beaten
100g gluten free plain flour
100g fine polenta
Enough gooseberry jelly-jam to cover the base of the tart
(or other jam/curd of your choice)

For the Icing
200g icing sugar
1 tablespoon warm water
50g gluten and dairy free chocolate

For the Filling
100 g stork block
100g caster sugar
2 free range eggs, lightly beaten
75g ground almonds
25g gluten free plain flour
1 teaspoon almond extract

Equipment
1 x 9" loose-bottomed flan tin or
1 x 12-hole muffin tin

Method

For the Pastry

1   Preheat oven to 190°c/170°c fan oven.

2   Grease a 9" round loose bottom flan tin, or a 12-hole muffin tin with stork block.

3   Put the polenta, flour, and caster sugar in a free-standing mixer and mix for a minute to blend. Add the stork, and mix slowly until you have something that looks like breadcrumbs. Add the egg and continue to mix until the mixture forms a soft pastry.

4   Empty the pastry onto a well-floured worktop (gluten free flour, of course), knead gently until smooth, then wrap in clingfilm and pop in the fridge for 30 minutes.

5   Remove the clingfilm and roll out the chilled pastry on a well-floured worktop until it is large enough to cover the base and sides of the flan tin (or cut out with a pastry cutter).

6   *Using a rolling pin, carefully transfer the pastry to the prepared tin(s). Smooth out any cracks and trim the pastry to be level with the top of the tin.*

7   *Line the pastry case with parchment paper, fill with baking beans, and blind bake for 10 minutes.*

8   *Once baked, remove from the oven, and take out the baking beans and parchment paper, but leave the pastry in the tin. Be careful, as the baking beans will be very hot.*

9   *Spread home-made gooseberry jelly-jam over the base of the pastry (or your choice of jam or lemon curd). Be generous but not too lavish here, or your chosen jam will ooze out of the tart once you add the filling.*

For the Filling

10   *Cream together the caster sugar and stork until light and fluffy.*

11   *Add the eggs slowly a little at a time, beating with each addition.*

12   *Stir in the ground almonds, flour, and almond extract.*

13   *Spread over the jam in pastry case, and bake for 25-30 minutes until golden brown and the filling feels firm to touch.*

14   *Leave to cool completely in the tin, then carefully remove and place on a serving plate*

For the Icing

15   *In a large bowl, mix the icing sugar with warm water to make an icing just thick enough to spread. Use this to coat the cooked and cooled tart.*

16   *Melt the chocolate over a bowl of gently simmering water. Once the chocolate has started to melt, remove from the heat and stir gently until all the chocolate has melted.*

17   *Pour the melted chocolate into a piping bag (no nozzle required), snip off the end of the piping bag, and pipe thin lines of chocolate across the icing.*

18   *Quickly before the icing and chocolate set, run a cake tester or pointed knife through the lines one way then the other, to create a feathered effect, and leave to set before serving.*

Disqualified from the Great Murphy Bake-Off!

Battenberg Cake has to be one of the most comforting cakes I can think of. Oh, the marzipan, the jam, and light sponge. What's not to love? Trust me here, although this looks like a complicated cake to make, it's easy if you take your time.

Sometimes called Church Window Cake, Checkerboard Cake, or Domino Cake, it's believed that this cake originated in the UK and was created to celebrate the marriage of Princess Victoria of Hesse to Prince Louis of Battenberg in 1884.

Before we opened the tearoom, I'd made a Battenberg cake on a couple of occasions, but in October 2014, Mr M and I had a bake-off making these, and the result still causes a bit of a debate.

I set the task for us to make a Battenberg with different coloured squares, using only home-made or natural ingredients. I'd made marzipan many times before and knew I'd be ok with that. The

Loiuse

sponges were easy enough, but how would I colour the cakes using only natural colours? I tried using pureed raspberries, but they didn't really colour the mixture enough, so decided to use some Ribena, as this is natural juice with no added sugar. I replaced the apricot jam that's usually found between the sponges and the marzipan with some of my home-made jam.

We both worked in secret, but I was a little concerned at how well Mr was doing in the task and was having a bit of a panic he might even win. Then I saw it! Mr M was using a jar of commercial apricot jam! I should have reminded him that everything had to be home-made or natural ingredients but 'forgot'. Oops!

A couple of hours later, we had between us two fabulous looking Battenbergs. At the time, we were running our training company, with our office in Kirkintilloch amongst lots of other offices and business. Next day we arrived with our Battenbergs and went to the office next door to get some independent judging carried out. We take our bake-offs very seriously, as you can see.

Judging took a little while and demanded several tastes and cups of tea, especially from Janice. The results were a mixed bag – some thought that one cake was the best looking, while others thought that one cake was better tasting, so it was beginning to look like a draw. To solve the problem, though, I was able to pull out the disqualification card and remove Mr M's Battenberg because he had ignored the rule about everything being hand-made or natural. 'That's not fair,' he cried (and I'm sure there was a tear in his eye and perhaps a glisten in mine).

Back to the tearoom, apart from the lemon drizzle cake, Battenberg has proved to be one of our most popular cakes, and disappears quickly once on display.

Giving this Battenberg a customer name was a tricky one, as so many people ask for it. It could even be given my daughter Chloe's name as she just loves this, but she already has the Orange Pepper Soup and Christmas Truffles named after her. The decision had to be to name it after Louise, who had this the first time she came into the tearoom and looks for it every week.

Janice the Judge

We like to think of Louise as being part of our tearoom family – a far cry from the girl who came in one day and hardly spoke to us. Now we have a laugh, discussions, banter, share crafts, and of course, always eat cake.

Louise's Battenberg Cake

Makes 1 Battenberg

My tip for making this cake is to get yourself a Battenberg baking tin. These tins are the right size and have the dividers for you to make four perfect cake sections. You could use an 8" square cake tin and make your own dividers with foil, but this can be a bit tricky and the cakes can sometimes be uneven. I make four Battenbergs at a time, as you can see from the photos, but I've given the recipe for just one. I keep saying, if you're going to have your oven on, fill it and then make use of your freezer. Battenbergs freeze perfectly and you can even slice them, wrap each slice in parchment paper, ready to take out just one piece at a time from the freezer (as if!).

Make sure you use a good quality food colouring gel rather than the cheaper liquids, as it really does make a difference to the look, taste, and texture of the cake. Be bold, though, as the colour fades a little during cooking even with the good quality gels.

You can make your own marzipan easily, but commercial marzipan is very good nowadays. I use commercial marzipan because of the high cost of ground almonds and the worry of using raw eggs in the tearoom.

Ingredients

For The cake

100g rice flour

50g ground almonds

150g stork block

150g caster sugar

1 teaspoon almond extract

1 teaspoon gluten free baking powder

2 tablespoons almond milk

3 free range eggs

Red and yellow food colouring

Equipment

8.5" x 7" Battenberg cake tin with 3 dividers

To Finish

Your favourite jam

500 g marzipan

Method

1   Preheat oven to 180°c/160°c fan oven.

2   Grease an 8" Battenberg cake tin and the dividers.

3   Put all the cake ingredients in a free-standing mixer (or use an electric whisk) and beat until well mixed and smooth.

4   Weigh the mixture into two bowls to make sure they are equal weights.

5   Put a few drops of pink food colouring into one bowl and yellow food colouring into the other. Mix each one until the colour is well blended, and put the mixtures into separate piping bags (no nozzle required).

6   Cut the end off the piping bags and squeeze the pink mixture into two of the sections and the yellow into the other two sections. Smooth the sections down with a teaspoon (using a clean teaspoon for each colour).

7   Put the tin into the pre-heated oven and bake for 20 minutes until well risen and firm to touch.

8   Remove from the oven and leave in the tins for 5 minutes.

9   Run a palette knife around all the sections just to make sure they are free from the edges. Carefully remove the dividers then tip the tin upside down and the four sections should come out. Leave to cool completely on a wire rack.

10   Roll the marzipan out on a work surface lightly dusted with cornflour. Shape to a rectangle 20cm x 30cm.

11   Warm a little of your chosen jam in the microwave for 20 seconds to soften it then spread over the rolled-out marzipan.

12   Using the remaining jam, sandwich together one yellow cake and one pink cake and, with the smooth side to the marzipan, place in the middle of the marzipan. Spread jam over the top of these cakes.

13   Sandwich together the remaining yellow and pink cakes with jam and place, smooth sides facing up, the pink cake on top of the yellow cake on the marzipan, and the yellow cake on top of the pink cake on the marzipan.

14   Carefully fold over the marzipan to form the Battenberg log.

15   Wet the joint with a little water on your finger and gently rub the joint to smooth.

16   Turn the cake over so that the joint is to the bottom, and gently mould to the perfect shape. Dusting your hands with icing sugar at this point helps.

17   Carefully slice a thin piece off each end to neaten the appearance, and make a pattern on the Battenberg of your choice. (I crimp the edges and make a criss-cross pattern.)

18   You could throw the off-cuts away or simply enjoy them with a well-deserved cup of tea whilst you admire your fabulous creation.

Oh no! Where has the track gone?

Does anyone actually like Brussel sprouts? I'm one of those people whose throat constricts at the idea of eating them, and it's like they grow and grow as I chew then. I'm not really sure why, but I force myself to have two sprouts on Christmas Day, much to the hilarity of anyone sharing Christmas dinner with me. I've heard of many different ways of cooking these horrors, which confirms my belief that they're just so nasty that the taste needs masking in any way you can think of. Whatever way you cook them, they're still a Brussel sprout.

So, you might well be surprised to find that one of my recipes is named after the Brussel sprout. Let me explain.

After the success of my gluten free and dairy free caramel shortbread, the next batch was not quite so successful. Whilst it tasted just as lovely as the previous bake, it was in fact toffee shortbread because the caramel was overdone, turning it into a lovely dairy free toffee. But I'm afraid this just couldn't be served in the tearoom without a dentist's warning! After dreaming about eating the whole batch myself (though Crafty Sal did offer to help with that task), I pulled myself together and thought about what it could be turned into.

The first glimpse of Ben Arthur (The Cobbler)

There was only one thing to do – blitz it in the food processor to make some sort of traybake. Using the basic recipe from our rocky road, I added a peppermint filling and finished with another chocolate topping. I was struggling with a name for this and was discussing this with a young man in the tearoom. Busy telling him that I wanted to keep it all to myself, as it was so nice, he suggested in his young wisdom that, having a green filling, if I called it Brussel Sprout Surprise, nobody would want any of it and I'd be able to eat it all myself without feeling too guilty. What a brilliant idea, I thought. Alasdair's Brussel Sprout Surprise it would be.

What fun there was in the tearoom listening to discussions about different vegetables going into cakes. Customers were saying they'd tried carrot cake, pumpkin pie, courgette and beetroot cake, but would never have thought to put Brussel sprouts into cakes. Oh, how I laughed. It didn't stop the customers eating it, though, and thoroughly enjoying it. One customer likened it to Viscount Biscuits and Dime Bars. And there was certainly no waste!

The extravagance of using blitzed caramel slice is just too costly for us in the tearoom, so now I make a simple base using our caramel shortbread recipe. The customers still love it, and the name gives everyone a good laugh.

The Brussel Sprout Surprise was also one of the highlights of one of my winter picnics on the Arrochar Alps, with Beatrix our Collie. The plan for this particular adventure was to climb up The Cobbler (Ben

Arthur) from Arrochar. I had a feeling there might be some snow and ice once I'd climbed up the valley, but didn't expect the day we had.

Monday morning arrived, and I found myself sitting in the motorway traffic on the M8 heading out towards the Erskine Bridge, but smirking a little to myself, thinking how I'd soon be free of the traffic and on the open roads.

An hour or so later, after a lovely drive along the side of Loch Lomond, passing the picturesque village of Luss and on to Tarbet, I arrived at the car park in Succoth. As is typical, the heavens opened as I got out of the car. But in the words of the comedian Billy Connolly, 'there's no bad weather, just bad clothing'. It did cross my mind that this rain might turn into snow higher up, but within 15 minutes, the rain had stopped and the sun was shining.

We had a lovely stroll up the forestry track at the start of the walk – a good path, but a bit of zig-zaggy pull. All was silent after the traffic of the M8, and the only sound really was the clickety-clackety of the West Highland train coming along from Helensburgh heading up to Fort William.

After a while, the track opens out onto the hills and it feels that the whole world is in front of you. Taking a glance back, you get a fabulous view of Ben Lomond and a terrific view down Loch Long. The real vista of the day, though, is the one that meets you as you come out of the forest and you get your first sighting of The Cobbler. This particular day was no disappointment, but there were the first signs of what was to come (though I ignored them).

The wind was no longer gently blowing on me, but rather starting to knock me over in places. Not to worry, though; the sun was still shining. Just as I took my first photos of The Cobbler in the sunshine, like a flash, the first of the snow showers arrived. Beatrix looked more like a polar bear at one point, but the snow quickly passed over us and out came the sun again.

Fooled by this short respite, I continued. A little further along, the route leaves the easy terrain and heads up the rocky peak. Oh, no! Where had the track gone! Suddenly we'd hit the real snow level and the going changed from just being blown by the wind, to slip-sliding along. And slip-slide I did. If I'd been on a sledge, I don't think I'd have gone much faster. Once I'd stopped sliding and found my feet again, I pulled my crampons out of my rucksack and fixed them to my boots. (Of course, Mr M was not told about that bit of the adventure!)

Heading further up the peak, I found myself balancing on the ice and trying to use my walking pole to keep myself upright, as the fierce wind had suddenly become twice as strong as before. Beatrix was by now almost at the top of the peak, not giving a jot about me.

Then, just as I was debating with myself whether to continue, the weather took a dramatic turn for

Lunch on the way back down looking towards Ben Lomond

the worse. The wind was now howling, and the snow came in so quickly it was difficult to breathe or see. As I realised that it would be dangerous for me (and for the rescuers who would need to come and get me) to continue, I allowed myself to slip and slide back down the peak to the path below.

Once down the peak, I knew the rest of the hike would be relatively easy as I'd soon be back below the snow level. A little further down, I found shelter from the wind in a large rock formation, where a lovely lunch was enjoyed looking across to Ben Lomond. I did also munch my way through some lovely Brussel Sprout Surprise – a bit like thick Kendal Mint Cake, I thought.

After this, the only scary bit was when I had to cross what's usually a bubbling beck (or burn). That day, it was a raging torrent. I looked at this fast-flowing water and the drop down the valley from it. I looked at Beatrix, who also looked at the fast-flowing water and the drop, and she quite simply refused to budge. Just imagine: me, the clumsiest person around, having to stand balanced on rocks in the fast-flowing water, holding Beatrix's lead as she trotted across the rocks and over the water. I swear she giggled at me when I finally got across myself!

We did survive to tell the tale and I had a great laugh about it in the car going home. 'Where will we go next week?' asked Beatrix. I told her not to tell her dad all about the day, and just to pick the nice bits or we'd find ourselves grounded for the rest of the winter.

All I can say is that if Peter Rabbit finds lettuce soporific, getting caught in a snow blizzard seemed to have the same effect on me and Beatrix, and the pair of us were soon sleeping at home in the warmth of the central heating!

Alasdair's Brussell Sprout Surprise

Makes a 16" x 12" traybake to cut into 28 pieces

My recipe is for a large 16" x 12" traybake, so if your tin is smaller remember to adjust your quantities depending on your tin size.

Ingredients

For Shortbread Base

350g fine polenta

310g caster sugar

250g rice flour

275g ground almonds

310g stork block, cut into small pieces

3 free range eggs

For the Mint Filling

100g very soft stork block

850g icing sugar

3 teaspoons peppermint extract

Green food colouring

6 tablespoons almond milk

For the Chocolate Topping

600g gluten and dairy free chocolate

Equipment

16 x 12" traybake tin

Alasdair

Method

For Biscuit

1   *Preheat oven to 180°c/160°c fan oven.*

2   *Line a traybake tin with parchment paper.*

3   *Put the polenta, sugar, rice flour, and ground almonds, into a free-standing mixer (or use a hand-held whisk) and mix to combine.*

4   *Add the stork and mix until you have no large lumps of stork.*

5   *Add the beaten eggs and mix until the mixture starts to come together, but don't get it to form a dough.*

6   *Empty the mixture into your prepared baking tray and press it down to cover the tray, making sure you get into all the corners. Smooth down with a palette knife or the back of a wooden spoon.*

7   *Bake for 25-30 minutes until lightly golden brown.*

8   *Remove from the oven, but leave in the baking tin.*

For the Mint Filling

9   *Put the stork in the free-standing mixer (or use an electric whisk) and beat until soft and smooth.*

10   *Add the icing sugar, almond milk, and peppermint extract. Beat until smooth (start slowly or you will have icing sugar all over you!).*

11   *Add a few drops of green food colouring and beat again until well blended.*

12   *Spread the filling evenly over the cooled shortbread base.*

For the Chocolate Topping

13   *Melt the chocolate over a bowl of gently simmering water. Once the chocolate has started to melt, remove from the heat and stir gently until all the chocolate has melted.*

14   *Pour the melted chocolate over the mint filling, spread with a palette knife, and leave to set (not in the fridge).*

15   *Once set, mark into 28 pieces and cut with a sharp knife.*

Let them eat cake

Marie Antoinette

When there just has to be more than one version

Caramel slice, millionaire shortbread, caramel shortbread – whatever you call it, who doesn't love this indulgent treat? With its crumbly shortbread base, gooey caramel centre, and thick chocolate topping, what's not to love? Ok, it's not the easiest or quickest recipe to make and, naturally, is not without calories. It is, however, a treat to be enjoyed over a cup of tea and a chat.

In the tearoom, I've been making caramel slice since we opened, and the customers just adore it. Firstly, there's the crumbly shortbread base, using my Empire Biscuit recipe. Then comes the gooey caramel filling. It took a little while for me to produce one I was happy with and could replicate time and again. Like the base, this loyal caramel never lets me down, even though it splashes and burns me every time I make it.

Finally, but perhaps most importantly, there is the chocolate topping. For me, it just has to be Cadbury's Dairy Milk. Some people say that this isn't really chocolate and there are lots of other superior makes, but for me, Cadbury's Dairy Milk hits the spot all the time. Even Mr M knows that if he wants to make me feel special (which he does all the time, of course!) he just needs to put Dairy Milk down in front of me.

Nicola

Which of our lovely customers would we name our caramel slice after? Well, it was no contest, really. It just had to be Nicola's Caramel Slice. Nicola's first visit to the tearoom was probably away back in 2017. We have a hairdresser next to the tearoom and Nicola was in desperate need of a cuppa as she waited for her aunty getting her hair done. It was late in the day and I was rushing away to take Beatrix for a walk, but Mr M took pity on the harassed young lady and served tea and cake after hours. It was only after eating the cake that Nicola saw the signs for our gluten free and dairy free cakes, and she thought about her nephew Charlie needing dairy free goodies. I think the Craft, Chat, and Cake signs may have also caught Nicola's interest, too.

It wasn't long before Nicola, her partner Craig (of Craig's Coconut Cake), and nephew Charlie became regulars and joined the tearoom family. It also transpired that Nicola is a crafty young lady and soon started to join us for the crafting sessions. You should see some of Nicola's cross-stitching. If I'd not seen her doing them myself, I would be easily convinced they were paintings and not done in cross-stitches. Everything she does is just perfection.

Nicola is working on her own business, Nicola's Cards and Crafts, and I'm sure she will be a household name before long. At the time of writing, Nicola was supplying the tearoom gift section with her fabulous hand-made cards.

Anyway, Nicola has a bit of a sweet tooth and is especially partial to a piece of caramel slice. She absolutely loves our original version, and if she can twist Mr M's arm a little, even when he is rushed off his feet (which is, of course, all the time), she enjoys nothing better than a piece of caramel slice with hot custard and a steaming pot of tea. We laugh as Nicola, ever the perfectionist, even cuts her caramel slice into four equal pieces before eating it!

Always aiming to cater for the gluten free and dairy free people, I had many attempts at making a gluten free and dairy free caramel slice, but just couldn't produce one to compare with our original version. After finally managing to make my empire biscuits gluten free and dairy free and finding Plamil's lovely gluten free and dairy free chocolate, I thought I'd have one last attempt to use this shortbread to make a caramel slice. The first dairy free caramel burned, and a few separated when set. One tasted wonderful, but was really dairy free toffee and came with a free dentist appointment. Then it happened – I had produced a gluten free and dairy free caramel slice. When I posted a picture of this on our Facebook page, the response was amazing – we even had one person offering to be our quality assurance taste-tester!

However, my rejoicing was short-lived as I quickly discovered that the dairy free caramel, lovely as it was, didn't have the same structure as the original version. In the heat of the tearoom, the dairy free caramel quickly became almost liquid again. Served as a pudding with custard, this was still lovely, but caramel slice it was not.

Back to the drawing board once more, and I had the brilliant idea to make it as a caramel tart. I used the gluten free and dairy free pastry from our Bakewell Tart recipe, added the dairy free caramel, and topped it with our lovely gluten free and dairy free chocolate. Perfection, I thought. However, what I'd not considered was that once the first piece had been taken out of the tart, the caramel would again be able to escape.

The drawing board again then! Finally, I came up with the idea of the mini caramel pie. Individual gluten free and dairy free pastry tarts, filled with the gluten free and dairy free caramel, and topped with the gluten free and dairy free chocolate. Oh my! These were divine, and when I topped them with meringue, they were heaven.

Now there is a saying, 'You can't please everyone all of the time.' And how true this is. No matter how hard I try to produce scrummy cakes and bakes that are gluten free and dairy free, there is always somebody who is not happy. Let me point out here that this is not a complaint, just an observation. And the saying is very appropriate when it comes to our caramel slice.

Some people preferred the new version, whilst others preferred the original version. There was also the problem that the evaporated milk and butter used in the original version had to be replaced by something to make it dairy free. My final choice was to replace this with soya, as soya cream has a creaminess that almost mimics the evaporated milk. Do you know how many people are unable to tolerate soya in their diet? I have a fairly good idea now!

In the tearoom, our 'Delicious Without' range is all gluten free and dairy free. It seems that being gluten intolerant often goes hand-in-hand with dairy intolerances, so it made sense to make the range both gluten free and dairy free. Baking dairy free is more problematic than baking gluten free, though, and I often despair that I can't make the fabulous looking cakes and bakes seen in other cafes and tearooms, using different sweets and chocolates as decoration. Then I get somebody in the tearoom overwhelmed by our choice of dairy free products, and it all feels worthwhile again.

Sometimes, though – just sometimes – we get customers who beg and beg and beg, and beg some more, for me to make something that sits somewhere between the gluten free and dairy free 'Delicious Without' and our 'Wi Nowt Tekken Owt' range (you need to say this with a Yorkshire Accent!). So, one week I succumbed to pleas from one of our regular customers, Beverley. Now, Bev is partial to a caramel slice, but isn't able to have our original one because of the gluten, and couldn't have the new version because of the soya. 'Please can you make the caramel slice with a gluten free shortbread but the original caramel,' said Bev, who has obviously been taking tips from her dog Trixie and our Beatrix for the puppy-dog eye trick.

Nicola at one of our craft sessions

How could I refuse?

So, Beverley with the puppy-dog eyes wanted a gluten free shortbread base but the non-dairy free caramel and chocolate topping. No problem, I thought. I'll just swap the shortbread to my now successful gluten free and dairy free Empire Biscuit mix, use my original caramel recipe, and top with Cadbury's Dairy Milk. Except, of course, now that I'm not Prime Minister and my manifesto was not passed, Mr Cadbury can still put 'may contain gluten' on his large bars of Dairy Milk. Shame on you, Mr Cadbury, and shame on you all for not voting for Mother Murphy as Prime Minister!

Anyway, I discussed with another long-standing member of the Tearoom family, Crafty Sal the coeliac, whether there were any gluten free chocolates to match Dairy Milk. No, was the short reply. A hunt around the chocolate aisles, looking at all the Cadbury's delights, came up with the answer – giant Cadbury's Chocolate Buttons do not contain gluten, and do not carry the 'may contain' warning. A bit of an expense, but for an exception, it would be worth it. Now I'm pleased to say that I use the fantastic chocolate from Plamil Foods which I believe is equally as good as Cadbury's milk chocolate. Who would have thought it!

I have included three different versions of the caramel slice – Original, Gluten Free, and then Gluten Free and Dairy Free.

Nicola's Caramel Slice - Original

Makes a 16" x 12" traybake to cut into 28 pieces

This was the first caramel slice I made in the tearoom, and the customers just loved it. This original version contains both gluten and dairy.

I make the shortbread base in the food processor but do it in two batches, because putting the full amount in just proves too difficult a task for my processor. Once you've made the two batches, simply knead the two doughs together and roll out as normal.

There is a little word of warning here, though. Don't forget that when making the caramel, you're dealing with boiling sugar. It WILL splash up and burn as you stir this, so make sure you use a long-handled wooden spoon and wear oven gloves to protect yourself.

The longer you heat the caramel and the darker you make it, the more solid the caramel will be when cooled. In summer, I cook the caramel a little longer than in winter, because the heat of the tearoom can sometimes melt it!

Once the caramel slices have been made, cooled, and cut into pieces, I wrap them individually with clingfilm and freeze them, taking them out as I need them. They only take an hour or so to defrost. This way, everyone is sure to be getting their caramel slice at its best (and you'll not be tempted to eat the whole lot yourself at one sitting!).

If your tin is smaller, remember to adjust your quantities to suit your tin size.

Ingredients

For Shortbread Base (Make two batches)
300g plain flour per batch
300g unsalted butter cut into cubes per batch
75g icing sugar per batch
75g cornflour per batch

For the Chocolate Topping
500g Cadbury's Dairy Milk Chocolate
A small knob of butter

For the Caramel
350g unsalted butter
230g caster sugar
200g golden syrup
2 x 397g tins condensed milk

132

Equipment

16 x 12" traybake tin

Method

For the Shortbread Base

1   *Preheat oven to 180°c/160°c fan oven.*

2   *Line a traybake tin with parchment paper.*

3   *Put one batch of the shortbread ingredients in a food processor and blitz until the mixture comes together as a soft dough. (Do this again for the second batch.)*

4   *Dust the worktop with flour and knead the two batches of dough together.*

5   *Roll out just about the same size as the baking tray and, using the rolling pin to help, transfer the dough to the prepared baking tray. Gently mould the dough to completely cover the base of the baking tray, making sure you get into all four corners and press down firmly. Prick the surface of the shortbread with a fork to help prevent it puffing up during baking.*

6   *Bake for 30 minutes until lightly golden brown.*

7   *Remove from the oven but leave in the baking tin.*

For the Caramel

8   *Put all the caramel ingredients in a large pan and gently heat on the hob until everything has melted and is well blended, stirring continuously.*

9   *Bring the mixture to the boil then reduce the heat and simmer, stirring continuously, for another 8-9 minutes until the caramel has turned golden brown.*

10   *Remove from the heat and continue to stir until the caramel has stopped bubbling.*

11   *Pour the caramel onto the cooked shortbread base, spreading out into all the corners, and leave to set.*

For the Chocolate Topping

12   *Melt the chocolate and butter over a bowl of gently simmering water. Once the chocolate has started to melt, remove from the heat and stir gently until all the chocolate has melted.*

13   *Pour the melted chocolate over the set caramel, spread with a palette knife, and leave to set (not in the fridge).*

14   *Once set, mark into 28 pieces and cut with a sharp knife.*

Caramel Slice - Gluten Free

Makes a 16" x 12" traybake to cut into 28 pieces

This is the version I made for Bev with the puppy-dog eyes. Although it's a gluten free version, it does contain dairy. The only difference customers noticed was that the base wasn't as crumbly as the original version, but most said they preferred it that way. Most didn't even realise it was gluten free.

I always say that there is no such thing as perfection, and I felt that the base of the gluten free caramel slice could still be improved. I tried and tweaked different recipes. I tried one that had ground almonds and nuts in it, which tasted lovely and the base had a lovely texture. Those who liked nuts loved it, but the nut taste was quite strong. The next batch I made, I used just ground almonds, giving the lovely texture, but not the strong nutty taste. I think I may now have my final version of gluten free caramel slice. Of course, never say never…

There is a little word of warning here. Do not forget that when making the caramel, you are dealing with boiling sugar. It WILL splash up and burn as you stir this, so make sure you use a long-handled wooden spoon and wear oven gloves to protect yourself.

The longer you heat the caramel and the darker you make it, the more solid the caramel will be when cooled. In summer I cook the caramel a little longer than in winter, because the heat of the tearoom can sometimes melt it!

Once the caramel slices have been made, cooled, and cut into pieces, I wrap them individually with clingfilm and freeze them, taking them out as I need them. They only take an hour or so to defrost. That way, everyone is sure to be getting their caramel slice at its best (and you'll not be tempted to eat the whole lot yourself at one sitting!).

If your tin is smaller remember to adjust your quantities depending on your tin size.

Ingredients

For Shortbread Base

350g fine polenta	275g ground almonds
310g caster sugar	310g stork block, cut into small pieces
250g rice flour	3 free range eggs

For the Caramel

350g unsalted butter

230g caster sugar

200g golden syrup

2 x 397g tins condensed milk

For the Chocolate Topping

500g gluten and dairy free chocolate

Equipment

16 x 12" traybake tin

Method

For Shortbread Base

1   Preheat oven to 180°c/160°c fan oven.

2   Line a traybake tin with parchment paper.

3   Put the polenta, sugar, rice flour, and ground almonds into a free-standing mixer (or use a hand-held whisk) and mix to combine.

4   Add the stork and mix until you have no large lumps of stork

5   Add the beaten eggs and mix until the mixture starts to come together, but don't get it to form a dough.

6   Empty the mixture into your prepared baking tray and press it down to cover the tray, making sure you get into all the corners. Smooth down with a palette knife or the back of a wooden spoon.

7   Bake for 25-30 minutes until lightly golden brown.

8   Remove from the oven but leave in the baking tin.

For the Caramel

9   Put all the caramel ingredients in a large pan and gently heat on the hob until everything has melted and is well blended, stirring continuously.

10   Bring the mixture to the boil then reduce the heat and simmer, stirring continuously, for another 8-9 minutes until the caramel has turned golden brown.

11   Remove from the heat and continue to stir until the caramel has stopped bubbling.

12   Pour the caramel onto the cooked shortbread base, spreading out into all the corners, and leave to set.

For the Chocolate Topping

13   Melt the chocolate over a bowl of gently simmering water. Once the chocolate has started to melt, remove from the heat and stir gently until all the chocolate has melted.

14   Pour the melted chocolate over the set caramel, spread with a palette knife, and leave to set (not in the fridge).

15   Once set, mark into 28 pieces and cut with a sharp knife.

Caramel Slice – Gluten Free And Dairy Free

Makes a 16 x 12" traybake to cut into 28 pieces

I still can't believe that I actually managed to make a gluten free and dairy free caramel slice that tastes so good. This doesn't suit everyone, though, because the condensed milk is replaced with soya. The caramel has a different taste and texture to the original version, but is equally as good.

I always say that there is no such thing as perfection, and I felt that the base of the gluten free caramel slice could still be improved. So, I tried and tweaked different recipes. I tried one that had ground almonds and nuts in it, which tasted lovely and the base had a lovely texture. Those who liked nuts loved it, but the nut taste was quite strong. The next batch I made, I used just ground almonds, giving the lovely texture, but not the strong nutty taste. I think I may now have my final version of gluten free caramel slice. Of course, never say never…

There is the same little word of warning here, though. Don't forget that when making the caramel, you are dealing with boiling sugar. It WILL splash up and burn as you stir this, so make sure you use a long-handled wooden spoon, and wear oven gloves to protect yourself.

Don't be tempted to over-cook this caramel or you will end up with dairy free toffee. I have found that the mixture, when cooked, is still quite runny. Don't worry, because once it cools and sets, it will firm up. I always place this version in the fridge to set.

If I'm honest, when I make the dairy free caramel in the tearoom, I do tend to make mini pies now, because the heat of the tearoom can make the caramel go quite runny.

Once the caramel slices have been made, cooled, and cut into pieces, I wrap them individually with clingfilm and freeze them, taking them out as I need them. They only take an hour or so to defrost. That way, everyone is sure to be getting their caramel slice at its best (and you'll not be tempted to eat the whole lot yourself at one sitting!).

If your tin is smaller, remember to adjust your quantities depending on your tin size.

Ingredients

For Shortbread Base

350g fine polenta	*275g ground almonds*
310g caster sugar	*310g stork block, cut into small pieces*
250g rice flour	*3 free range eggs*

For Caramel

600 g stork block

600g caster sugar

500 ml soya single cream

4 tablespoons golden syrup

1 teaspoon salt

For the Chocolate Topping

500 g gluten and dairy free chocolate

Equipment

16 x 12" traybake tin

Method

For Biscuit

1   Preheat oven to 180°c/160°c fan oven.

2   Line a traybake tin with parchment paper.

3   Put the polenta, sugar, rice flour, and ground almonds, into a free-standing mixer (or use a hand-held whisk) and mix to combine.

4   Add the stork and mix until you have no large lumps of stork.

5   Add the beaten eggs and mix until the mixture starts to come together, but don't get it to form a dough.

6   Empty the mixture into your prepared baking tray and press it down to cover the tray, making sure you get into all the corners. Smooth down with a palette knife or the back of a wooden spoon.

7   Bake for 25-30 minutes until lightly golden brown.

8   Remove from the oven but leave in the baking tin.

For the Caramel

9   Put all the caramel ingredients in a large pan, and gently heat on the hob until everything has melted and is well blended, stirring continuously.

10   Bring the mixture to the boil then reduce the heat and simmer, stirring continuously, for another 8-9 minutes until the caramel has turned golden brown.

11   Remove from the heat and continue to stir until the caramel has stopped bubbling.

12   Pour the caramel onto the cooked shortbread base, spreading out into all the corners, and leave to set.

For the Chocolate Topping

13   Melt the chocolate over a bowl of gently simmering water. Once the chocolate has started to melt, remove from the heat and stir gently until all the chocolate has melted.

14   Pour the melted chocolate over the set caramel, spread with a palette knife, and leave to set (not in the fridge).

15   Once set, mark into 28 pieces and cut with a sharp knife.

Is this one of your five-a-day?

It's no big secret that I'm not a vegetable lover and now, being in my 50s, this is probably never going to improve, despite Mr M's valiant attempts to change my eating habits.

Creating lovely cakes and bakes for the tearoom has found me using vegetables in more recipes than I'd ever have imagined. There's Craig's Coconut Cake made with courgettes and Popeye's Chocolate Cake made with spinach and avocado. But my favourite has to be carrot cake. A hint of warm spices, sweet carrots, and a not-too-sweet frosting, makes for a delicious teatime treat.

Bev

Carrot cake has been around for many, many years. It's thought that it originates from way back in medieval times. During these times, sugar was very expensive and scarce, whilst carrots were much more plentiful and easier to get hold of. As they contained more sugar than most other vegetables, carrots became a great substitute. Does this mean you're having one of your five-a-day eating a portion of carrot cake? I like to think so.

In the tearoom, carrot cake was a customer favourite with the original recipe, using the traditional cream cheese frosting. Adapting our cakes to make them gluten free and dairy free, it was soon time to tweak the carrot cake. Changing the sponge to gluten free and dairy free didn't pose a problem and the resulting cake was indeed yummy, but the filling and topping were a different matter. Making the cream cheese frosting using a vegan substitute meant the taste and texture were nowhere near as good as the original version, so our carrot cake now has a dairy free frosting without out cream cheese. It must be ok, though, as I've seen customers nearly crying because they've finished their slice!

Naming our carrot cake after one of our customers happened during a Craft, Chat, and Cake session. The tearoom gingernuts originally had Bev's name against them, but in an act of kindness, Bev gave away hers to Gina, who really only ever eats gingernuts. There was one condition, though, Bev declared. 'Gina can have the gingernuts as long as I can have the carrot cake, because it's the nicest carrot cake I've ever tasted.' And that's how our carrot cake became Bev's Carrot Cake.

It would be rude not to introduce Bev, or Beverly to give her Sunday name. I met Bev at a ladies' group and her ears pricked up when she heard me putting cake, gluten free, and craft into the same sentence. Bev is Dashing Tom's daughter, and after our first meeting it didn't take her long to find the tearoom and bring along her dad to show his crafting skills (and have gluten free cake). Bev quickly became part of the tearoom family, joining us for chat, craft, cake, more cake, more chat, and more craft. Many a pleasant Sunday afternoon is spent in the tearoom chatting away to Bev and doing some sneaky crafting – and getting me into trouble with Mr M. (Sunday is not a craft day, of course!).

Bev with her Dad, Dashing Tom

Bev's Carrot Cake

Makes a two layer 9" round cake or 24 individual cakes

Ingredients

For the Cake

350g light brown sugar

350ml vegetable oil

6 free range eggs

280g carrots, topped, tailed, peeled, and grated

200g sultanas

Juice and zest of one large orange

350g gluten free self-raising flour (I use Dove's)

2 teaspoons bicarbonate of soda

2 teaspoons ground ginger

2 teaspoons ground mixed spice

¾ teaspoon xanthan gum

For the Icing

235g stock block

470g icing sugar

1 teaspoon vanilla extract

2 teaspoons lemon juice

Orange and green fondant icing (optional)

Equipment

2 x 9" round deep loose-bottomed cake tins or

2 x 12 hole loose-bottomed mini sandwich tins

Method

For the Cake

1   Preheat the oven to 180°c/160°c fan oven.

2   Grease and line two 9" round deep cake tins with parchment paper or grease, or two 12-hole mini sandwich tins.

3   Put the flour, bicarbonate of soda, ginger, mixed spice, and xanthan gum into a large bowl and stir to combine.

4   Place the eggs into the free-standing mixer (or use a hand-held whisk) and beat for a couple of minutes until the eggs are light and fluffy.

5   Add the sugar and continue to beat until the mixture is again light and fluffy.

6   With the mixer still running, slowly pour in the oil and mix until well combined.

7   Turn the mixer to a slow speed and gradually add the flour mixture until everything is well blended.

8   Add the grated carrots and sultanas, along with the orange juice and zest, and mix until just combined.

9   Divide the mixture between the prepared cake tins and bake in the pre-heated oven for 40 minutes until the cake is well risen, firm to touch, and a cake tester pressed into the centre of the cake comes out clean.

10 Place the tins on a wire rack and leave to cool for 15 minutes before removing them from the tins and leaving to cool completely on the wire rack. If you are making individual cakes, slice the cold cakes horizontally.

For the Icing

11 Place the stork, icing sugar, lemon juice, and vanilla extract into the free-standing mixer and beat until the icing is light and fluffy (start slowly or you will have icing sugar all over your kitchen!).

12 Put one of the cooled cakes on a serving place, flat side down, and spread with a good helping of the icing.

13 Carefully place the second cake on top of this, flat side down, and spread the rest of the icing over the top and sides of the cake.

14 If you wish, make some carrots from the orange and green fondant icing, but this is just for decoration.

15 Make yourself a cup of tea, put your feet up, and enjoy a large piece of this and tell yourself you're having one of your five a day!

Completed homework gets you the cake

Bringing the idea of my book together took many years of collecting recipes, ideas, and tales, gathering photos, and generally enjoying the whole writing process. There was never a rush to finish the book, but finally a target was set to at least get it written, if not published, by Easter 2020. All was going well, with the computer document beginning to look like a book and the target date looking a possibility, until along came the Corona virus, or Covid-19 as it became known. Friday, 20th March, 2020 saw the Prime Minister, Boris Johnson, close all none-essential workplaces, including tearooms, forcing Mother Murphy's Magical Tearoom on the Hill to close for the foreseeable future.

Ellie

Concerned that many of our customers would be very isolated in lockdown without their tearoom to visit, Mr M and I decided we'd do a live Facebook chat every night from our home. The content of the chats was never planned, but provided an avenue for us to let people know we were still there for them, still talking to them, and still listening to them. They couldn't physically join in the chat, but could leave comments as we chatted away. It was the next best thing to being in a discussion with us and other tearoom family members.

Still working on my book, I thought it would be nice to offer up the naming of a couple of the remaining cakes to those joining the chats. I tried this for the first time during our live chat on 7th April, as I was writing up the recipe for our new Apricot and Ginger Loaf which, being a fairly new cake, had not been named after anyone. Before the evening chat, I baked myself an Apricot and Ginger Loaf, then took a large slice of this just before the chat started, showed it to the viewers, and asked who would like it named after them and why. Of course, I then had to eat the cake. Oh, the things I do for my job!

There was a bit of a battle between Linda, Norma, and Alan. We even had my cousin Adrian and my daughter Chloe joining in. Linda tried to convince us she should have the cake because she'd had apricots that day for pudding, had apricots in jelly, and loved ginger. She said she was drooling over the view of the cake, and it just had to be hers. Norma argued that it had to be hers because it was like her – a wee bit fruity and a wee bit spicy. Cousin Adrian was just begging to have a cake named after him, but I've still not forgiven him for the peppermint incident a few years ago! Alan offered to adopt the cake as he used to have a similar one with his Nan at home.

I was almost set on giving the cake to Norma because her answer made me smile, but was also being swayed by Alan's answer as he mentioned his Nan, and I built the tearoom around what my own Grandma would like.

But then Chloe jumped in, saying Ellie, her 14-year-old stepdaughter, wanted it to be hers. Needing more than just family emotional blackmail, I demanded a better reason. The reply was that Ellie had completed all the homework set by school for her during the lockdown.

That did it, with everyone in the debate agreeing it had to be Ellie's cake, because finishing her homework, especially in lockdown, had to be rewarded. Even Norma and Linda finally agreed, although I could imagine Norma downing her large gin and tonic as she handed over the cake, and Linda stuffing herself with all her apricot goodies in Birmingham.

Thanks to the Covid-19 lockdown, our Apricot and Ginger Loaf became Ellie's Apricot and Ginger Loaf.

Ellie's Apricot And Ginger Loaf

Makes a 2lb loaf

This cake is an adaptation of our popular Cherry Cake. If you are going to add a topping of icing to the cooled cake, omit the sprinkling of demerara sugar before you bake the loaf.

This is perfect just as it comes, spread with butter or jam, or as a pudding with a good helping of hot custard. How will you enjoy yours?

Ingredients

250g dried apricots, chopped into quarters
100g ground almonds
185g gluten free self-raising flour (I use Dove's)
1½ teaspoons ground ginger
1 teaspoon xanthan gum
200g very soft stork block
200g light brown sugar
3 free range eggs
1 tablespoon lemon juice
2 tablespoons demerara sugar

Icing Topping (optional)
100g icing sugar
Enough cold water to make a thick but spreadable icing

Equipment

1 x 2lb loaf tin

Method

For the Cake

1   Preheat the oven to 180°c/160°c fan oven.

2   Grease and line a 2lb loaf tin with baking parchment paper.

3   Mix the ground almonds, flour, ginger, and xanthan gum together in a bowl.

4   Put the stork and sugar into a free-standing mixer (or use a hand-held whisk) and whisk until light and fluffy.

5   With the mixer running, gradually add the beaten eggs until well combined, light, and fluffy.

6   Turn the mixer to a slow setting and add the flour mix until well combined.

7   Finally mix in chopped apricots, along with the lemon juice.

8   Spoon the mixture into the prepared loaf tin and level the top.

9   Sprinkle the demerara sugar over the top of the loaf and bake in the pre-heated oven for 60 minutes. The loaf should be well risen and golden brown.

10   Remove from the oven and leave in the loaf tin for 30 minutes before taking the loaves from the tin and leaving to cool completely on a wire rack. Leave the loaf in the parchment paper to cool, though.

Icing Topping

11   Mix the icing sugar with enough cold water to make a thick but spreadable icing, and pour this over the top of the cold cake and allow it to drip down the sides. Leave to set before serving.

There's nothing better than cake but more cake.

President Harry S. Truman

Posh folk in the tearoom

Who doesn't love a traditional cake? And there's nothing more traditional than Cherry Loaf. It's delicious just as it comes, and it's a great energy boost when out walking or cycling. And if you add some hot custard, you have yourself an amazing pudding.

For me, the best bit of the loaf is the crispy end. Some people don't like this, and there have been times when the offending end has had to be removed in the tearoom. On those occasions, you know how much I hate waste, so there's really only one thing to do with it! I like to call it quality assurance.

Naming the different cakes after our lovely customers, I realised some people were going to be disappointed as many people love the same ones. Just as in Bev's Gingernuts that became Gina's Gingernuts, there was a problem with the lemon drizzle cake, which was quickly claimed by Margaret and anyone would have a battle on their hands to steal the name away from her.

The problem was that Nicky the Posh Lady, married to Brian (of The Posh Woman's Husband's Omelette), comes to the tearoom especially for the lemon drizzle. Nicky comes a fair distance from the other side of the Kincardine Bridge to visit us, usually giving plenty warning that she's coming. I like to think this is because she's just excited about thinking of her visit, but in reality, it's probably just to give ample time for lemon drizzle cake to be made.

Nicky is a girl after my own heart and will have hot custard at any opportunity; the highlight of her visit always being her pudding of lemon drizzle cake with lashings of hot custard. I'm not ashamed to say that we enjoy her visits so much that a double portion of custard always seems to end up in Nicky's bowl.

Nicky

What was I to do then, as there was no way I could steal the name back from Margaret? My dilemma was solved one day when Nicky didn't give me ample warning of her visit, resulting in there being no lemon drizzle cake in the tearoom. She was persuaded to try our Cherry Loaf – and she loved it. Phew! Of course, she had it with lashings of hot custard, and that's how our Cherry Loaf became Nicky's Cherry Loaf.

Nicky's Cherry Loaf

Makes a 2lb loaf

Ingredients

   250g glace cherries, rinsed and quartered

   285g gluten free self-raising flour (I use Dove's)

   ½ teaspoon xanthan gum

   200g very soft stork block

   200g caster sugar

   3 free range eggs

   1 tablespoon lemon juice

   2 tablespoons demerara sugar

Equipment

   1 x 2lb loaf tin

Method

1. *Preheat the oven to 180°c/160°c fan oven.*

2. *Grease and line a 2lb loaf tin with baking parchment paper.*

3. *Rinse the cherries in cold water and allow them to drain before mixing them with 2 tablespoons of the flour. This helps to stop them sinking during cooking (not that it matters if this happens, though).*

4. *Mix the remaining flour and xanthan gum together in a bowl.*

5. *Put the stork and sugar into a free-standing mixer (or use a hand-held whisk) and whisk until light and fluffy.*

6. *With the mixer running, gradually add the beaten eggs until well combined and light and fluffy.*

7. *Turn the mixer to a slow setting and add the flour with the xanthan gum until well mixed.*

8. *Finally stir in the lemon juice.*

9. *Spoon the mixture into the prepared loaf tin and level the top.*

10. *Sprinkle the demerara sugar over the top of the loaf and bake in the pre-heated oven for 60 minutes. The loaf should be well risen and golden brown.*

11. *Remove from the oven and leave in the loaf tin for 30 minutes. Then remove from the tin and leave to cool completely on a wire rack, but leave the loaf in the parchment paper to cool.*

12. *Don't try cutting this loaf until it is completely cold or it will be too crumbly. Of course, being the baker, you can cut yourself the scrummy end of the loaf before you share the rest of this traditional delight with your friends and family.*

Poetic licence without the crusts

One of the marvellous things about the tearoom is that we never know who is going to step through the door or what will happen during the day.

We regularly hold Afternoon Tea for 16 events, when the tearoom's closed and only those with the golden tickets can attend. You have to be quick to get a ticket, I can tell you.

In May 2019, it was to be a Britain at War Afternoon Tea for 16. As always, tickets for this sold very quickly and there was a notice in the tearoom advising everyone that the event was fully booked. The week before this event, we were having a busy afternoon getting to know some new customers, Colin and his lovely wife, Chris. As Colin was leaving, he happened to mention that he was a poet with some war-themed poems we could use at our Britain at War event. I thanked him, but didn't expect him to remember our little tearoom once he'd left us.

However, checking my emails that night, Colin had indeed emailed across a whole host of his poems for me to choose from. The most difficult part was selecting just a couple of poems to use – they were all so poignant and moving that I'd have liked to have used them all. I showed the poems to Elaine, now our fabulous lead singer at the Afternoon Tea Events, and asked if she'd like to read one. I'd chosen mine and had one in mind for Elaine. Can you believe she picked one for herself and suggested one for me – the same two I'd selected!

Colin very kindly allowed me to show all his poems on the day and to read out the two we had chosen. (By the way, Colin has published several poetry books in which you can read his terrific words. Take a look at his website, https://cmpoetry.webs.com, or find him on Facebook at Poetic Thoughts). During our Covid-19 live chats, Colin also wrote more poems for us and very kindly allowed me to read his poems out to cheer up our customers. Thank you, Colin.

Our Britain At War Afternoon Tea was a great success, with Colin's poems bringing tears to a few people as we recited A Place of Safety and The Garden Shed. So well received were his poems that we asked him to run a poetry evening for us at the tearoom, and what a fabulous evening it was.

Colin had written a poem about Mother Murphy's Tearoom that made me swell with pride (there may a have been a little tear, too). He read out lots of his other poems from his new book, Of Sadness And Of Joy – some sad, some moving, and some humorous. He also did a little workshop, getting everyone to give a few words about the tearoom and explaining why they come to us.

One customer attending that night was a tearoom regular, Anne – a lecturer at the local college. Anne's comments during the workshop were along the lines of 'Don't come to the tearoom to sit in a corner and read your book, because it just won't happen! I tried it once. I still bring my book with me, but it never gets opened!'

At the end of the evening, Colin and Chris took away all the suggestions, and a few weeks later sent me a fabulous new poem about the tearoom. It's made all the more special, of course, because some of our wonderful customers helped write it.

Anne's comments at the poetry evening made me think back to when she first came into the tearoom.

She did indeed come along with her book, making a very good attempt to read it. The problem in the tearoom is that I like to talk, Mr M likes to talk, and all the customers like to talk. It didn't take long for Anne to start listening to the conversations, chuckling at the conversations, and then joining in with the conversations.

Nowadays, Anne is just as likely to start up a conversation. She still brings along a book or her Kindle, but never reads it. She is now a well-loved member of our tearoom family, has joined our Tearoom Book Club, and comes along to different events, including some of our Afternoon Teas for 16 and, of course, our poetry evening. So, if you come into the tearoom and see somebody pretending to read a book whilst eating crustless fish finger butties, followed by buttered fruit tea loaf, that'll be Oor Anne.

Inspired by the poetry evening, Anne wrote her own poem about the tearoom – and what a lovely poem it is, too. At our Victorian Afternoon Tea in December 2019, Anne was persuaded to recite not only Colin's poem about the tearoom, but also her own one.

Anne's Fruit Tea Loaf

Makes a 2lb loaf

Whether you call it fruit tea loaf, Welsh Bara Brith, or Borrowdale tea loaf, this is quite simply a lovely light fruit loaf made with dried fruit soaked overnight in cold tea. The choice of tea is up to you: perhaps a simple breakfast tea, but why not be a little more daring and use Earl Grey or a whisky tea? Just make sure it's strong tea, made with no milk or sugar.

Fruit tea loaf is usually served cut into thick slices, with lashings of butter and sometimes a slice of cheese. I like mine toasted with jam (and have even been known to have hot custard with it, but you know me and my hot custard).

As our tea loaf is the favourite of our poet Anne, Anne's Fruit Tea Loaf it has to be.

Ingredients

375ml cold strong tea made without milk or sugar
(I use Earl Grey tea, but any tea will be fine)
125g raisins
125g currants
125g sultanas
150g dark brown sugar
1 free range egg, lightly beaten
250g gluten free self-raising flour (I use Dove's)
1 teaspoon gluten free baking powder
1 teaspoon xanthan gum
1 teaspoon mixed spice
Grated zest of 1 orange

Equipment

1 x 2lb loaf tin

Method

1   Start the night before you want to bake the loaf. Make up your chosen tea and leave it to cool.

2   Mixed the raisins, currants, and sultanas together in a large bowl and stir in the cold tea. Cover the bowl with clingfilm and leave overnight for the fruit to soak up the tea.

3   The following day, preheat the oven to 180°c/160°c fan oven.

4   Grease and line a 2lb loaf tin with baking parchment paper.

5   Mix the flour, baking powder, xanthan gum, and spice in a bowl.

6   Add the beaten eggs and sugar to the fruit mixture and stir until blended.

7   Now add the flour mixture and stir until everything is well mixed.

8   Spoon the mixture into the prepared tin and bake in the pre-heated oven for 75 minutes or until the loaf is well risen and a cake tester comes out almost clean.

9   Remove from the oven and leave to cool completely in the tin.

10 Once cooled, cut yourself a thick slice, add lashings of butter, make a steaming pot of tea, and read A Wee Poem by Anne Reid.

A Wee Poem

Come to Mother Murphy's on the hill if you would like some cake.
(Anne's) Tea loaf, ginger sponge, caramel slice, and Battenberg
are just a few that Debra makes.

Now don't worry if you are gluten free
because Mother Murphy's is THE place to be.
You can enjoy ALL the scones and cakes happily
and if you look on the wall you will see
Debra's published recipe for biscuits
to enjoy with your coffee or tea!

It won't be long before you start to meet
the regulars who come along each week.
You will find books, art, sewing, and dominoes,
card making, Christmas wreathes, tea leaf reading
–anything goes! And oor Jim the musician,
who will strum all our favourite songs under the sun.

Afternoon teas and special nights
for book club, songs, and poetry.
Making new friends with arts and crafts
Mother Murphy's is the place to be.
Plenty of hugs and company...
but NOT a quiet place to sit,
as there's always a project on the go
with someone nearby to help you to crochet or to knit!

The 'flippin' bandstand was a lot of work
that nearly caused oor Debra to flip.
Lots of folk pitched in and the old folks home benefitted from the gift!
It all looked braw, we did agree, but now it's back to making blankets
for the wee ones in Maternity (tee).

Over 100 at the last count – definitely a success.

Trying to sort them into piles left Mother Murphy's tearoom in quite a mess!

So, to Mother Murphy's on the hill for the craft, the coffee,

and don't forget to try some… cakes!

Look forward to learning new skills, and of course,

try out the braw food that Jim and Debra make!

Too many things to mention coz we would surely miss and fail

to capture the real reason so many people make the trip.

For it's more than ALL of this that makes this wee place close to our hearts:

the WELCOME, the sense of belonging, the laughter, and the fun,

and yeah, okay, as well as the jam tarts… Empire biscuits, sponges, lemon curd,

and just about everything else under the sun!

So, I am sure that we will all agree

That Jim and Debra have filled a space in this wee community (tee)

For a welcome, a hug, a song, or a coffee or a tea

To be enjoyed with friends and family (ee)

Mother Murphy's surely is THE very, very best place to be!

By Anne Reid, September 2019

Where there is cake, there is hope. And there is always cake.

Dean Koontz

Lycra-clad Murphys

One of my favourite ever things to eat in life has got to be a Terry's Chocolate Orange. Growing up, there would always be one of these delights in my Christmas stocking, along with a satsuma. I loved (and still love) the way the wrapper cuddles the orange segments underneath the foil, giving the impression of a real orange. In the advert with Dawn French, she said to 'tap it and unwrap it'. I put mine in the fridge to make sure that the segments really do fall apart when you tap the orange on the table. When the chocolate's cold from the fridge, you also end up with a chocolate orange core! Who needs satsumas when you can have these!

I'm with Ms French here when she says, 'It's not Terry's, it's mine.' It's a rare day that I'll share my chocolate orange! Then, of course, there was the year I bought a whole load of chocolate oranges to make into little gifts for everyone at our table on Christmas Day, and crocheted different covers for them. Naturally, I made sure I bought more chocolate oranges than needed!

Anyway, moving on from dreaming of the chocolate orange, the next best thing has to be a chocolate orange cake. It does, though, need to be moist, contain chocolate, and must, absolutely must, taste of freshly squeezed oranges. Chocolate must be coated or be drizzled thickly over the cake to finish it off to perfection.

I'd like to take you back to May 2016, to the month I spent living as a coeliac to see how well the tearoom was catering for those with coeliac disease, and also to experience how it felt to have to hunt down safe gluten free food when eating out. In my Facebook posts, I wrote daily notes from my diary to let everyone know how it was going and what I'd experienced each day. There were many grim days, with Monday, 30th May, 2016 being one of the worst – and it did indeed involve a chocolate orange cake. I'd like to share my Facebook post from that day, as this is what ultimately led me to create our very own Chocolate Orange Cake.

Debra's Gluten Free Month – Monday, May 30th, 2016

Thirty days into the month and I've just had the worst experience of the whole month – or perhaps I've just had the perfect experience of how it feels to be coeliac and trying to eat out.

Today, being Monday, was our playing out day with no baking, and a well-deserved bike ride was planned. A round trip of 40 miles would take us from Kirkintilloch, along the old railway path to Strathblane, up to Killearn, across to Fintry, then over the Crow Road down into Lennoxtown and back to Kirkintilloch.

Being a sunny day, the legs were shaved (mine, not Mr M's!) and the Lycra dug out. By the way, you may mock Lycra, but it really is the best material when cycling. The shorts have lots of padding and don't ride up your leg when pedalling; the leggings don't get caught in the chain. It's very good when racing as Lycra is far less wind resistant than a big thick tweed coat and, of course, shows off our fabulous figures!!

Our picnics were made – mine gluten free and Mr M's not. Can I just point out here that I found out at lunchtime I had one tiny gluten free sandwich and Mr M had two massive rolls!

Anyway, we cycled along the old railway line out to Strathblane. This provides a nice easy start to the day but is a little flat, and I was glad to get out onto the road to do some real cycling. We made our way up to Killearn and decided, as it was a hot, sunny day, to treat ourselves to morning coffee and cakes. I'll not name the place we went into! When we first got there, I went in (as I waited for Jim to cycle up the hill to catch up with me) and asked the waitress if she had any gluten free cakes. ‘We have*

a flourless chocolate cake,', was the reply. ‘Is it *gluten free?' I asked.* 'It's made with almonds, *so yes it must be gluten free,' was the reply. The alarm bells were ringing but I ignored them.*

Smiling to myself, I went back out to tell Jim it was ok to go in as I could indeed get a gluten free cake. Bikes locked up outside, we made our entrance, with the whole cafe watching these two sweaty, Lycra-clad folks sliding and clipping across the shiny wooden floor in cycling shoes with cleats (metal bits for fastening your shoes to the pedals).

We slunk our way to the table and the waitress brought us a menu. ‘You can only sit there until 1pm as it's booked from then,' she informed us. *'You'll only be wanting a cake and drink, though, won't you?' Obviously we were not the most welcome customers in their establishment!*

'I'll have the gluten free chocolate cake and a cup of tea please,' I said, with Jim just opting for the tea – there being no biscuits to choose from, and the scones were uncovered.

The tea arrived, and very welcome it was, too. The lovely looking chocolate cake was put down in front of me. Drooling, I again asked if it was totally gluten free. ‘Yes, it's made with almonds,' was the reply.

As I was just about to dig in, I noticed the piece of Terry's Chocolate Orange on the top. I couldn't remember if this was one of the chocolates I was able to eat in my role as a coeliac. Mr M took great delight in telling me that if I was doing this experiment, I had to be absolutely thorough with it. So reluctantly, I asked the waitress, ‘Is this chocolate gluten free?' *She went away to check.*

By this time, the people at the other tables were obviously having a good giggle at us. I saw the waitress asking somebody who looked to be the boss (she didn't have an apron on and was leaning against the counter, so she must have been!). The waitress came back and told me that they thought it was gluten free. I asked her if she could double check for me (more giggles from the table next to us). I watched her ask this person again, who looked over at us, rolled her eyes, sighed, and marched off into the kitchen.

The waitress finally came back and said that the chocolate may in fact contain gluten. I said that in that case I couldn't eat the cake. The waitress took the cake back to the counter and the Terry's Chocolate Orange Cake was taken away from me! A discussion was obviously taking place between the waitress and her very informed manager, then the waitress came marching back to us. Wait for it... 'Can't you just take the chocolate off the cake and then you could eat it?'

Within minutes, we were sitting outside, as Mr M ate his banana and I ate my nut bar.

What poor service, poor staff training, and even more poor knowledge from the person running the place (they claim to do their own baking and should know what is in each item). It was very clear to me that they had no understanding of what gluten is or the consequences for people with an intolerance eating it.

I am starting to understand how people must feel every time they go out to eat somewhere. It's one thing to say that people must voice their complaints at the time in an establishment if something is not right, but once you already feel the laughing stock of the place, the only thing you want to do is to leave.

I can honestly say that the first time anybody is made to feel like this in Mother Murphy's Tearoom will be the day I close my business!

Laura

With this experience fresh in my mind, I set about making my own chocolate orange cake that was light, moist, chocolatey, and tasting like freshly squeezed oranges.

It was round about this time that we had some new customers – Laura and her mum – who came looking for gluten free delights. On one of the first visits, we did indeed have Chocolate Orange Cake on the menu and Laura fell in love with it. As she declared that it was her Chocolate Orange Cake, it just had to become Laura's Chocolate Orange Cake. We even made Laura a full cake for her birthday one year. Happy customers indeed, I think.

This terrible experience for me on a cycle trip gave me the opportunity to ensure this would never happen in our tearoom.

Laura's Chocolate Orange Cake

Makes a 9" round cake

Ingredients

For the Cake

200g stork block, melted

Zest of 4 oranges

Juice of 2 oranges

1.5 teaspoons orange oil

4 free range eggs

200g granulated sugar

2 teaspoons gluten free baking powder

200g ground almonds

100g fine polenta

100g mixed chopped nuts

200g gluten and dairy free dark chocolate chips

For the Orange Drizzle

2 tablespoons granulated sugar

Juice of 2 oranges

To Finish

50g gluten and dairy free dark chocolate, melted

Equipment

1 x 9" deep loose-bottomed cake tin

Method

1. Preheat the oven to 180°c/160°c fan oven.

2. Grease and line a 9" round cake tin with baking parchment.

3. Grate the zest from four oranges and squeeze the juice from two of them.

4. Put the sugar, baking powder, ground almonds, mixed nuts, and polenta into a free-standing mixer and mix to blend.

5. Put the eggs into a large bowl and beat lightly.

6. Melt the stork in the microwave and add to the beaten eggs, along with the orange zest, orange juice, and the orange extract. Add this mixture to the dry ingredients in the mixer and beat until light and smooth.

7. Add the chocolate chips and mix on a slow speed until well blended.

8. Pour the mixture into the prepared tin and bake in the pre-heated oven for 40 minutes until well risen and a cake tester comes out clean.

9. While the cake is baking, squeeze the juice from the remaining two oranges and add this to a bowl with two tablespoons of granulated sugar. Stir to dissolve the sugar.

10. Once the cake is cooked, remove from the oven but leave in the tin. Use cake tester or pointed knife to make holes across the top of the cake and pour the orange and sugar mixture over the cake whilst is still hot.

11. Leave to cool completely in the tin then remove from the tin.

12. Melt the chocolate over a bowl of gently simmering water. Once the chocolate has started to melt, remove from the heat and stir gently until all the chocolate has melted.

13. Drizzle the melted chocolate liberally over the top of the cake and leave to set.

14. Enjoy!

Courgettes in a cake!

Coconut sponge cake sandwiched together with a layer of home-made strawberry jam and coconut buttercream, then coated with more coconut buttercream. Heaven!

It didn't take long for this to become a customer favourite for Craig, the lovely partner of another one of our customers, Nicola (of Nicola's Caramel Slice). Craig would pick this cake over anything else, and would even make a special trip to the tearoom if I posted pictures of it on Facebook, with Nicola using this as an excuse for an extra trip to the tearoom to squeeze in some crafting.

When this cake was first made for the tearoom, it wasn't gluten free or dairy free, and contained condensed milk, giving it a lovely moist sponge. Would it be spoilt trying to adapt this? Eventually, by combining a couple of recipes, our Coconut and Courgette Cake was created, with courgettes

Craig with his Coconut Cake and nephew Charlie

ensuring the cake remained equally lovely and moist (and even lighter). Customers can't believe that the cake is made with grated courgettes. The real test was whether Craig would still like his cake. Last year one of Craig's Christmas presents was a whole coconut cake for himself, which answers the question.

Craig's Coconut Cake

Makes a 2-layer 8" round cake

Ingredients

For the Cake

260 desiccated coconut

4 medium free-range eggs

235g caster sugar

325g courgettes, topped, tailed, peeled, and grated

1 tablespoon vanilla extract

160g rice flour

3 teaspoons baking powder

1 teaspoon bicarbonate of soda

Strawberry or raspberry jam

For the Coconut Frosting

500g icing sugar

150g stork block

50g desiccated coconut

3 tablespoons almond milk

Extra desiccated coconut for sprinkling

Equipment

2 x 8" round deep cake tins

Method

For the Cake

1   *Preheat the oven to 160°c/140°c fan oven.*

2   *Grease and line two 8" round cake tins with baking parchment.*

3   *Put the coconut in the food processor and whizz for a few minutes to get this as fine as possible.*

4   *Put the coconut, flour, baking powder, and bicarbonate of soda in a bowl and mix until well blended.*

5   *Put the eggs and sugar into the free-standing whisk (or use a hand-held whisk) and beat until pale and fluffy. This will take a few minutes.*

6   *Beat in the grated courgette and vanilla extract.*

7   *Add the flour mix to the courgette mixture and beat until well combined.*

8   *Pour into the two prepared cake tins.*

9   *Bake in the preheated oven for 45 minutes.*

10   *Remove from the oven and leave to cool in the tins for 10 minutes. Remove from the tins, take off the parchment paper, and leave to cool completely on a wire rack.*

For the Coconut Frosting

11   *Put the frosting ingredients in a free-standing mixer (or use a hand-held whisk) and beat (slowly at first!) until all the ingredients are mixed and the icing light and fluffy.*

12   *Place one of the cooled cakes on a serving plate and spread with a good dollop of the coconut frosting.*

13   *Turn the other cake over and spread a good coating of your favourite home-made jam.*

14   *Place this cake, jam-side down on the bottom cake.*

15   *Cover the cake sides and top with the remaining coconut icing, and smooth with a palette knife.*

16   *Sprinkle more coconut around the sides and top to finish.*

17   *Enjoy, knowing that you are having one of your five-a-day in your cake.*

Yorkshire friendship hanging on a shaky nail

Sometimes people come into the tearoom, and straight away you know there's something just a little bit special about them. Away back in 2016, when Mother Murphy's Tearoom was still building a reputation as the place for gluten free and dairy free cakes, in walked two girls. As soon as they started to speak and I heard the lilt of their Yorkshire accents, I knew these two people were going to become my friends. And Salena and her sister Danielle are still special people in my life.

It turned out that Salena is a coeliac and had seen a couple of my posts on a gluten free Facebook page. 'I hear you do gluten free cakes,' she said. She was amazed with the choices in the tearoom that day and I'm convinced was nearly crying at one point.

Salena had a proper toasted gluten free sandwich with our own gluten free bread and our home cooked ham. That was before she even got onto the cakes. The expression 'like a kiddie in a candy store' was probably written about Salena that day!

Crafty Sal

Not only was Salena a Yorkshire girl but, like me, she also happens to be left-handed. Salena noticed our small craft section in the tearoom and started to talk about all the crafting she loved to do. Crochet was her big thing. We had a discussion about how I had been trying for many years to learn to crochet, but couldn't get the hang of it as nobody could show me how to do it left-handed. 'I'll show you,' she announced.

Meanwhile, Danielle tucked into her non-gluten free food (or so she thought) and rolled her eyes at our heightened conversation over crafting ideas. Danielle is not a crafter!

It was quickly arranged for Salena to attend one of our Craft, Chat, and Cake sessions to teach me how to crochet. Thanks to her patience and left-handed skills, by the time she left the tearoom on her second visit, I could crochet and had my new best friend.

Salena is now part of our tearoom crafting family and is a big part of my life outside the tearoom. I'm convinced that if anyone should happen to read our on-line conversations, we would be either locked up for our own safety or the safety of others! We do happily call ourselves the two Mad Left-Handed Yorkshire Birds. One day I'm sure we'll have a tearoom/crafting shop together and the world will be a better place. We might call it 'She Baked It and I Made It'. Danielle will still roll her eyes at us and our crafting.

That first day in the tearoom, Salena had our coffee cake, and I had to pull her away from the cake to make sure she didn't lick the whole cake to stop others having it (it's a Yorkshire thing!). Salena said that it had to be best coffee cake she'd ever tasted.

It's no surprise then that our coffee cake quickly became Salena's Coffee Cake. I asked her to give me a little quote to go alongside the cake in my book and she said, 'Delectable, delicious, divine, oh… and mine!'

What do I think is the secret of my coffee cake? Lots of good quality coffee. A coffee cake needs to taste of coffee, with coffee in both the sponge and the frosting. It's also important to use a good quality coffee. I use Nescafe in my cake.

Of course, if you read some of my adventures on the hills, you'll see that, as the saying goes, Salena's friendship membership is now hanging on a shaky nail. Twice I've tried to contact her in my hour of need on the mountains, and twice she's not answered the phone. (Although we have now been able to laugh about this, Salena is determined to get me the best GPS system available. Just in case!)

Salena's Old-Fashioned Coffee Cake

Makes a 9" round cake or

15-18 mini individual cakes

'Delectable, delicious, divine, oh… and mine!' said

Salena, the Left-Handed Yorkshire Crafty Coeliac

Ingredients

For the Cake

350g soft stork block

350g light brown sugar

350g gluten free self-raising flour (I use Dove's)

2 teaspoons gluten free baking powder

1 teaspoon xanthan gum

6 free range eggs

8 teaspoons instant coffee dissolved in 5 teaspoons boiling water

For Coffee Frosting

150g very soft stork block

300g icing sugar

4 teaspoons instant coffee dissolved in 4 teaspoons boiling water

50g gluten and dairy free plain chocolate (I use Plamil's)

Equipment

2 x 9" round loose-bottomed cake tins or

2 x 12-hole mini sandwich tin

Method

For the Cake

1. *Preheat oven to 180°c/160°c fan oven.*

2. *Line two 9" round cake tins with parchment paper, (I use a parchment paper liner) or grease 2 x 12-hole mini sandwich tins.*

3. *Put all the ingredients in the free-standing mixer (or use a hand-held mixer) and beat together until light and smooth.*

4. *Divide the mixture between the baking tins, and smooth the top.*

5. *Bake in the pre-heated oven for 30 minutes.*

6. *Remove from the oven and leave in the tins to cool for 30 minutes before turning out of the tins and leaving to cool completely on a wire rack. (If making individual cakes, cut the cakes in half horizontally once cold.)*

For the Coffee Frosting

7. *Put all the frosting ingredients in a free-standing mixer (or use a hand mixer) and beat until smooth.*

8. *Place one of the cooled cakes, flat side down, on s serving plate and spread over half of the frosting.*

9. *Top with the other cooled cake, flat side down, and spread the remaining icing over the cake.*

10. *Drizzle the melted chocolate over the cake.*

Let's face it, a nice creamy chocolate cake does a lot for a lot of people;
it does for me.

Audrey Hepburn

The girl who would be Hannah

Today's hike was to go up Ben Ledi in the Trossachs, which is the hill you see when driving to Callander. Standing at 879 meters, it's a Corbett rather than a Munro, but still a good hike to the top. I knew I was going to have a good day when my lost Maltesers from last week's walk were found in the bottom of my rucksack. First morning snack sorted!

It should be a 40-minute or so drive from my house to the car park just past Callander. Do you know how many people work at the Prudential offices just off the A9? Well, after this morning's rush-hour drive and long wait along the A9, I can hazard a good guess!

Anyway, all that was soon forgotten once Beatrix our Border Collie and I had parked the car by the Strathyre Lodges off the A85. We were soon strolling along the track, me munching my newly-found Maltesers and Beatrix finding herself a new stick. I was chuckling to myself at the weather warnings issued this week for temperatures of minus ten degrees, along with snow and ice. Looking at the fells, there did look to be some snow on the tops, but nothing to shout about. It was so mild, and I was soon stopping to take off my gloves and neck warmer, and tucking them safely away in the rucksack for later if needed.

After a bit of a pull up the forest, the climb eases for a while as you meander your way up through Stank Glen. It's so peaceful up through this glen that you can practically feel all of life's stresses and anxieties falling away as you stroll along.

Before long, the climbing started again, and the snow level was soon reached. It was time to put on my crampons and an extra layer of clothing under my jacket, as the wind was starting to bite a little. The photo I never managed to get today as I was busy getting my crampons on was Beatrix finding the bones of a dead sheep and running round it with its leg in her mouth. I'm glad that BBC News was not following me today as this would have made for a strange film – Yorkshire Lass, who would be Hannah Hauxwell, chasing her Border Collie to stop her eating a dead sheep's leg. Fortunately, I had one of my Fab Slices with me and Beatrix is quite partial to my baking, so I was able to bribe her away from the leg.

I've walked up Ben Ledi many times, and was looking forward to reaching the top slopes to be rewarded with a good view of the many Munros you can usually see, and imagining they would be all be dusted with snow today. The forces of nature had other ideas for me, though. Clouds were soon heading my way, but I thought nothing of it.

However, very quickly these thick, freezing clouds descended on us, enveloping us in a coldness I'd never experienced before. It reminded me of a scene out of the film, The Day After Tomorrow. Beatrix was starting to look like a polar bear, my purple jacket was turning white, and ice had suddenly formed on my walking poles.

Debra and Beatrix planning their route

I knew the summit couldn't be far away so made the decision to continue upwards, following in footsteps of previous walkers, with my adrenaline just shy of turning into fear.

Turning round wasn't really an option, as the route back was now so ill-defined in the clouds. My thinking was that if I could reach the top, I'd soon be out of the clouds, and once at the summit trig-point I'd be able to get my bearings and start the relatively straightforward descent.

Thankfully, like some sort of miracle, in the distance I could just make out the summit trig-point and made a bit of a spurt for this before it disappeared

Is it a polar bear or is it Beatrix

into the clouds again. Sitting behind the stone pillar out of the wind, I grabbed a quick cup of tea and a sandwich and gave Beatrix the lovely ham Mr M had packed for her. She did, of course, have half of my tuna butty, too. Have you ever tried to resist Border Collie begging eyes – especially ice-covered Border Collie begging eyes?!

Sitting there, I realised I could only see just past the end of my arm and had absolutely no idea which was the correct route off the mountain. Beatrix told me to take a deep breath, get out the map and compass, and work out the direction. This I did, but as I stood up, my foil-backed mat blew away. I asked Beatrix if she'd go and get it for me, but she just laughed.

I worked out the direction of travel required, but was so unsure about my decision that I had a bit of a panic. I looked at my phone. A full signal! Heck, I can't even get a signal in my front room, and here I was in white-out conditions on a mountain in the Trossachs with a full signal. Now, normally I'd ring Mr M and have a chat to him, but thinking he'd just have a major panic and have the mountain rescue called out to me, I did the next best thing and phoned my pal Crafty Sal. Salena's phone rang and rang but no answer. Salena's friendship membership was cancelled there and then!

Suddenly out of the clouds appeared two icy figures in exactly the same direction I had planned to go. Chatting with the two men about which way they'd come from, it was obvious they had indeed come up the route I needed. Next time compass reading skills are needed, I'll have more faith in myself.

We set off again with Beatrix taking the lead as usual, calling her back when she was getting too far in front for me to see her. Even in my anxious state, I was able to find the funny side of watching my ice dog slide herself down the hills as though she was on a sledge, run back up to me and then do it all again, having a roll in the snow just for good measure. And there was me worrying that I was going to kill Beatrix with the cold!

Away from the summit, we were soon able to start descending at a fair rate, and the clouds began to open out a little, giving glimpses of the route ahead. Before long, we found ourselves out of the clouds and below the snow level. Stopping to take off my crampons, I took the opportunity to enjoy a break with my now lukewarm tea and the rest of my lunch.

Sitting there looking down on Loch Lubnaig in all its glory, I sighed to myself with relief at surviving another one of my adventures, and started to contemplate which bits I'd share with Mr M. A couple of hours later, I was home, showered, changed, and being pampered by Mr M. If only he knew!

Why did our Fab Slice that I enjoyed on the hill become Charlotte's Fab Slice, you might ask? Making these many years ago, long before we opened the tearoom, it was an adaptation of a recipe for something called energy bars. I found the bars way too sweet and sticky, so put in less honey, sugar, and butter. These became one of our favourite snacks for our cycle trips, with a big stash of these made for our five-week cycle tour of Scotland. They lasted a good couple of weeks but only thanks to me being very strict with Mr M, as he would have had them eaten within the first few days!

When we later opened the tearoom, I was sure these would be one of the popular bakes. When the customers didn't seem interested in these delights, I couldn't understand it and discussed it with a few people. It turns out it was the name that was putting people off, as it sounded like something way too healthy.

As a trial, I changed the name to Fruit and Nut Slice, and would you believe they sold like hot cakes? It's amazing that what we call something in the tearoom can have a huge effect on whether it's popular or not.

Not long after we started our Craft, Chat, and Cake sessions in the tearoom, in popped this smiling, chatty young lady, Charlotte, who very quickly became part of our tearoom family. If we could give an award for the friendliest, happiest, most helpful person, Charlotte would win hands down.

Charlotte the Temptress

Charlotte is an incredibly talented crafty person, and we are often in awe of her creations at the sessions. Embroidery, sewing, drawing – all freehand – are just some of her talents. She does lead us into temptation, though, by showing us new things every time she comes along, leading to her nickname being The Temptress. Charlotte likes nothing better than to have a pot of very weak leaf tea to accompany her crafting, chatting, and cake. I could list hundreds of cakes that she loves, but the fruit and nut slices were one of her favourites and when they were drizzled with chocolate, she described them as just fab! That's it! Fab Slice for the name; and of course, Charlotte's Fab Slice.

They still sell like hot cakes in the tearoom, and it's not the first time I've hidden a couple away for myself for my walking or cycling trips.

Charlotte's Fab Slice

Makes 28 squares

My recipe is for a large 16" x 12" traybake. If your tin is smaller, remember to adjust your quantities depending on your tin size.

Ingredients

350g stork block

350g runny honey or golden syrup

525g gluten free porridge oats

350g soft light brown sugar

2 pinches salt

175g dried chopped apricots

175g dried dates chopped

175g raisins

175g cherries, rinsed and chopped

100g chopped nuts

100g sunflower seeds

100g pumpkin seeds

175g desiccated coconut

Equipment

1 x 16" x 12" traybake tin

Method

1 *Preheat oven to 180°c/160°c fan oven.*

2 *Grease and line a traybake tin with parchment paper.*

3 *Put the stork and honey into a pan and heat gently on the hob until melted.*

4 *Once everything has melted, bring the mixture to the boil and cook for a further two minutes, stirring continuously. Remove the pan from the heat and leave to cool.*

5 *Put the remaining ingredients in a large bowl and mix well to combine.*

6 *Add the cooled honey mixture and mix well until everything is well combined.*

7 *Tip the mixture into the prepared baking tray and spread with a spatula to level the surface.*

8 *Bake in the pre-heated oven for 20-30 minutes until golden brown.*

9 *Remove from the oven, mark into squares, and leave to cool in the tin.*

10 *Once cool, cut into squares.*

11 *For a special treat, drizzle some melted chocolate over your fab slices and leave to set before cutting.*

12 *Enjoy with a hot cup of tea and think of Debra and Mr M cycling over the Applecross Bealach na Ba Pass to earn an extra Fab Slice.*

Flapjacks

Makes 24 squares

My recipe is for a large 16" x 12" traybake. If your tin is smaller remember to adjust your quantities depending on your tin size.

Flapjacks were always one of my favourite treats around bonfire night at home. The only thing that disappointed me was that often there would be fruits or nuts in some of them, which I never liked as a youngster.

I decided I'd have my flapjacks in the tearoom just as they come (or with a little extra chocolate) and save the fruit and nuts for our Fab Slices.

For something a little different, especially at bonfire night, you could replace the golden syrup with black treacle or try half syrup and half treacle.

Ingredients

750g gluten free oats
375g stork block
375g dark brown sugar
375g golden syrup
200g gluten and dairy free chocolate (optional)

Equipment

1 x 16" x 12" traybake tin

Method

1. Preheat oven to 180°c/160°c fan oven.

2. Grease and line a traybake tin with parchment paper.

3. Put the stork, sugar and syrup into a pan and heat gently on the hob until melted and combined. Stir frequently to ensure the mixture does not stick to the pan.

4. Once everything has melted and is well combined, add the oats.

5. Stir until all the oats are combined then scrape the mixture into the prepared tin.

6. Smooth the mixture with a palette knife and bake in the pre-heated oven for 20 minutes until golden brown.

7. Remove from the oven, mark into squares and leave to cool in the tin.

8. Once cool, cut into squares.

9. For a special treat, melt the chocolate in a microwave and dip the cooled flapjacks in to partly coat or simply drizzle the melted chocolate over the them.

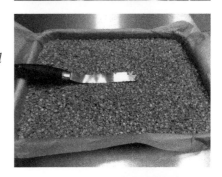

Remember, no matter what life throws at us, we can always bake a cake!

Sarah Ban Breathnach

It's not a fly cemetery!

I do love something sweet that has juicy mixed fruit in it, and a fruit slice ticks all the boxes. The jury is still out as to whether the slice should be simply sprinkled with sugar or finished with a covered of icing. If the fruit is plentiful and there is sweet spice, then a sprinkling of sugar is enough. Oh, but then the icing covered one… Really, the choice is yours.

It's not just the topping of this bake that causes debate, it's also the name. I've always just called this a fruit slice but have discovered in Scotland they call this a fly cemetery. No! A fly cemetery to me is an Eccles Cake or a Chorley Cake which has lovely little pockets of currants wrapped in either flaky or shortcrust pastry.

Chorley and Eccles are towns in Lancashire, and many a time I cycled through these on a Sunday run with my local cycle club when I still lived in England. Maybe this is why I just love the fruit and pastry combination (whatever that combination may be) as when you're out cycling, perhaps doing 60-80 miles that day, you can't beat an energy boost of fruit and sugar.

I'm often reminded of these memories as I travel the train journey back and forth from Scotland to Halifax to visit my children, and I wrote about this in one of my blogs. (You can sing Simon and Garfunkel's Homeward Bound as you read it).

So, there I was on the Northern Rail train from Halifax to Preston, heading back up to Scotland. Was I homeward bound or was I leaving home?

The train was almost empty. I had the whole carriage to myself and my thoughts, very different from the journey on Sunday down from Scotland. On that train, there were only two carriages but enough people with suite cases to fill at least four carriages. Sweaty sardines would be an apt description.

This journey, though, was very peaceful. The train pulled away from Halifax station, leaving behind the large Nestle factory and the giant poster stating, 'Quality Street, Proudly made in Halifax since 1936'. The view from the train is limited at first, with steep embankments on either side along the valley bottom to Sowerby Bridge (pronounced Sorby). The luscious hills of the Calder Valley soon begin to appear. On the hillside on the right, like a knight guarding over Calderdale, stands Wainhouse Tower. This impressive tower was originally built in the 1800s as a chimney for the local dye works to meet the Smoke Abatement Act, but was never actually used as a working chimney. Whatever the reason was that this tower was built, it is certainly impressive. It has always been, and still is, my guiding beacon to tell me when I'm arriving at or leaving Halifax.

The train journey trundles gently along and very soon reaches Mytholmroyd. This area is one of my favourite cycling areas, with the hills up from Mytholmroyd taking you over Cragg Vale. This beautiful valley came into the national news with the Tour de France route going up it in 2014. Cragg Vale from Mytholmroyd proudly claims to be the longest continual ascent in England, with 968 feet of climbing in 5.5 miles. It's not a steep climb by anyone's imagination but more a long, long drag. Some cyclists like short, steep climbs, but this is my type of hill and I'm still in my element riding this type of route.

Aged 14 or 15 years old, I would often take myself off over Cragg Vale to the reservoir at the top, turning right at Blackstone Edge, descending down the sweeping road to Littleborough, back along the Calder Valley to return to Halifax. The valleys and open moors were a safe haven for me, providing the solace and solitude I craved. I often wondered what my headmistress, teachers, and fellow school pupils would think if they knew about my cycling. This was an all girls' grammar school where we were taught to be ladies, and from where I was once sent home for being indecently dressed for wearing sandals without socks! There was I clad in cycling gear (not quite Lycra in those early days, but still tight-fitting), sweating from the effort, swigging water from my bottle, and munching on Mars bars from my back pocket in public!

Along the valley bottom, the train line follows the canal and the new flood defences now in place as you approach Hebden Bridge. This village has suffered terrible floods over the years, especially in 2012, 2015 and 2019. All along the valley, the stone-built houses are quite obviously built from Yorkshire stone, and I'm sure if you were blindfolded and dropped in any area in Calderdale, you could describe the stone buildings and everyone would say, 'Oh, you must be in Calderdale.'

Leaving Hebden Bridge, the views start to subtly change. The moors come into view, the valley widens, and the houses start to change. There are streets upon streets of terraced houses built on hillsides at what look like a totally impossible angle to be safe (but have been there for a lifetime). There are different trees, bushes, and flowers along the train line, with so many different greens reminding me of an artist's paint palette. The valley closes in on the railway again. Hills climb steeply at either side and you can feel the slowing of the train as it climbs, almost crawling, up the valley.

Then it happens. The line levels, the Calder Valley is gone, and the open moors of Lancashire await. There's always been a friendly rivalry between Yorkshire and Lancashire folk (though it was not always friendly in the past!). Growing up, I remember a TV advert aimed at encouraging youngsters to drink milk. Two young boys arrive home covered in mud, still in their football strips. One boy gets the glass milk bottle from the fridge and starts to drink it. He tells the other boy his dad says that if you don't drink your milk, you'll end up playing football for Accrington Stanley! 'Where's Accrington Stanley?' asked the other boy. 'Exactly,' comes the reply!

My sadness of once again leaving Halifax is gradually replaced with anticipation of the onward journey through the Lake District, the borders of Scotland, and finally back home to Kirkintilloch, with the pot of gold at the end of my rainbow journey being in the form of Beatrix (and Mr M, of course).

In the tearoom, I'd developed a fruit slice that I was very happy to serve (and eat), with customers coming in especially for this little square delight; cold, hot, with custard, with ice cream. One customer found it so delicious she immediately ordered a second bowl of this fruit slice with custard!

My next challenge was to convert my Fruit Slice to be gluten free and dairy free. Could I replicate my usual recipe for my fruit slice to have a gluten free and dairy free shortcrust pastry that would still literally melt in your mouth? The filling wasn't a problem, as it was naturally gluten free and dairy free. But the first version of our gluten free and dairy free fruit slice was a little disappointing. The filling was exactly the same, but the pastry was a bit difficult to cut, even though it tasted not too bad.

Our now almost resident gluten free taste-tester, Bev, was very happy to sample this, along with Louise, who can eat gluten and dairy. Bev's opinion was that even though the pastry was a little soft, it was still better than any bought gluten free fruit slice. Both Bev and Louise tucked happily into their bowl of fruit slice served with a big helping of hot custard, and I did at one point think they were both going to lick the bowls. All in all, not a total failure, but not a fruit slice I was happy to serve and ask people to part with their money for.

Bev, of course, was quite happy with my decision, as she left the tearoom that afternoon armed with a whole batch of fruit slices to go in her freezer. For days afterwards, I would receive photos in messages, showing her eating the fruit slices, and did wonder at one point if she was having a fruit slice for every meal, including breakfast!

Fruit Slice

Makes a large 16" x 12" traybake to cut into 24 squares

My recipe is for a large 16" x 12" traybake. If your tin is smaller, remember to adjust your quantities depending on your tin size.

Ingredients

Fruit Filling

600g raisins

300g currants

400g caster sugar

400ml cold water

2 tablespoons cornflour

2 teaspoons ground All Spice

Pastry

875g gluten free self-raising flour (I use Dove's)

3 teaspoons xanthan gum

463g stork block

Cold water

1 free range egg, lightly beaten (optional)

Caster sugar to sprinkle

Icing (optional)

300g icing sugar

Cold water

Equipment

16" x 12" traybake tin

Method

Making the fruit filling

1 *Preheat oven to 190°c/170°c fan oven.*

2 *Grease and line a large traybake tin with parchment paper.*

3 *Put all the fruit filling ingredients in a large pan and bring to the boil.*

4 *Boil for about 5 minutes, stirring constantly, until the mixture has thickened.*

5 *Remove from the heat and leave to cool.*

Making the pastry

6 *Put the flour, baking powder, and xanthan gum into a free-standing mixer (or a large bowl) and whisk to mix.*

7 *Cut the stork into small cubes and add to the flour mix. Have the mixer running at low speed and mix until you have rough breadcrumbs (or rub in with your fingers).*

8 *Add cold water, a little at a time, with the mixer still running (or mixing with a knife) until you have a soft but not sticky dough.*

9 *Cut the dough into two equal pieces and roll out each piece until it is large enough to cover the baking tray.*

10 *Carefully lift one of the pieces (use the rolling pin to help you to lift the rolled-out pastry) and place in the baking tray, making sure you press it into the four corners.*

11 *Cover the pastry with the cooled fruit mixture and spread out covering all the pastry.*

12 *Carefully lift the second piece of pastry (again, use the rolling pin to help here) and place this over the fruit.*

13 *Prick the pastry all over with a fork and then brush with beaten egg (or milk/almond milk if you need to avoid egg).*

14 *Bake in the pre-heated oven for 30 minutes until lightly browned.*

15 *Remove from the oven and (if you are not coating it in icing later) sprinkle with sugar.*

16 *Leave to cool completely in the tin before cutting into 24 equal pieces.*

17 *If you are adding icing to this, wait until completely cold. Mix the icing sugar with enough cold water to make a thick paste and carefully spread over the pastry, and leave to set before slicing.*

The breeze blew around the open-topped car

I've lived in Scotland now for over 15 years, and truly feel at home here. Of course, this doesn't mean I've forgotten my roots, as I'll always be a Yorkshire girl at heart. I even have a mug in the tearoom that reads 'You can take the girl out of Yorkshire, but you can't take Yorkshire out of the girl'. Very true indeed.

Yorkshire's a great central place to go travelling in any direction. I've been lucky enough to have fabulous holidays, both walking and cycling, in Devon, Cornwall, Wales, and of course, the beautiful Lake District.

In my teens, my love of cycling took me all over Yorkshire, but my own cycle runs and club runs never really managed to get beyond Horton-in-Ribblesdale or Ingleton in North Yorkshire. I was introduced to the Lake District by my son's father, long before Benjamin even came along, and can still remember my first journey up to beautiful Cumbria.

The magnificent Langdale Pikes

I was a troubled soul growing up and had lots of demons to fight, but never had the strength or confidence to allow anyone to fight them with me. Sometimes, out of the blue things just seem to happen to help you cope with life. In the early 80s, one early summer evening found me as a passenger in a Triumph   Vitesse convertible with the roof down, travelling up the A65 through Keighley, Skipton, Kirby Lonsdale, and finally onto the dual carriage way towards the Lakes.

The early evening sun was shining, and as the road dipped and twisted leaving Kirby Lonsdale, the views of the Lake District hills started to come into view. I was in awe. There in front of me was the most beautiful backdrop of hills I'd ever seen (and coming from Yorkshire, that's saying something!). I now know that these were the magnificent profiles of the Langdale Pikes, Wetherlam, and The Old Man of Coniston.

There was a cassette player in the car (some younger people may need to Google what a cassette player is) and I selected *Born to Run* by somebody called Bruce Springsteen. As I listened to the tracks on the cassette, they just seemed to blend into each – *Thunder Road*, through to *Born to Run*, and finally *Jungleland*. The music, the wonderful singing voice, the breeze blowing around the open-topped car, the golden evening sunshine, and the vision of the Lake District appearing in front of me, all seemed to be warming my soul. Gradually, I could feel the heavy load that I carried constantly on my young shoulders start to lift and transport me into an unknown world of peace, calmness, and of unbelievable solace. For the first time in many years, I was able to be at one with myself.

That memory has stayed with me and has been a lifeline for me over many years. Now when my demons try to take over my mind, I find myself a quiet space, turn out the lights, draw the curtains, block out the

world, turn on the album *Born to Run*, and take my mind back to that journey. That album can now transport me to that moment in time and the sense of peace, calmness, and safety. For me, this works. Everyone needs their own way of coping when life becomes too much to handle, and you should look for yours.

I've spoken to Mr M about this, and he's grateful for the love that has grown between us and which allowed me to let him slowly into my deepest and darkest world. Now when he sees me disappear with Bruce, he knows that the demons are tapping me on the shoulder, and he understands a little more.

Many years later, I introduced Mr M to the Lake District and he, too, has fallen under its spell. For me, it's wonderful that his favourite place in the Lakes is also one of mine – Grasmere, a small village between Ambleside and Keswick. The poet William Wordsworth lived in Grasmere for 14 years and called it 'the loveliest spot that man hath ever found', and I would totally agree with him. One of Mr M's favourite poems is by Wordsworth, 'I Wandered Lonely as a Cloud', and you'll often hear him reciting this in the tearoom. I've even managed to get a daffodil planted for him in the Daffodil Garden next to the church-yard where Wordsworth and his family are buried.

Next door to the church is the amazing Grasmere Gingerbread Shop, selling the most fantastic ginger-bread, invented by Sarah Nelson in 1854. This is a spicy-sweet cross between a cake and a biscuit. As you walk the road down to the church through the village, you get the wonderful smell drifting from the small shop where it is baked fresh each day. I tasted this delight when visit-ing Grasmere all those years ago, and just love it. Grasmere Gingerbread is still to this day made to the same secret family recipe, and is not sold anywhere other than in this tiny shop in Grasmere.

Over the years I've tried to replicate this gingerbread, with varying degrees of success. I finally thought I'd created a good recipe that tasted great, but it was still not a patch on the real thing. Then once we started to expand our gluten free and dairy free range in the tearoom, I had to start exper-imenting again. Again, I altered the ingredients, changed the texture, and added different spices. Once again, I thought I had a good recipe, with Mr M even saying that he preferred my version to Sarah Nelson's!

Myles learning to crochet

The problem in the tearoom in Scotland was, though, that not many people had tasted the original Grasmere Gingerbread so didn't really understand exactly what I was trying to achieve. They couldn't understand why I kept trying to change the recipe, as they liked each version I made. That was until one Friday afternoon, when into the tearoom strolled two young men.

'I hear you do gluten free cakes,' said one of them, who I now know to be the lovely Myles. Since that day, he and his husband Garry quickly became regulars in the tearoom. We've shared ideas about books, this and that, and I've even taught Myles to crochet as it turns out that he is a left-hander like me.

Not only that, but Myles and Garry love the Lake District, especially Grasmere and, of course, Grasmere Gingerbread. Being coeliac, Myles can no longer have the lovely gingerbread, so he was very keen to try my version. He agreed that it was lovely, but not quite like the real thing. Myles gave me a link to a recipe by a certain Mr Oliver, which was described as the next best thing to the original Grasmere Gingerbread, and said he had every faith in me to reproduce this in a gluten free version. The challenge was set.

In Mr Oliver's recipe, he uses ready-made shortbread. Hmmm! Using ready-made gluten free shortbread would ensure that my next version of the gingerbread would be dire. But what if I used my new gluten free and dairy free Empire Biscuit recipe for the shortbread, changed the remaining flour to gluten free flour, used stork block instead of butter, and added a touch of xanthan gum? It was obvious while it was baking that this was a much-improved version, and really did look and smell like the real thing. But what would it taste like? Oh my! It was amazing, even though I say it myself.

Myles and Garry returned to the tearoom and were my official taste-testers for this. They both agreed it was pretty awesome but still needed a tweak or two to be just perfect. What was it that was missing? I was running out of ideas for the missing flavour until one day when Mr M was reading through a book, *Dining with the Wordsworths*, and there it was: caraway seeds! Could that be the missing spice?

A new batch of gingerbread was made and caraway seeds added. The smell when it was cooking was just like being transported back to Grasmere, and I could hardly wait for it to cool down to taste it. It was fabulous – a strong smell of ginger and nicely browned. It didn't snap when I bit into it, but had a slightly chewy centre, and the crumble topping, which is the most important part, was just right. I thought my version was the closest thing to the real thing.

Never one to rest on my laurels, though, I wondered if there was something I could use instead of caraway seeds, as they are quite difficult to grind. Scouring the internet for different substitutes, anise, aniseed, and fennel were all suggested, as they all give the lovely liquorice flavour. Liquorice in the Grasmere Gingerbread? I wondered. Well, let's just try it. I figured that a liquorice flavour would not spoil the bake, and if it took away from the authentic taste of the original Grasmere Gingerbread, I could always go back to using caraway seeds.

Well, if you ask me, I think I've really cracked it this time, with the gingerbread thinner and cut into rectangles rather than my usual squares. If I didn't know better, I could be fooled into believing I was already back in Grasmere. Of course, the real test will be the verdict of the customers in the tearoom, especially those who have tasted the real thing.

Perhaps I'll bring some of the original Grasmere Gingerbread back with me from our holidays – though of course, those needing gluten free and dairy free will only be able to taste my version. Even better, maybe I'll take a batch of mine down with me, sit outside the Grasmere Gingerbread shop, and share my own gluten free and dairy free version.

Myles' Grasmere Gingerbread

Makes a large 16" x 12" Traybake to cut into 24 squares

My recipe is for a large 16" x 12" traybake. If your tin is smaller, remember to adjust your quantities depending on your tin size.

Ingredients

For the shortbread

(you will need two batches of this)

150g gluten free plain flour

½ teaspoon xanthan gum

75g cornflour

75g icing sugar

200g stork block

For the Grasmere Gingerbread

340 g demerara sugar

6 teaspoons ground ginger

80g mixed peel

4 stem ginger lumps

140g gluten free plain flour

2 pinches gluten free baking powder

80g golden syrup

80g black treacle

140g stork block

1 teaspoon carraway seeds or

2 tsp anise extract

Equipment

16" x 12" traybake tin

Method

For the Shortbread

1   Preheat oven to 200°c/180°c fan oven.

2   Line several baking trays with parchment paper.

3   Put all the shortbread ingredients in a free-standing mixer or food processor, and beat/whizz until the mixture comes together as a soft dough.

4   Repeat stage 3 to give you two lots of the shortbread dough.

5   Dust the worktop with gluten free flour, roll the dough out to about the thickness of a pound coin, and cut with a cutter dipped in flour to stop it sticking. (Don't worry about being too neat here, as you are going to crumble the biscuits in the Grasmere Gingerbread.)

6   Re-roll the dough that's left and cut more biscuits until all the dough has been used.

7   Use a fish-slice or palette knife to lift the cut dough onto the prepared baking trays.

8   Bake for 15 minutes (you do not want them to brown).

9   Remove from the oven. Leave on the baking trays for 10 minutes, and then transfer to a wire rack to cool completely.

For the Grasmere Gingerbread

1   Lower the oven to 180°c/160°c fan oven.

2   Grease and line a large traybake tin with parchment paper.

3   Put the cooled biscuits, demerara sugar, and 4 teaspoons of the ground ginger into a food processor and whizz until you have fine crumbs.

4   Take 200g of the crumbs and set aside.

5   Add the other two teaspoons of ground ginger, stem ginger, mixed peel, flour, and baking power to the crumb mix in the food processor, and blitz again until it is well mixed.

6   Put the golden syrup, black treacle, and stork into a pan, and melt over a low heat on the hob.

7   Remove from the heat, add in the crumb mix from the processor, and stir well to combine.

8   Tip this mixture into the prepared baking try and press down firmly.

10 Bake in the pre-heated oven for 10 minutes until golden brown. Sprinkle the reserved crumbs over the gingerbread and bake for another 10 mins.

11 Remove from the oven and mark the squares on the hot gingerbread, but leave in the tray to cool completely.

12 Once cooled completely, cut the gingerbread into your marked pieces.

13 Sit back, relax with a piece of Grasmere Gingerbread and a steaming cup of tea, imagining you're sitting on the banks of Rydal Water, enjoying the view over Helm Crag.

Two friends, laughter, chat, gossip, and cake

Who doesn't love the simplicity of a lemon drizzle cake? This is an easy cake to make and is moist, full of lemon flavour, with a crunchy, sugary topping to finish. It's important to use the best quality lemons you can buy and to make sure that they're un-waxed, as you'll be using the zest in your bake. Also, make sure you put the lemon drizzle on the cake whilst the cake is still warm, to ensure you get a lovely crisp topping.

Of all the cakes and bakes served in the tearoom, this lemon drizzle is one of the most popular. I only make a gluten free and dairy free version of this now, but nobody seems to realise. We serve it just as it comes, but it's also very popular served warm with hot custard.

When Margaret first came into the tearoom, she was as quiet as a mouse, but was just amazed with the choices she could have that would be ok for her coeliac disease – pancakes with bacon and maple syrup, toasted sandwiches made with home-made gluten free bread, French toast made with home-made gluten free bread.

Why is it Margaret's Lemon Drizzle, though? Margaret started coming into the tearoom after her good friend Fiona discovered that we did gluten free food (Fiona of Fiona's Stem Ginger Cake). The two women meet up every Thursday for a good old gossip and for something to eat. Being a coeliac, though, Margaret finds it difficult to find places where she feels she can safely eat out. Widowed several years ago, she was also quite nervous about going to places by herself.

It's with enormous pride that I can say Margaret is now so much at ease in our tearoom that she comes along by herself if Fiona is unable to meet her. She is happy to chat to Mr M and myself, and she is very comfortable talking, laughing, and joking with all the other customers.

Margaret's favourite cake is the lemon drizzle cake, and the first thing she does when she arrives is to walk up and down the cake display to see what we have. She is often in my mind when planning the cakes and bakes for the week. Knowing that there are very few cakes Margaret will try, I always aim to make sure that there will be the Lemon Drizzle or the Cherry Cake for her. Mind you, I'm pretty sure that Margaret could have her name after Salena's Coffee Cake, too.

Often in the tearoom I have to cut a thin slice off the end of loaves, because so many people don't like that bit; it's something I can't quite get my head around, as in Yorkshire we love the ends of loaves.

Margaret

188

That's the best bit – all crispy and crunchy. In fact, if I could have a whole cake made from ends, that would be perfect for me. Well, Margaret is the same, and her face is a picture if she turns up and the end has already been taken. It's not the first time I've had to cut the crust from the other end of the loaf just for her!

Margaret and Fiona are two friends who know how to laugh, chat, gossip, and enjoy a good pot of tea and cake, and they really do brighten up my Thursday mornings.

Margaret's Lemon Drizzle Loaf

Makes a 2lb loaf

Ingredients

For the Loaf
250g very soft stork block
250g caster sugar
250g rice flour (I use Dove's)
2 teaspoons gluten free baking powder
4 free range eggs, lightly beaten
Grated rind and juice of 1 un-waxed lemon

For Lemon Drizzle
Grated rind and juice of 2 un-waxed lemons
100g granulated sugar

Equipment

2lb loaf tin

Method

For the Loaf

1   *Preheat oven to 180°c/160°c fan oven.*

2   *Line a 2lb loaf tin with parchment paper. (I use a parchment paper loaf liner.)*

3   *Put all the loaf ingredients in a free-standing mixer or food processor, and beat/whizz until smooth, light, and fluffy.*

4   *Spoon the mixture into the lined tin, and bake in the pre-heated oven for 60 minutes until golden and firm to the touch and a cake tester comes out clean.*

5   *Remove from the oven, but leave in the tin.*

For the Lemon Drizzle

6   *Prick holes all over the loaf with the cake tester or a cocktail stick.*

7   *Mix together the drizzle ingredients in a bowl, then drizzle over the warm loaf.*

8   *Leave in the tin until completely cold then serve sliced.*

Surely not yellow food colouring!

Lemon Meringue Pie is another of my favourite puddings. A crisp pastry base with a lemon custard filling, all topped with meringue – but the lemon filling needs to make your mouth tingle, and the meringue has to be crispy on the outside but soft in the middle. Over the many years I've been baking, both for myself and for the tearoom, I couldn't begin to guess how many lemon meringue pies I've made (and eaten!). A gluten free and dairy free option is very hard to find, though.

My big disappointment when making this has always been that, even when using the freshest lemons, my filling always looked a pale yellow and not the bright, vivid colour I saw in all the recipe books I drooled over. Then one day whilst scrolling the internet, I saw somebody saying that they add a little yellow food colouring to their filling to give it a vibrant colour. Surely not? I thought. However, after making another batch of Lemon Meringue Pie, my filling turned out lovely and tasted great, but again didn't have the bright yellow colour I was looking for. There was only one thing for it. Yes, I went for it and added a couple of drops of yellow food colouring. Instantly my lemon meringue filling looked like all the pictures in my different recipe books. If only I'd read about this years ago!

Once I'd mastered my gluten free and dairy free pastry for the Bakewell Tarts, I realised that I could very easily come up with a gluten free and dairy free Lemon Meringue Pie. A couple of attempts later, I'd put together a combination that works perfectly and this is now one of our popular bakes in the tearoom. There is even an early Lemon Meringue Pie warning on our Facebook page to let customers know when this delight will be available.

Ours is now named Evelyn's Lemon Meringue Pie, as it is the all-time favourite of one of our lovely customers from the Ayrshire Coeliac Group. As Evelyn comes such a long distance to sample our cakes and bakes, it's only right that she has this named after her. Mind you, it would be just as fitting to name Jim's gluten free bread after Evelyn, or poached eggs and toast, as she comes to our tearoom especially for our safe gluten free food. Mr Evelyn, Terry, dutifully does the driving, picking up Evelyn's dropped cameras, phones, and bags on the way, to give him the

Evelyn and Mr M

opportunity to then tuck into our freshly cooked breakfast, washed down with a couple of cups of our freshly ground Caffia coffee.

We may not see Evelyn and Terry as often as our other customers, but Evelyn follows us closely on Facebook – just another example of the far-reaching arms of our tearoom family.

Evelyn's Lemon Meringue Pie

Makes a 9" round tart

Ingredients

For the Pastry Base
100g stork block

50g caster sugar

1 free range egg, lightly beaten

100g gluten free plain flour (I used Dove's)

100g fine polenta

For the Lemon Filling
5 free range egg yolks

6 tablespoons cornflour

267g caster sugar

¼ teaspoon salt

355ml cold water

Juice and zest of 7 lemons

(you will need 115ml lemon juice)

30g stork block

For the Meringue Topping
1 tablespoon cornflour

80ml cold water

¼ teaspoon cream of tartar

130g caster sugar

5 free range egg whites

½ teaspoon vanilla extract

Equipment

9" round loose-bottomed flan tin

Method

1   *Preheat oven to 190°c/170°c fan oven.*

Making the Pastry

2   *Grease a 9" round loose bottom flan tin with stork.*

3   *Put the polenta, flour, and caster sugar in a free-standing mixer, and mix for a minute to blend. Add the stork and mix slowly until you have something that looks like breadcrumbs. Add the egg and continue to mix until the mixture forms a soft pastry.*

4   *Empty the pastry onto a well-floured worktop (gluten free flour, of course), knead gently until smooth, then wrap in clingfilm and pop in the fridge for 30 minutes.*

5   *Remove the clingfilm and roll out the chilled pastry on a well-floured worktop until it is large enough to cover the base and sides of the flan tin.*

6   *Using a rolling pin, carefully transfer the pastry to the prepared tin. Smooth out any cracks and trim the pastry to be level with the top of the tin.*

7   *Line the pastry case with parchment paper, fill with baking beans, and blind bake for 10 minutes.*

8   *Once baked, remove from the oven, and take out the baking beans and parchment paper, but leave the pastry in the tin. Be careful, as the baking beans will be very hot. Do not put them back into a plastic container until they have cooled down.*

9   *Lower the oven to 150°c/130°c fan oven.*

Making the Lemon Filling

10   *Whisk the egg yolks in a bowl and put to one side.*

11   *Put the cornflour, sugar, salt, and water into a heavy-based pan, stirring with a balloon whisk to combine.*

12   *Bring the mixture to a boil on a medium heat on the hob, whisking constantly. Let the mixture simmer for 1-2 minutes until the mixture bubbles and starts to thicken, then remove from the heat.*

13   *Take a spoonful of the cornflour mixture and whisk it into the beaten egg yolks. Continue to whisk in spoonfuls of the cornflour mixture to the egg yolks until you've added about half of it.*

14   *Add the egg yolk mixture back to the pan with the remaining cornflour mixture. Return to a boil on medium heat on the hob, whisking constantly, and cook for a further 3 to 4 minutes.*

15   *Remove from heat and stir in the lemon juice, lemon zest, and stork.*

16   *If you want your lemon filling to be bright yellow, you can mix in a couple of drops of food colouring at this point, then spoon the lemon mixture into the prepared pastry case.*

17   *Spread the lemon filling over the prepared pastry case.*

Making the Meringue

18   *Mix the cornflour with the water in a small pan, and cook on a medium heat until the mixture bubbles and thickens. Remove from the heat and put to one side.*

19   *In a bowl, mix together the sugar and the cream of tartar.*

20   *Put the egg whites and vanilla extract in a free-standing mixer (or use a hand-held whisk) and whisk until the mixture is frothy.*

21   *With the mixer still running, add the sugar and cream of tartar, one spoonful at a time.*

22   *Continue whisking until the mixture forms soft peaks but is not too stiff at this point.*

23   *Again, with the mixer still running, add the cornflour mixture one spoonful at a time, then whisk until the mixture forms stiff peaks.*

24   *Spoon the mixture onto the lemon filling (or you could pipe this on if you feel adventurous). Make sure the meringue goes right to the edges and touches the pastry all the way round.*

25   Bake in the pre-heated oven for 60 minutes.

26   Remove from the oven and leave to cool completely before you carefully remove from the baking tin.

27   Sit down with a large piece, a hot steaming cup of tea, and think of Evelyn travelling across the country for a slice of this delight.

Watching them blossom

I think chocolate and mint are a perfect combination; you just have to think of After Eight Mints.

Sometimes chocolate cakes are a little too sugary, even for my sweet tooth, but this recipe makes a lovely light chocolate cake which is transformed into an indulgent treat with the mint frosting and melted chocolate.

This delight is a favourite of two of our younger customers, best friends Kirsty and Jade, and where you see one, you usually see the other. They first came into the tearoom as shy teenagers not long after we opened, and barely spoke to us, just keeping their heads down and eating cake. One of the first they had was this mint chocolate cake, and it has remained their firm favourite.

We have seen these two young girls grow into fine young ladies, watching with interest as their new adult lives develop. The whole of the tearoom family has taken these two under their wings, loving to see them blossoming.

Kirsty and Jade

Kirsty And Jade's Mint Chocolate Cake

Makes a 2 or 3-layer 9" round cake

This mint delight can be made into a 3-layer cake, with thin layers of cake separated with the mint frosting. You can, of course, just make this as a two-layer cake, but you will need less frosting. Sometimes I pipe the frosting in-between the cake layers, which looks pretty. Other times, I cover the whole cake in frosting. The frosting can be piped, or you can just cover the whole cake and smooth with a palette knife.

Ingredients

For the Cake

75g cocoa powder

100ml boiling water

½ teaspoon xanthan gum

263g gluten free self-raising flour

1.5 teaspoons gluten free baking powder

413g caster sugar

150g stork block softened

75ml almond milk

5 free range eggs, lightly beaten

For the Mint Frosting

200g very soft stork block

600g icing sugar

3 tablespoons almond milk

2 teaspoons peppermint extract

Green food colouring

For the Chocolate Covering

50g gluten and dairy free chocolate, melted

Equipment

2 or 3 x 9" round loose-bottomed sandwich tins

Method

For the Cake

1   *Preheat oven to 180°c/160°c fan oven.*

2   *Grease and line your cake tins with parchment paper.*

3   *Dissolve the cocoa powder in the boiling water.*

4   *Put the xanthan gum, flour, baking powder, and sugar into a free-standing mixer (or use a hand-held mixer) and mix until combined and there are no lumps left.*

5   *Add the cocoa mix, beaten eggs, almond milk, and stork to the flour mix. Beat until you have a well-blended smooth mixture.*

6   *Divide the mixture between the three prepared cake tins, and smooth the surface.*

7   *Bake in the pre-heated oven for 30 minutes, or until a cake tester/knife inserted into the centre of the cakes comes out clean.*

8   *Remove from the oven, but leave the cakes in the tins for 20 minutes before removing them from the tins and placing on a wire rack to cool completely.*

For the Mint Frosting

9   *Put all the frosting ingredients in a free-standing mixer or large mixing bowl, and beat until you have a smooth batter.*

10   *Once the cakes have cooled completely, place one of the sponges on a cake stand/plate, bottom side down, and spread with a layer of the frosting.*

11   *Spread the bottom of another of the sponges with your favourite jam. Place this sponge, jam side down, on top of the first sponge and spread some more icing over the top of this cake.*

12   *Spread the bottom of the final sponge with jam, and carefully place this on top of the other two, jam side down.*

13   *Spread the remaining icing over the top and sides of the cake, smoothing with a palette knife.*

14   *Melt the chocolate in the microwave and pour over the top of the cake, allowing it to drip down the side (or lightly sprinkle cocoa powder over the top).*

15   *Make yourself a cup of tea, lock all the doors, cut yourself a large slice, and enjoy!*

The curse of Glen Lyon

Today was the day. I was going to climb one of my favourite Munros, Stuchd an Lochain, starting with a drive through one of Scotland's finest remote glens, Glen Lyon. To add to the enjoyment, Mr M was coming with me and Beatrix. 6am and the sky was clear. It was still dark, but I could see the sky was cloudless. It was going to be a fabulous day.

By the time breakfast was finished, lunch and flasks of tea packed into rucksacks with warm clothes and waterproofs, daylight had arrived, and the sky was clear blue.

The drive up to Glen Lyon is a bit of an adventure in itself, and today was no exception. It started with a tootle along the M9 motorway to the Callander exit, then the wonderful drive along the A84, past the impressive Ben Ledi and alongside Loch Luibnaig. The views were amazing. The loch was glass-like and so clear it was difficult to decide which was the reflection or the real thing.

Driving on through Lochearnhead and up to Glen Ogle, I glanced over at the old railway bridge, remembering the many different cycling adventures I've had on that cycle track. The road from here sweeps down, passing all the newly harvested trees, giving a glimpse of the twin Munros of Ben More and Stob Binnein towards Crianlarich, then down to the small village of Killin, passing the impressive tumbling Falls of Dochart. A mile or so beyond the village, we took the small single-track road towards Ben Lawers and Bridge of Balgie. At least there'd be no snow today to make the journey hazardous.

It's been a few years since I drove all the way down this glen, and the map is a bit vague: 'Drive to the end of the single-track road to the dam.' What could go wrong? Well, this is me, of course! Five minutes along (or up) the single-track road came my first hazard – a large timber lorry coming down the winding hill. Oh flip! Now, I'm the girl who can drive quite well forwards, but reversing is not really my thing. I panic if I've got to reverse the length of Ladysmill outside the tearoom! And today was made even worse because I had the joy of Mr M, the back-seat driver.

'You'll have to reverse down the hill a bit,' he informed me. No kidding! I thought to myself. 'Left a bit, right a bit, straight back…' You get the picture. Finally, I managed to reverse down the windy single-track road to a passing place large enough to allow the lorry to pass me, which he did with a smile, a nod, and a friendly wave. Perhaps even he could feel the tension in our car!

But back to my route. 'Start at the end of the road below the dam of Loch an Daimh,' said my guide-book. The road continues in the same vein, twisting, rising, and getting narrower as you pass the Ben Lawers range on your right and the Tarmachan ridge on the left. As we passed the first dam, we both agreed this was not 'the dam', as this was not the end of the road and we'd certainly not driven far enough.

I continued on the road, ever conscious of Mr M gripping his seat, sighing, gasping, and I'm sure I even saw him mopping his brow! I was only going 20mph at some points! This road had been blocked by deep snow for a long time during the winter and now bore evidence of this. The road surface was terrible; there were potholes the size of houses, grit, gravel, and deep ditches down the side of the narrow strip of road I was driving on. The sign at the bottom of the road said Bridge of Balgie 9 miles, meaning I just had a few more miles to drive towards the end of the glen. At least the sun was shining and the views were amazing.

Can you tell I'm cross?

We eventually arrived at Bridge of Balgie and took the turning to the left, with the sign indicating this was a dead end after 10 miles. 'This is the road,' we both agreed. Can I just emphasise the word 'both' here! Now, this road was a little better, with no high drops at the side of the road, and it even felt wide enough for my car. We passed another dam. No, not this one, we both agreed, as it still wasn't the end of the road.

We drove on, enjoying the scenery, with my back-seat driver relaxing a little but becoming the 'I think I need the toilet. I'm getting hungry' passenger instead. Beatrix, of course, was just sitting in the back with her head resting between the headrests. What she was thinking? I wonder.

At last we did indeed come to the end of the road, with a huge dam towering over us. Mr M very proudly announced that this was not the right dam, as he clearly remembered there should be a large parking area with signs all around. As he got out of the car and did what he needed to do, I turned the car around and yes, I did contemplate leaving him there!

'You'll just have to go back and find the right one. You've obviously gone the wrong way,' he advised me. Obviously!

We set off back towards the Bridge of Balgie. Time was now marching on, and I decided to drive back to the Ben Lawers car park, from where we could go for a shorter walk. In my mind, though, my short walk was to go up Beinn Ghlas (the Munro you climb on the way to Ben Lawers).

From the Bridge of Balgie, I had to drive back up the dreaded narrow road. The steep drops were now on my side of the car, which added to my excitement a little, and I've already told you that the road was covered in potholes, gravel, stones, and ditches down either side. Driving very cautiously, my passenger side wheel suddenly managed to go down one of the soft ditches. The car twitched and twisted, and the steering wheel pulled in my hand.

I have to admit my heart was in my mouth (I think at this point, it was running alongside the car), but I managed to catch the skid and carry on my merry way. My back-seat driver was now almost in the passenger footwell, and I could hear lots of sharp intakes of breath. To his credit, he never said a word! Finally, we arrived back safely to the Ben Lawers car park.

Excitement over, it was now nearly lunchtime, so we had some of our picnic lunch in the car before donning our walking boots ready for the walk. I pointed out Beinn Ghlas to Mr M, advising him that's where we were going. Again, to be fair to him, he never said anything.

Just as everyone else in Scotland was enjoying the glorious weather, our sunshine disappeared at the same time as we got out of the car! The temperature had dropped and the wind was building up. Nevertheless, we had a great walk to the top of Beinn Ghlas. The rain came down in heavy showers, but fortunately, it was falling horizontally because of the force 10 wind.

Mr M did make lots of comments on the way to the summit, such as, 'This is steep; this wind is too strong; my hearing aid is whistling; I need another jacket on; I need a rest.' Beatrix, meanwhile, was chasing after every stone she could find, barking at people to throw the stones to her, and generally making a nuisance of herself.

The turning point was when I told Mr M and Beatrix in no uncertain terms that if they didn't stop their behaviour, I would quite simply leave them on the hill and go back to the car. In hindsight, I should have said this at the start of the walk, because their bad behaviour ceased very quickly after that.

Shona

Again, in fairness to Mr M, it was incredibly windy, and I was blown off my feet a couple of times heading towards the summit. We managed to find a sheltered spot in the dip between the top of Beinn Ghlas and the start of the final ascent to Ben Lawers, where we had a lovely lunch and peace reigned once more – helped by the lovely Candy Road I had in my lunch pack.

I decided to take us down the old Shepherd's trail around Beinn Ghlas, giving us an easy descent, and eventually we were back to the safety of the car.

'Do you want me to drive from here?' asked Mr M.

The Candy Road we enjoyed on the hill was created after the success of our awesome Rocky Road. Dairy Milk Chocolate, McVities digestive biscuits, and Maltesers, are what makes our Rocky Road awesome, but they are also the things that make it a no-go treat for those who need or want gluten free and diary free goodies. I was a little scared to make a different version of our Rocky Road in case our customers would be disappointed. It's been a little bit of a long journey to get this perfected, but it's now a lovely, different version of Rocky Road that even more people can enjoy.

What did I do then? Firstly, the lovely crisp, tasty McVities digestive biscuits had to be replaced. That became easy once I'd started making my own Wannabe Digestive Biscuits. What could I do about the Maltesers, though? A little light bulb moment came when making some cinder toffee (puff candy) and I realised this was a very good substitute for the Maltesers. The final piece of the jigsaw was to be able to replace the lovely Cadbury's Dairy Milk Chocolate with a gluten free and dairy free version.

Everything just fell into place once I discovered the chocolate made by Plamil Foods, who make gluten free and dairy free versions of plain, milk, and white chocolate. Who even knew that dairy free chocolate could taste so good? With all my ingredients identified, I set about making a tray of deliciousness.

I didn't want to call this new traybake Rocky Road, because we need to be very clear which of our products are gluten free and dairy free, so we came up with the name Candy Road. In the tearoom, customers know that the Rocky Road is the one with everything in it, and the Candy Road is the gluten free and dairy free version.

Is it just as good, though? Oh boy, it is that! Never did I think I'd choose something over my favourite Dairy Milk, but this Candy Road does it for me. Just to prove the point even further, our Candy Road is now named Shona's Candy Road, because this is just her absolute favourite even though Shona can eat gluten-free or non-gluten free!

So, who is Shona? Shona came into the tearoom a couple of years ago, shuffling her way to an empty table, pulling out her magazine, ordering her food, and sitting quietly, talking to nobody. We, of course, chatted to Shona. The following Wednesday, the same thing happened. In came Shona with a glimmer of a smile. The magazine still came out, but this time it wasn't really being read. A couple of weeks further down the line, Shona was a regular on a Wednesday, always with a magazine in her hand, and always ordering a cheese omelette, finishing with Rocky Road.

Shona started to join in with the conversations, but still liked to sit on her own table. One week, we were discussing crafting and cross-stitching. "I like to do cross-stitching," Shona told us, so I suggested that she bring in her cross-stitching at her next visit.

Lo and behold, the next week Shona came along with her cross-stitching kit and started to work on this (still not joining the crafting table). The following week, though, we managed to get her to join us at the crafting table. And that was it. Now Shona is well and truly part of the tearoom family and comes along to the crafting every Wednesday and Saturday.

We've seen Shona do some amazing cross-stitching, sewing, and card-making, and we have even turned Shona into a crochet queen. She doesn't like to have her photo taken, and when I take photos of the crafters, it's usually only Shona's fantastic craft projects you see. My hope is that one day I'll able to take a photo of Shona with her great smile and post this along with photos of the other crafters and customers.

Shona still has her cheese omelette, but will now try different cakes like the White Chocolate Fudge Cake, Caramel Slice, and the Chocolate Orange Cake. One week, when Candy Road was replacing our Rocky Road, Shona came in and looked suspiciously at the Candy Road, but reluctantly agreed to try a piece.

And, would you believe it? Our Rocky Road lover was converted, and said she prefers the Candy Road to the Rocky Road. So, Shona's Candy Road it had to be.

Shona's Candy Road

Makes a large 16" x 12" traybake to cut into 24 pieces

My recipe is for a large 16" x 12" traybake. If your tin is smaller, remember to adjust your quantities depending on your tin size.

Ingredients

For the Wannabe Digestive Biscuits
160g gluten free oats

60g pumpkin seeds

60g sunflower seeds

620g gluten free plain flour

200g dark brown sugar

200g stork block (cut into cubes)

1 teaspoon salt

4 tablespoons gluten free baking powder

200ml almond milk

For the Cinder Toffee (makes three batches)
1 teaspoon bicarbonate of soda

75g caster sugar

2 tablespoons golden syrup

For the Candy Road Base
45 wannabe digestive biscuits

3 batches of cinder toffee

300g stork block

225g golden syrup

600g gluten and dairy free chocolate

For the Candy Road Topping
600g gluten and dairy free chocolate

gluten and dairy free mini marshmallows

Equipment
16" x 12" traybake tin200g

202

Method

Making the Wannabe Biscuits

1   Preheat oven to 200°c/180°c fan oven.

2   Line several baking trays and a traybake tin with parchment paper.

3   Put the oats, sunflower seeds, and pumpkin seeds in a food processor and blitz until fine.

4   Put the oat mixture, flour, baking powder, stork and sugar into a free-standing mixer and mix until well mixed.

5   Add the almond milk, and mix until you get a stiff dough.

5   Dust the work surface with a little gluten free flour and gently knead the dough until smooth, then cut the dough in two halves (this makes it easier to roll out).

6   Roll the dough out to about 5mm thick and cut with a 3-inch round cutter dipped in flour to stop it sticking. (There is no need to be neat and tidy with these, as you are going to blitz them into crumbs later.)

7   Re-roll the dough left, and cut more biscuits until all the dough has been used. You should get about 60 biscuits.

8   Use a fish-slice or palette knife to lift the cut dough onto the prepared baking trays.

9   Bake for 15 minutes until golden and just firm to touch (they'll become crisper once cold).

10 Remove from the oven, leave on the baking tray for 10 minutes, then transfer to a wire rack to cool completely.

11 You will need 45 biscuits for your Candy Road, so you can decide what to do with the remaining biscuits. I'd suggest mixing them with a quiet afternoon, a large teapot of steaming tea, and a good book.

Making the Cinder Toffee (Puff Candy)

You will need to make three batches of this. Don't be tempted to try and make one large batch or you will have boiling sugar pouring over the top of your pan!

12 Put the sugar and golden syrup in a large heavy-based pan and allow to melt slowly over a low heat, stirring gently with a long-handled wooden spoon to make sure all the sugar grains are melted.

13 Once melted, turn the heat up and allow to boil until the mixture changes colour and becomes a deep golden brown (not black!). This will only take a couple of minutes.

14   Take the pan off the heat and stir in the magical bicarbonate of soda. The mixture will explode into life like a volcano. Quickly mix to make sure all the bicarbonate of soda is blended, then pour the mixture immediately into a tray lined with parchment paper.

15   Leave to cool and set for about 15 minutes. The final cinder toffee will either be very crunchy or maybe a little chewy, depending on how hot you allowed the melting sugar to become.

Making the Candy Road Base

16   Take 45 of your Wannabe biscuits and whizz in the food processor to make fine crumbs.

17   Crumble the cinder toffee with your hands into a large bowl until there are no large pieces.

18   Put the stork block, chocolate, and golden syrup for the base into a large pan. Allow to melt over a low heat, stirring gently, until everything is blended.

19   Add the wannabe biscuit crumbs and the crumbled cinder toffee, and mix until everything is combined.

20   Put the mixture into the prepared traybake tin, pushing the mixture into all four corners, and pressing the mixture down with a spatula to level. Leave to set for about thirty minutes.

Making the Candy Road Topping

21   Put the chocolate for the topping in a bowl over a pan of gently simmering water on a low heat on the hob, until the chocolate starts to melt. As the chocolate begins to melt, turn the heat off and allow the heat of the hot water to continue to melt the chocolate. Once nearly all the chocolate has melted, take the bowl off the hot water and allow the heat of the chocolate to melt the remaining chocolate.

22   Pour the melted chocolate over the set Candy Road base and spread with a spatula.

23   Sprinkle generously with the mini marshmallows and allow to set.

24   Cut into portions.

Building a snowman with Beatrix

January 22, 2018. Last week Scotland saw snow, rain, hail, sunshine, and gales – sometimes it seemed like all of them within half an hour! Twice last week we decided to close the tearoom early due to the snow, and twice we just made it home from Falkirk to Kirkintilloch before the roads were blocked.

With the usual post-Christmas weight loss campaign starting, I decided to take Beatrix out on one of her favourite walks. The Meikle Bin is the highest peak in the Kilsyth Hills, but with a modest height of 570m (1,870 ft), it's classified as a Marilyn rather than a Munro. It's also the site of a fatal air accident in January 1950, when a Fairey Firefly Royal Airforce plane crashed just below the summit in low cloud, killing both crewmen. Wreckage from this can still be seen on the north and east slopes of the peak.

Mr M was mortified at the idea of me going up the Carron Valley in the snow and, not for the first time, declared I had totally lost my mind. I assured him I'd be fine and would turn back if the snow was too bad.

So off I went, armed with food, a flask of tea, crampons, and an excited Border Collie. The road up from Lennoxtown was not too bad, but once I reached the narrow B818 up from Fintry it was a different matter altogether! Of course, the problem then was that there was nowhere for me to turn the car around to head back home.

The temperature gauge on my dashboard was showing -0.5 degrees, but it was raining, and another car did come down the road in the opposite direction so I decided things couldn't be that bad. A few breath-holding moments later, I managed to get to the little space where everyone parks to start the walk. Not a soul was there, and clearly hadn't been since the snow came!

As I discussed our options with Beatrix, a gritter and plough came along the road. Phew! Decision made. It would take a good couple of hours for us to complete the walk, giving the road a chance to clear and more traffic to drive along it. We were there now, and with no more snow forecast, the road home shouldn't get any worse.

The walk up the Meikle Bin is usually an easy stroll up the forestry track, with a bit of a hike up the last bit of the hill. Today was different, though. There was a good three to four inches of snow at road level, meaning my crampons were needed as soon as I left the car. It took me a good fifteen minutes to remember how they fitted onto my boots, but before long I was togged up in my Gore-Tex gear, crampons secured, and provisions safely in my rucksack.

It was completely silent apart from the crunching of snow as I walked. A couple of birds were singing to us and a gentle breeze was blowing through the trees, causing the snow to fall off the branches and scare Beatrix. It was hard-going walking in the deep snow, but thankfully a forestry wagon had been up before me, providing a little track to walk in and making the going slightly easier. Beatrix, of course, was off bounding, jumping, eating, and rolling in the snow.

Further up the forest, the track became covered with virgin snow with no tyre tracks to walk in. The going was really hard work now, and my thighs were aching like never before. I couldn't believe that what was usually just the warm-up for the main peak was turning into such a challenge.

With the forestry work going on, many of the lovely trees had been cut down, which further exposed the track to the fierce, biting gale force wind now blowing up from the Carron Valley. I zipped up my jacket further and snuggled into my hood.

Beatrix and I debated the merits of climbing to the top of the hill. She said we should, as it would be fun in the snow and wind. I explained that I was already tired and that, as it was raining, cloudy, and there was a bitter wind blowing, the experience may not be quite so much fun as usual. Yes, I do have these conversations with my dog!

Believe it or not, just as you leave the forest track to start the final ascent, there's a well-positioned picnic bench – although it was no longer quite as sheltered because the trees here had also been cut down. Decision made again. We'd have a short lunch break here, then head back to the car without going up the main climb. A flask of hot tea, turkey and cranberry sandwiches, and bakes from the tearoom – perk of the job!

Starting the walk back down, my left heel was beginning to rub in my boot, even though they were well-worn boots and I was wearing my usual walking socks. It was time to pull out my small first aid kit, containing paracetamol for aches, pains and headaches; plasters; bandage to stop a major bleed; Compeed for blisters; 2 foil survival blankets (one for me and one for Beatrix); a well-charged mobile phone; some emergency chocolate and Kendal Mint Cake.

Taking a break to apply some Compeed to my sore heel, I suddenly realised how tired I was. There was nothing else for it: we needed to build a snowman. A few minutes later, we'd built ourselves Michael the Snowman – the only person we spoke to all day!

Looking at the Rocky Road I'd placed in Michael's hand, the tell-tale signs of real tiredness crept upon me. Even though I love chocolate (especially Cadbury's Dairy Milk), I found myself not wanting to eat the Rocky Road. I'm old and wise enough now to understand that this can be a sign of tiredness and fatigue.

We bade our farewells to Michael, stole the Rocky Road back from his hand, and I forced myself to munch this treat as we set back off again. Another ten minutes down the hill, with my heel being cuddled by Compeed, the ill-fitting crampons adjusted around my boots, and the Rocky Road doing its job, I was back to enjoying our snowy walk – although the return walk took us twice as long as usual.

Today's Rocky Road is one of the most popular traybakes in the tearoom. Russell, a local washing machine mechanic, calls into the tearoom most weeks for a chat, soup, a hazelnut latte, and a piece of Rocky Road. At his first visit to the tearoom, he found himself in hot water by helping himself to a piece of Rocky Road from the cake display – though he very quickly learned the error of his ways. So, who better to name the Rocky Road after then? Russell's Rocky Road it is.

Our Rocky Road has been described as awesome by some customers, and is the same recipe we used at our Charity Afternoon Tea when starting Mother Murphy's Home Baking and Afternoon Teas. This is all down to the good quality ingredients we use in it – always McVities Digestive biscuits (the only time we use a bought-in biscuit at the tearoom), Cadbury's Dairy Milk, Maltesers, golden syrup, real butter, and mini marshmallows.

Before the sugar police come along to arrest us, I know it contains sugar, but if you're only having this as a treat every now and again (or when hiking in the snow), I'm sure it's not going to kill you.

Russell

Russell's Rocky Road

Makes a large tray 16" x 12" bake
to cut into 24 pieces

My recipe is for a large 16" x 12" traybake. If your
tin is smaller, remember to adjust your quantities
depending on your tin size.

Ingredients

For the Base

300g unsalted butter

225g golden syrup

600g Cadbury's Dairy Milk chocolate

35 McVities Digestive biscuits

600g Maltesers

For the Topping

600g Cadbury's Dairy Milk chocolate

200g mini marshmallows

Equipment

16" x 12" traybake tin

Method

For the Base

1   *Line a traybake tin with baking parchment.*

2   *Break the chocolate into squares and add to a large pan with the butter and syrup.*

3   *Melt on a gentle heat on the hob, stirring regularly, until everything is melted and blended.*

4   *Blitz the digestive biscuits in a food processor until biscuit crumbs are made and there are no large pieces remaining. (You can also do this by putting the biscuits in a plastic bag and bashing them with a rolling pin.)*

5   *Add the biscuit crumbs and Maltesers to the chocolate mixture, and stir until everything is well mixed and coated with chocolate.*

6   *Spoon the mixture into the prepared tin and press smooth with a wooden spoon.*

7   *Leave to set (not in the fridge or the butter can separate).*

For the Topping

8   *Put the chocolate for the topping in a bowl over a pan of gently simmering water on a low heat on the hob until the chocolate starts to melt. As the chocolate begins to melt, turn the heat off and allow the heat of the water to continue to melt the chocolate. Once nearly all the chocolate has melted, take the bowl off the hot water and allow the heat of the chocolate to melt the remaining chocolate.*

9   *Pour the melted chocolate over the set Rocky Road base and spread with a spatula.*

10   *Sprinkle generously with the mini marshmallows and allow to set.*

11   *Once set, remove from the tin and cut into portions.*

There's nothing like a fresh scone.

Gillian Armstrong (Movie director)

Scones

Is there anything more traditional for a British teatime treat than the humble scone? Golden brown, slightly crispy on the outside, yet light and fluffy on the inside, scones are just perfect for serving with butter, jam, and cream. But this dainty little treat can cause so many debates.

Firstly, there's the pronunciation. Do you say scone to rhyme with gone or scone to rhyme with tone? Then there's the order of the jam and cream. Does the cream go on first then the jam, or the jam on first and then the cream?

I say scone to rhyme with tone, with just a good dollop of home-made jam or home-made lemon curd. Mind you, I'm partial to a fresh scone with nothing on (the scone – not me, of course!). Let's get real here, though. It doesn't matter how you pronounce or serve this little delight, as long as you enjoy eating it.

Many years ago, I dreaded making scones, as mine were not so much light and fluffy as hard and heavy. By chance, during my time as a Vocational Award Assessor, I was working with a lovely man who made the scones for a cafe in Carluke. He kindly shared a few of his tips with me, and I'm proud to say we now have customers coming to the tearoom just for my scones.

Another improvement in my scones came about by accident. I was always of the opinion that a proper scone had to be made with real butter. One morning making the scones in the kitchen at home, I realised I'd run out of the usual Graham's butter we use for the tearoom, and wondered what would happen if I used the stork block I use for our dairy free baking. Well, just let me tell you what happened. The lightest scones I had ever made floated their way out of the oven. No surprise then that all my scones are now made with stork block.

Whilst I'm on my high horse about scones, let's just mention the size of scones. Have you ever been somewhere and been presented with a gigantic scone? At first glance, your eyes light up and you drool at the idea of this delight. Then you cut into it. It's heavy, doughy, and stodgy; the butter's too hard to spread; the jam is in one of those silly little plastic packs that take the effort of two people to open; and the cream… well!

After many disappointing scone outings, I decided my scones would be a moderate size, not too large but not too small. The scone cutter I use is 2.5"/6cm. For our afternoon teas, though, I make smaller scones, 2"/4.5cm, and each person gets two scones. Our jam in the tearoom is always home-made, and we use good quality butter and fresh Scottish double cream. Don't let your lovely scones be spoiled by poor quality butter, jam, and squirty cream.

Continuing to develop our gluten free and dairy free range, I was often asked for a gluten free scone. Could this lovely scone be replicated using gluten free and dairy free ingredients? I sampled many gluten free scones

Rosemary

outside of the tearoom, and they were just not a scone. They were a strange texture, and heavy, with a nasty after-taste. My work was going to be cut out to make a scone that would actually taste like a scone.

Initially I tried to make a gluten free version by simply replacing the wheat flour for gluten free flour. But these were probably the worst scones I'd ever made, so it was back to the drawing board. I looked at different recipes in books and on the internet. Then one day, by chance, I was looking at the back of the Dove Farm's rice flour packet and saw a recipe for sultana scones containing no eggs and no butter or margarine. This recipe seemed so impossible I just had to try it.

The first attempt came out not too bad, but didn't have a particularly good rise. However, a few attempts later and after a few tweaks, I produced some great little scones. These passed the seal of approval with members of the Forth Valley Gluten Free Group, who couldn't get enough of them. One lady was actually reduced to tears at being a given a choice of gluten free scones.

What was the trick to these scones then? Forget all the tips about making a traditional wheat scone. Don't make a dough to roll and cut out, but rather make a thick batter-type mixture and use an ice cream scoop to measure the mixture out. Remember also that how they look when they go in the oven is just about how they look when they come out. As they don't rise or brown like traditional wheat-based scones, spend a little time brushing them with the milk and smoothing them into a nice, presentable shape.

As good as these scones were, though, I still didn't feel they were just right. They were tasty and certainly looked like scones, but the texture still needed improving. I decided that I needed to go back to adding egg into my scones, so I looked around for different recipes and tried lots of different ones. Eventually I came up with a recipe that was a combination of lots of different ones I'd seen, with my best ones being apple and cinnamon, treacle, or cherry scones.

For my gluten free scones, I make mini scones and serve everyone two. I've found that way they stay light and fluffy. Any type of scone is best eaten on the day of baking, and this applies even more to gluten free scones. These scones are best if they're frozen as soon as they've cooled down from baking, then defrosted in the microwave or warmed/toasted a little on the griddle.

When it came to naming our scones, the traditional wheat scone was easy. Just up the road from the tearoom is the Toyota Garage, and every day Brian from the garage would pass the tearoom on the way to put a bet on at the local bookies. He would only ever take a plain scone, telling us they were the best he'd ever tasted, so our wheat scones became Brian's Plain Wheat Scones.

Our gluten free scones just had to be Rosemary's Scones. Rosemary had been a customer in the tearoom for some time, coming along to try our lovely gluten free offerings, then joined our book club, and attended different events in the tearoom.

One day, Rosemary booked afternoon tea for her social group. I'd just made my new version of gluten free and dairy free scones, and served these on Rosemary's afternoon tea. I don't think Rosemary has stopped talking about these scones since, and I was proud as punch when she posted on Facebook that my scones were better than those at the wonderful Willow Tearooms in Glasgow. Praise indeed! So, Rosemary's Scones they have to be.

Brian's Plain Wheat Scones

Makes about 18 scones

These first scones are my traditional wheat-based scones. You can make your own flavours – just keep the flour/fat/liquid ratio the same. Remember that if you add fresh fruit to your scones, you'll be adding extra liquid. If you've never made scones before, I'd suggest you try these plain ones first, then experiment with your own flavours. I'm sure, though, that whatever scones you make, yours will be lovely and much better than the shop-bought, absolutely identical packets of sad-looking ones you can buy.

Try to be as gentle as possible and don't over-knead the dough, as this can make them tough. When brushing them with the extra milk or egg, just brush the tops to allow them to rise fully in the oven.

I use a 2.5"/6cm cutter and get about 18 scones from this mixture. Make yours whatever size you prefer – larger or smaller – but don't roll the dough out too thinly or they will not be lovely, tall, well risen scones.

Ingredients

800g plain flour
10 teaspoons baking powder
150g stork block (or unsalted butter) cut into small pieces
100g caster sugar
2 free range eggs, lightly beaten
500ml skimmed milk
Extra milk or a beaten egg for brushing

Method

1. Preheat the oven to 220°c/200°c fan oven, and cover two baking trays with baking parchment.

2. Mix the flour and baking powder in a large mixing bowl.

3. Rub the stork or butter pieces into the flour until there are no large lumps left and you have what looks like breadcrumbs.

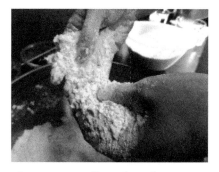

4. Mix the sugar into the flour mixture, using your hands to make sure it is all combined.

5. Add the beaten eggs to the flour mix and stir with a knife until mixed.

6. Add the milk to the mixture and stir again with a knife until well combined and you are starting to get a dough forming. This should only take a minute or two.

7. Empty the mixture out onto your work surface and gently knead the mixture until you have a soft, but not sticky, dough. If it is very sticky, just add a little more flour.

8. Roll out the mixture gently to the same depth as your scone cutter.

9. Dip your cutter into flour and then cut out your scones. Press down firmly with the cutter and, just before lifting it back up, give a little twist to release the scone. You should then be able to lift the scone cutter and your scone from the dough.

10. Place the scones well apart on the baking trays.

11. Gently re-knead and re-roll the dough until you have used it all.

12. Brush the tops of the scones with extra milk, or lightly beaten egg if you prefer.

13. Bake in the pre-heated oven for 10-15 minutes until well risen and golden brown.

14. Remove the scones from the oven, take them off the baking trays, and place on wire racks to cool.

I worship scones and danishes. If I never had another meal, I wouldn't care as long as I could eat pastries and jelly doughnuts.

Gene Simmons (Musician)

We've been waiting for a tearoom like you!

Our very first two customers at the open day of the tearoom on 1st April, 2015 were Tommi and Nanna. Students from Finland staying around the corner from the tearoom, they'd been in Scotland for nearly a year and had been searching all that time for a traditional tearoom. They couldn't believe that a proper tearoom had now opened on their doorstep. One of their regular treats was to have tea and scones, with jam and butter (and a good chat), with our cherry scones being their favourite.

Long before we started our Craft, Chat, and Cake sessions, I was always dabbling in some form of craft or another, showing the customers what I was working on. One day I was making pompoms, and before I knew it, I'd arranged a pompom-making session with Tommi and Nanna spending a lovely morning in their favourite tearoom making a whole bunch of multi-coloured pompoms.

These two lovely people have now returned to their native Finland, but we still feel they are part of our tearoom family as they continue to follow us on Facebook. I thought it only right that our cherry scones became Tommi and Nanna's Cherry Scones.

Nanna and Tommi

Tommi And Nanna's Cherry Wheat Scones

Makes about 18 scones

When making cherry scones, to make sure your cherries don't sink in your scones (not that it really matters if they do) it helps if you rinse them in cold water and drain them before cutting them into quarters.

Try to be as gentle as possible, and don't over-knead the dough as this can make them tough. When brushing them with the extra milk or egg, just brush the tops to allow them to rise fully in the oven.

I use a 2.5"/6cm cutter and get about 18 scones from this mixture. Make yours whatever size you prefer – larger or smaller – but don't roll the dough out too thinly or they will not be lovely, tall, well risen scones.

Ingredients

800g plain flour

10 teaspoons baking powder

150g stork block (or unsalted butter) cut into small pieces

100g caster sugar

200g glace cherries, rinsed, drained, and chopped into quarters

2 free range eggs, lightly beaten

500ml skimmed milk

Extra milk or a beaten egg for brushing

Method

1. Preheat the oven to 220°c/200°c fan oven, and cover two baking trays with baking parchment.

2. Mix the flour and baking powder in a large mixing bowl.

3. Rub the stork or butter pieces into the flour until there are no large lumps left and you have what looks like breadcrumbs.

4. Mix the sugar and cherries into the flour mixture, using your hands to make sure they are well combined.

5. Add the beaten eggs to the flour mix and stir with a knife until mixed.

6. Add the milk to the mixture and stir again with a knife until well combined and you are starting to get a dough forming. This should only take a minute or two.

7. Empty the mixture out onto your work surface and gently knead the mixture until you have a soft, but not sticky, dough. If it is very sticky, just add a little more flour.

8. Roll out the mixture gently to the same depth as your scone cutter.

9. Dip your cutter into flour and then cut out your scones. Press down firmly with the cutter and, just before lifting it back up, give a little twist to release the scone. You should then be able to lift the scone cutter and your scone from the dough.

10. Place the scones well apart on the baking trays.

11. Gently re-knead and re-roll the dough until you have used it all.

12. Brush the tops of the scones with extra milk, or lightly beaten egg if you prefer.

13. Bake in the pre-heated oven for 10-15 minutes until well risen and golden brown.

14. Remove the scones from the oven, take them off the baking trays, and place on wire racks to cool.

Fireman Friday

Mark

The local fire station is around the corner from the tearoom, and shortly after opening in 2015, some of the firemen found their way to visit us. It became a bit of a talking point that on a Friday morning you might find a host of firemen and firewomen at the tearoom. Mark was one of those firemen, and he always had a sultana scone and a strong black coffee. There was nothing else for it but to call our Sultana Scones, Fireman Friday Sultana Scones.

Mark then seemed to go missing for a couple of years, until lo and behold he appeared back at our tearoom on a Friday morning for his Sultana

Scone and strong black coffee. Not just Mark the Fireman, though. He is now proudly Mark the Commander at the local fire station in Falkirk. Fireman Friday was back.

Fireman Friday's Sultana Wheat Scones

Makes about 18 scones

I think our Sultana Scones are probably the tearoom's most popular scone, besides the lovely plain version. Just as when making the plain scones, try to be as gentle as possible and don't over-knead the dough, as this can make them tough. When brushing them with the extra milk or egg, just brush the tops to allow them to rise fully in the oven.

I use a 2.5"/6cm cutter and get about 18 scones from this mixture. Make yours whatever size you prefer – larger or smaller – but don't roll the dough out too thinly or they will not be lovely, tall, well risen scones.

Ingredients

> 800g plain flour
> 10 teaspoons baking powder
> 150g stork block (or unsalted butter) cut into small pieces
> 100g caster sugar
> 300g sultanas
> 2 free range eggs, lightly beaten
> 500ml skimmed milk
> Extra milk or a beaten egg for brushing

Method

1   Preheat the oven to 220°c/200°c fan oven, and cover two baking trays with baking parchment.

2   Mix the flour and baking powder in a large mixing bowl.

3   Rub the stork or butter pieces into the flour until there are no large lumps left and you have what looks like breadcrumbs.

4   Mix the sugar and sultanas into the flour mixture, using your hands to make sure they are well combined.

5   Add the beaten eggs to the flour mix and stir with a knife until mixed.

6   Add the milk to the mixture and stir again with a knife until well combined and you are starting to get a dough forming. This should only take a minute or two.

7   Empty the mixture out onto your work surface and gently knead the mixture until you have a soft, but not sticky, dough. If it is very sticky, just add a little more flour.

8   Roll out the mixture gently to the same depth as your scone cutter.

9   Dip your cutter into flour and then cut out your scones. Press down firmly with the cutter and, just before lifting it back up, give a little twist to release the scone. You should then be able to lift the scone cutter and your scone from the dough.

10 Place the scones well apart on the baking trays.

11 Gently re-knead and re-roll the dough until you have used it all.

12 Brush the tops of the scones with extra milk, or lightly beaten egg if you prefer.

13 Bake in the pre-heated oven for 10-15 minutes until well risen and golden brown.

14 Remove the scones from the oven, take them off the baking trays, and place on wire racks to cool.

Is that thunder and lightning?

Arriving in Scotland all those years ago, I hadn't even heard of treacle scones but, loving treacle, these were a wonderful find for me. It was my late father-in-law, Jim, who introduced me to them. Every Friday night Mr M and I would go to see his lovely parents, Renee and Jim. One week, Old Jim had bought in treacle scones, and I just loved them. And I think I had a treacle scone every Friday for the next year! As Mr M and me have both had previous lives, sadly I didn't have the pleasure of knowing Renee and Jim for many years, but treacle scones still give me lovely memories of them.

Obviously, once I'd realised just how loved the treacle scones were in Scotland, we had to make them for the tearoom. Researching treacle scones further, I came across something called Thunder and Lightning – a treacle scone served with fresh cream, drizzled with black treacle, and sprinkled with icing sugar. Oh my! If I thought treacle scones were good, then Thunder and Lightning scones were amazing.

Not many months after the tearoom had opened, in popped Bill and Pat, who it turned out seemed to be spending their lives visiting as many different places in search of the perfect scone. Chatting to them as we prepared their order, they told me about their blog, https://www.allaboutthescones.com/scones/. No pressure then when they ordered scones at our little tearoom!

Rene and Jim at our wedding

They were disappointed not to be able to sample our Thunder and Lightning scones on their first visit, but as I pointed out, they'd just have to return. And I was chuffed to bits when they wrote a lovely blog about their visit to Mother Murphy's, and sang their praises about our plain and blueberry scones. Here's a little snippet of what they wrote about us in August 2015 on their blog:

> *'The best thing about Mother Murphy's Tearoom is Jim and Debra. They are very friendly and seem really enthusiastic and genuinely happy with what they are doing, and so they should be! We wish them every success, and one day we might get to sample that elusive thunder and lightning scone. If we do, you will be the first to hear about it. In the meantime, we think all that talent and ingenuity deserves a top-scone award. So it is like Gleneagles, after all!'*

I felt it only proper that I let them know when our treacle scones were going to be in the tearoom a couple of days later. I think I could hear their car tyres screeching as they arrived at the tearoom, and their follow-on blog about our Thunder and Lightning scones tells everyone how much they enjoyed them:

'A veritable extravaganza of treacle, cream, and icing sugar. Scoffing could get a bit messy, if it was not for the fact that it comes complete with a dedicated 'thunder and lightning' scone scoffing kit – a knife and fork. The picture hopefully describes adequately how good it was... divine even!"

If you're making treacle scones at home, for an extra special treat turn them into Thunder and Lightning and you'll have no shortage of people wanting to try them.

Thunder and Lightning

Old Jim's Treacle Wheat Scones

Makes about 18 scones

Just like when making the plain scones, try to be as gentle as possible and don't over-knead the dough, as this can make them tough. When brushing them with the extra milk or egg, just brush the tops to allow them to rise fully in the oven.

I use a 2.5"/6cm cutter and get about 18 scones from this mixture. Make yours whatever size you prefer – larger or smaller – but don't roll the dough out too thinly or they will not be lovely, tall, well risen scones. Treacle scone dough is a little sticky and they don't rise quite as much as the other scones.

Ingredients

800g plain flour
10 teaspoons baking powder
3 teaspoons ground cinnamon
3 teaspoons ground mixed spice
150g stork block (or unsalted butter)
cut into small pieces
100g caster sugar
240g black treacle
2 free range eggs, lightly beaten
500ml skimmed milk
Extra milk or a beaten egg for brushing

Method

1. Preheat the oven to 220°c/200°c fan oven, and cover two baking trays with baking parchment.

2. Mix the flour, spices, and baking powder in a large mixing bowl.

3. Rub the stork or butter pieces into the flour until there are no large lumps left and you have what looks like breadcrumbs.

4. Mix the sugar into the flour mixture, making sure they are well combined.

5. Add the beaten eggs to the flour mix and stir with a knife until mixed.

6. Put the milk and treacle into a jug and mix to combine, then add this to the flour mixture. Stir with a knife until well combined and you are starting to get a dough forming. This should only take a minute or two.

7. Empty the mixture out onto your work surface and gently knead the mixture until you have a soft, but not too sticky, dough. If it is very sticky, just add a little more flour.

8. Roll out the mixture gently to the same depth as your scone cutter.

9. Dip your cutter into flour and then cut out your scones. Press down firmly with the cutter and, just before lifting it back up, give a little twist to release the scone. You should then be able to lift the scone cutter and your scone from the dough.

10. Place the scones well apart on the baking trays.

11. Gently re-knead and re-roll the dough until you have used it all.

12. Brush the tops of the scones with extra milk, or lightly beaten egg, if you prefer.

13. Bake in the pre-heated oven for 10-15 minutes until well risen and golden brown.

14. Remove the scones from the oven, take them off the baking trays, and place on wire racks to cool.

Rosemary's Plain Gluten Free Scones

Makes about 20 small scones

Ingredients

225g gluten free plain flour (I use Dove's)

225g rice flour (I use Dove's)

5 teaspoons baking powder

2 teaspoon xanthan gum

100g stork block

50g caster sugar

2 free range eggs, lightly beaten

200ml almond milk

Extra beaten egg to brushing

Method

1. Preheat the oven to 220°c/200°c fan oven, and cover two baking trays with baking parchment.

2. Mix the flour, xanthan gum, and baking powder in a large mixing bowl.

3. Rub the stork into the flour until there are no large lumps left and you have what looks like breadcrumbs.

4. Mix the sugar into the flour mixture, making sure they are well combined.

5. Add the beaten eggs to the flour mix and stir with a knife until mixed.

6. Make a well in the centre of the mixture and pour in the milk. Stir with a knife until well combined and you're starting to get a dough forming. This should only take a minute or two.

7. Empty the mixture out onto a well-floured work surface and gently knead the mixture until you have a soft, but not too sticky, dough. If it's very sticky, just add a little more flour.

8. Roll out the mixture gently to the same depth as your scone cutter.

9. Dip your cutter into flour and then cut out your scones. Press down firmly with the cutter and, just before lifting it back up, give a little twist to release the scone. You should then be able to lift the scone cutter and your scone from the dough.

10. Place the scones well apart on the baking trays.

11. Gently re-knead and re-roll the dough until you have used it all.

12. Brush the tops of the scones with extra lightly beaten egg.

13. Bake in the pre-heated oven for 10-15 minutes until well risen and golden brown.

14. Remove the scones from the oven, take them off the baking trays, and place on wire racks to cool.

Mr M enjoying a chat in the sunshine with Rosemary

Sultana Gluten Free Scones

Makes about 20 small scones

Ingredients

225g gluten free plain flour (I use Dove's)

225g rice flour (I use Dove's)

5 teaspoons baking powder

2 teaspoon xanthan gum

100g stork block

50g caster sugar

300g sultanas

2 free range eggs, lightly beaten

200ml almond milk

Extra beaten egg to brushing

Method

1. Preheat the oven to 220°c/200°c fan oven, and cover two baking trays with baking parchment.

2. Mix the flour, xanthan gum, and baking powder in a large mixing bowl.

3. Rub the stork into the flour until there are no large lumps left and you have what looks like breadcrumbs.

4. Mix the sugar and sultanas into the flour mixture, making sure they are well combined.

5. Add the beaten eggs to the flour mix and stir with a knife until mixed.

6. Make a well in the centre of the mixture and pour in the milk. Stir with a knife until well combined and you're starting to get a dough forming. This should only take a minute or two.

7. Empty the mixture out onto a well-floured work surface and gently knead the mixture until you have a soft, but not too sticky, dough. If it's very sticky, just add a little more flour.

8. Roll out the mixture gently to the same depth as your scone cutter.

9. Dip your cutter into flour and then cut out your scones. Press down firmly with the cutter and, just before lifting it back up, give a little twist to release the scone. You should then be able to lift the scone cutter and your scone from the dough.

10. Place the scones well apart on the baking trays.

11. Gently re-knead and re-roll the dough until you have used it all.

12. Brush the tops of the scones with extra lightly beaten egg.

13. Bake in the pre-heated oven for 10-15 minutes until well risen and golden brown.

14. Remove the scones from the oven, take them off the baking trays, and place on wire racks to cool.

Treacle Gluten Free Scones

Makes about 20 small scones

Ingredients

225g gluten free plain flour (I use Dove's)

225g rice flour (I use Dove's)

5 teaspoons baking powder

2 teaspoon xanthan gum

2 teaspoons ground cinnamon

2 teaspoons mixed spice

100g stork block

50g caster sugar

2 free range eggs, lightly beaten

200ml almond milk

180g black treacle

Extra beaten egg to brushing

Method

1. Preheat the oven to 220°c/200°c fan oven, and cover two baking trays with baking parchment.

2. Mix the flour, xanthan gum, spices, and baking powder in a large mixing bowl.

3. Rub the stork into the flour until there are no large lumps left and you have what looks like breadcrumbs.

4. Mix the sugar into the flour mixture.

5. Add the beaten eggs to the flour mix and stir with a knife until mixed.

6. Put the milk and treacle into a jug and mix to combine, then add this to the flour mixture. Stir with a knife until well combined and you're starting to get a dough forming. This should only take a minute or two.

7. Empty the mixture out onto a well-floured work surface and gently knead the mixture until you have a soft, but not too sticky dough. If it's very sticky, just add a little more flour.

8. Roll out the mixture gently to the same depth as your scone cutter.

9. Dip your cutter into flour and then cut out your scones. Press down firmly with the cutter and, just before lifting it back up, give a little twist to release the scone. You should then be able to lift the scone cutter and your scone from the dough.

10. Place the scones well apart on the baking trays.

11. Gently re-knead and re-roll the dough until you have used it all.

12. Brush the tops of the scones with extra lightly beaten egg.

13. Bake in the pre-heated oven for 10-15 minutes until well risen and golden brown.

14. Remove the scones from the oven, take them off the baking trays, and place on wire racks to cool.

Becoming 'The Magical Tearoom on the Hill'

Over the few years Mother Murphy's tearoom has been opened, it has become a community hub; a place for people to come along, meet new friends, and enjoy the peace, tranquillity (and often madness) of our traditional tearoom.

Catering for people with different dietary requirements, including those with coeliac disease and dairy intolerance, there are always new customers coming along who are looking to see if it's really true that most of our lovely cakes and bakes are gluten free and dairy free.

One Saturday a few years ago, we were getting ourselves geared up for one of our first Craft, Chat and Cake Sessions, doing some encaustic art painting. You've never heard of this? Well, until the fabulous Norma came along, neither had I. Encaustic art is painting with beeswax, using a travel iron. And believe me, it is one of the best crafts I've ever tried; even Mr M had a go!

Anyway, that Saturday lunchtime, into the tearoom walked Sharon and Frances with their gorgeous little blonde-haired baby Sofia. They'd heard good reviews from colleagues about our baking, and were looking for somewhere that was safe for a coeliac, but also family friendly. Talk about kiddies in a candy shop! I think they wanted to take home one of each of the cakes they saw that day.

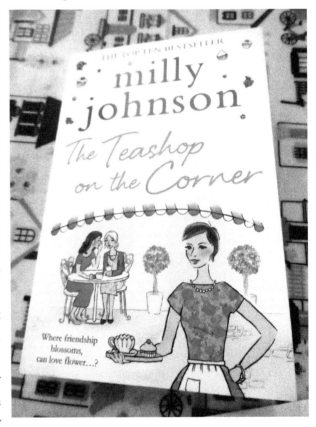

Later that afternoon, just as the craft session was coming to a close, Frances ran in again asking for takeaway soups because they'd enjoyed their lunch time visit so much. Let's just say that some time later, Frances, Sharon, and Sofia left the tearoom once again, armed with Frances' encaustic art painting, soup, and some cakes. 'But I only came in for soup,' giggled Frances.

At one of their next visits, they unknowingly made all the hard work of setting up the tearoom worth every penny and sweat bead, when they told me that Mother Murphy's Tearoom reminded them of the Teashop on the Corner, a book by Millie Johnson. They said this book had some sort of magic about it, and that same magic was in our little tearoom.

Wanting to understand fully what they meant, I went out and bought the book for myself, and was bursting with pride as I read it thinking that people should associate our tearoom with the one in the novel.

After reading the book, I started to refer to our tearoom in our Facebook posts as The Tearoom on The Hill, and this quickly became our nickname, even receiving post addressed to the Tearoom on the Hill. This has developed further, and we now get referred to as the Magical Tearoom on the Hill.

As autumn drew to a close in 2017, Sharon popped in with a sack full of wonderful apples from their garden. Scouring recipe books for some sort of apple delight, I came across a Dorset Apple Traybake. I pondered over this and thought about how to adapt it to make it both gluten free and dairy free, and as a large round cake rather than a traybake, and I created our very own Spiced Apple Cake.

Throughout December 2017, we had a Christmas Quiz in the tearoom, with the deciding question being, 'We like to name our cakes after our customers. Which cake should we name after you and why?'

Sharon and Frances obviously did some major cheating along the way, as they were the only people to get every single question correct. The deciding question was not needed, but their answer was so good that the apple cake had to be named after them.

What was their answer, I hear you cry?

'Spiced Apple Cake, because we donate fabulous, home-grown, organic apples. We adore spices that compliment and balance the fabulous apples. We could be described as "fruity" and spicy" too.'

Spice Girls' Apple Cake

Makes a 9" round cake

Sweet spices turn this simple apple cake into a wonderful treat. The apples on the outside of the cake become caramelised and toffee-like. Serve it warm and the spices are enhanced. Add a good helping of hot custard and this simple treat is transformed into a delicious pudding.

Ingredients

900g cooking apples (unpeeled weight)

50ml lemon juice

225g stork block

280g soft brown sugar

4 free range eggs

2 teaspoons vanilla extract

350g gluten free self-raising flour (I use Dove's)

2 teaspoons gluten free baking powder

1 teaspoon xanthan gum

½ teaspoon ground cinnamon

½ teaspoon freshly grated nutmeg

½ teaspoon ground cloves

Demerara sugar to sprinkle

Equipment

9" deep loose-bottomed cake tin

236

Method

1. Preheat oven to 180°c/160°c fan oven.

2. Grease and line a 9" round deep cake tin with parchment paper. (I use a parchment paper liner.)

3. Peel, core and thinly slice the apples, squeeze the lemon juice over them, and put to one side.

4. Put all the other ingredients in the free-standing mixer (or use a hand-mixer) and beat together until light and smooth.

5. Spread half of the mixture over the bottom of the prepared cake tin.

6. Arrange half of the apples over the top of this, then repeat these two layers with the remaining mixture and apples.

7. Sprinkle demerara sugar over the top.

8. Bake in the pre-heated oven for 45-50 minutes or until golden and springy to touch.

9. Leave in the tin until almost cold, then cool completely on a wire rack.

Frances, Debra, Sharon and Sofia

I eat cake every day.

Adriano Zumbo (Chef)

But the ginger cake isn't gluten free!

Not long after Mother Murphy's opened, Fiona found her way into the tearoom, sometimes with her friends, sometimes with her daughter or her granddaughter, but always with a smile. Fiona soon became a regular at the tearoom, liking nothing better than to sit and relax, chat, enjoy the tearoom and, of course, try all the different cakes. Very quickly, Fiona found her favourite, Stem Ginger Cake with Ginger Frosting, and if anyone came in and was trying to decide on which cake to have, Fiona would quickly jump in and recommend the ginger cake.

Long after Fiona's first visit to the tearoom, I was having a chat to a new customer about all the different cakes and bakes, explaining that DW was short for 'Delicious Without', indicating the cake or bake was gluten free and dairy free. Fiona joined in the chat at this point and said, 'Yes, but the ginger cake isn't gluten free, is it? Because I don't like gluten free cakes.' It took some convincing to get Fiona to believe that for the last year or so she had in fact been tucking into gluten free and dairy free delights every time she came into the tearoom.

Fiona and Margaret

Fiona then mentioned that she had a friend with coeliac disease, and would bring her in next time they were meeting, because they always struggled to find somewhere for her friend to get good food in cafes.

Fast forward another year, and on a Thursday morning in the tearoom you'll usually find Fiona and Margaret (of Margaret's Lemon Drizzle) whiling away the hours, chatting, laughing, having a late breakfast/early lunch, more chatting, more laughing, persuading Mr M to serenade them with his guitar playing, and of course, eating cake.

Never have there been two more lovely, friendly ladies. They've become part of our magical tearoom family, loving nothing better than getting to know all our customers. They really do make everyone feel like they're long lost friends when they talk to them, even if they've never met before.

Fiona's Stem Ginger Cake

Makes a two-layer 9" round cake

'The ginger cake's not gluten free, though, because I don't like gluten free cakes,' said Fiona.

Of all the spices, ginger is my favourite. Add some black treacle into the mixture, and the smell as you prepare this mixture is heavenly. This is a lovely moist cake with ground ginger, stem ginger, and ginger syrup – a ginger lover's heaven – perfect with morning coffee or afternoon tea… or anytime.

Ingredients

For the Cake

200g stork block

175g dark brown sugar

75g black treacle

150ml almond milk

2 free range eggs, lightly beaten

4 pieces of stem ginger, chopped finely

300g gluten free self-raising flour

½ teaspoon xanthan gum

1 teaspoon gluten free baking powder

2 tablespoons ground ginger

Pinch salt

For Ginger Frosting

4 tablespoons stem ginger syrup from the jar

300g icing sugar

150g very soft stork block

2 teaspoons lemon juice

Equipment

2 x 9" loose-bottomed cake tins

Method

For the Cake

1   *Preheat oven to 160°c/140°c fan oven.*

2   *Line two 9" round cake tins with parchment paper. (I use a parchment paper liner.)*

3   *Melt the stork, sugar, and treacle gently in a pan on the hob.*

4   *Remove from the heat and allow to cool for a few minutes.*

5   *Slowly pour in the almond milk, stirring continually.*

6   *Beat in the eggs using a whisk.*

7   *Mix the flour, xanthan gum, salt, and ground ginger together in a bowl, then add this to the treacle mixture and whisk until smooth.*

8   *Stir in the chopped stem ginger.*

9   *Pour the mixture into the prepared tins, smooth the tops, and bake in the pre-heated oven for 30 minutes or until firm to touch.*

10 *Remove from the oven and cool for about one hour in the tins, then remove from the tins, remove the parchment paper, and place on a wire rack to cool completely.*

For the Ginger Frosting

11 *Prick holes all over the cakes with a cake tester or cocktail stick, spoon over one tablespoon of the stem ginger syrup on each cake, and allow to soak in for a couple of minutes.*

12 *Put the icing sugar, stork, two tablespoons stem ginger syrup, and lemon juice, in a free-standing mixer or bowl, and beat well until very soft and creamy.*

13 *Put one sponge flat-side down on a serving plate and spread half of the ginger frosting over it.*

14 *Carefully place the second sponge, flat-side down, on top of this, and spread or pipe the remaining frosting on top of the cake.*

15 *Put the kettle on, cut yourself a large slice, and be amazed, just like Fiona, that something so yummy can be gluten and dairy free.*

Strawberry Heaven

Makes a large 16" x 12" traybake to cut into 24 squares

My recipe is for a large 16" x 12" traybake. If your tin is smaller, remember to adjust your quantities depending on your tin size.

When I introduced this to the tearoom, customers said it tasted like a strawberry toffee crisp.

Ingredients

For the Biscuit Base
240g ground almonds
180g rice flour
100g dark brown sugar
210g cold stork block
3 teaspoons vanilla extract

For the Strawberry Cream Filling
100g very soft stork block
700g icing sugar
150g Nesquik Strawberry Milk Shake Powder
Pink food colouring
6 tablespoons almond milk

For the Chocolate Finish
500g gluten and dairy free milk/dark chocolate of your choice (or a mixture)

Equipment
16" x 12" traybake tin

Method

For the Biscuit

1   *Preheat oven to 190°c/170°c fan oven.*

2   *Grease and line a traybake tin with parchment paper.*

3   *Put all the biscuit ingredients, except for the vanilla extract, in a free-standing mixer or food processor and beat/whizz until you have rough crumbs. Don't mix it so much that you get a dough.*

4   *Add the vanilla extract and mix again gently until combined.*

5   *Tip the mixture into the prepared tin and use the back of a spoon or palette knife to press down and make a smooth base.*

6   *Bake in the pre-heated oven for 20 minutes.*

7   *Remove from the oven and leave to cool in the tin.*

For the Strawberry Cream Filling

8   *Put the stork in the free-standing mixer (or use an electric whisk) and beat until soft and smooth.*

9   *Add the icing sugar, Nesquik, and milk, and beat until smooth.*

10   *Spread evenly over the cooled biscuit base.*

For the Chocolate Finish

11   *Melt the white chocolate over a bowl of gently simmering water. Once the chocolate has started to melt, remove from the heat and stir gently until all the chocolate has melted.*

12   *Pour over the strawberry cream and smooth with a palate knife, and leave to set before repeating with the milk chocolate.*

13   *If you are just using white chocolate, you could add a dash of pink food colouring and swirl into the chocolate with a cake tester/cocktail stick.*

14   *Leave to set completely before slicing into 24 pieces.*

When you can't decide what to have with your
Strawberry Heaven

Can thee park thi' parkin?

Growing up in Yorkshire, this wonderful dark, spicy cake brings back fond memories of plotting (gathering wood) for the bonfire, watching fireworks, and writing my name in the air with a sparkler held at arm's length. Hallowe'en wasn't a big celebration in Yorkshire, but Bonfire Night was a different matter. Every year the local neighbourhood seemed to magically come together for a bonfire evening.

For weeks before plot night, the local children all went around the neighbours asking for anything they wanted to get rid of that would burn on the bonfire. We happily took this away for them on a hand-made bogie cart, taking the wood to the large field behind the houses, ready to be built into a giant bonfire. Of course, we had to be on guard with our wood stash, as the rival gangs would try to set fire to our structure before the night. We also had to check that there were no hedgehogs or other little animals building a home in our bonfire.

On the Saturday night closest to 5th November, the community would somehow just come together. There were no written invites or long planning meetings. One of the responsible grown-ups (!!) would come along long with a can of petrol to pour over the bonfire to make it easier to light. Stacks of jacket potatoes, wrapped in silver foil, would be tucked in around the bottom of the bonfire, ready to cook once the fire started. Then the bonfire would be lit.

Of course, the petrol made sure the bonfire went up in flames in a flash. Once the neighbours saw the fire was lit, they'd all start to gather in the field. Bonfire treats of parkin, bonfire toffee, flapjacks, coconut tarts, cinder toffee, toffee apples, hot dogs and, of course, the jacket potatoes from the fire, were shared out. It just wouldn't be a good night if everyone didn't have soot around their face from the burned jacket potatoes!

All the children were handed sparklers, and we wrote our names in the air or chased each other, waving the sparklers around. Then the fireworks started, flying everywhere. This was not just one organised demonstration but an hour of everyone setting off their own fireworks in the one field.

People you never spoke to all year were all gathered together, wrapped in hats, gloves, scarves, and wearing Wellington boots. I still don't know who organised these events, but it certainly wasn't the local Health and Safety officer!

Long before I'd moved up to Scotland, I was working for a training company in Halifax that did a lot of work with Standard Life in Edinburgh. One year, I was invited to their award ceremony, and found myself sitting with a group of people I didn't know and listening to strong Scottish accents I couldn't understand. I was chatting to a lovely lady, Nadia, when the conversation turned to Hallowe'en and bonfire night celebrations.

'Do you have parkin up here?' I asked Nadia.

'Oh, yes, we get a space each in the car park,' replied Nadia.

How we laughed when Nadia realised from my expression that I wasn't talking about parking but parkin.

It still amazes me how many customers in the tearoom in Scotland have never heard of or tasted parkin. I'm pleased to say I'm successfully introducing this wonderful treat to more and more people each Bonfire Night.

Parkin is made with old-fashioned ingredients such as black treacle, oatmeal, ginger, cinnamon, and nutmeg. To be enjoyed at its best, it should be made at least a week in advance, wrapped in parchment paper and foil, then stored in a cool place. If you can resist it that long, when you finally unwrap it the smell is just wonderful.

I've now adapted my parkin recipe to have this as a gluten free and dairy free cake. It took me many attempts to get this to be as good as the wheat version, but I'm happy to say that this version is now the only one I now make in the tearoom.

Traditionally, parkin is served sliced thinly and buttered. I prefer a thick piece just by itself, but it's equally good served with hot custard for a special bonfire pudding.

I wonder, which customer has the parkin been named after? Me! It's my parkin! I have to say that I really struggle each year serving customers with my parkin. The smell when I'm carefully unwrapping each piece is just wonderful.

In an attempt to persuade customers to have a different cake, I've been known to tell the customers that parkin is not very nice, and even resorted to claiming that I've licked each piece (a Yorkshire trick to stop your siblings eating your cake). Nobody seems to believe me, though.

Debra's Yorkshire Parkin

Makes a 9" round cake/8" square cake

Ingredients

- 120g golden syrup
- 120g black treacle
- 120g stork block
- 120g dark brown sugar
- 220g gluten free oats
- 120g gluten free self-raising flour
- 1 teaspoon xanthan gum
- 1 teaspoon bicarbonate of soda
- 3 teaspoons ground ginger
- 2 teaspoons ground cinnamon
- 1 teaspoon ground nutmeg
- 1 pinch salt
- 100ml almond milk
- 1 free range egg, lightly beaten

Equipment

9" round deep loose-bottomed cake tin or 8" square deep loose-bottomed cake tin

Method

1. Preheat oven to 160°c/140°c fan oven.

2. Grease and line a 9" round/8" square cake tin with parchment paper.

3. Melt the golden syrup, black treacle, stork, and brown sugar in a pan over a low heat on the hob until the sugar has dissolved, stirring frequently until the mixture is smooth and blended.

4. Remove from the heat and allow the mixture to cool for a few minutes.

5. Put the gluten free oats in a food processor and blitz for a couple of minutes until fine. (You now have gluten free oatmeal.)

6. Put ground oats, flour, spices, and salt into a large bowl and stir to mix.

7. Pour the treacle mixture in the flour mixture and stir until well blended.

8. Lightly beat the almond milk and beaten eggs together and add these to the mixture, then mix well until fully blended and the mixture is smooth and glossy.

9. Pour the mixture into the prepared tin and bake in the pre-heated oven for 45-50 minutes, or until firm to touch and a cake tester or sharp knife inserted into the centre of the cake comes out clean.

10. Remove from the oven and leave to cool completely in the tin.

11. When cold, remove from the tin, wrap the cake in fresh parchment paper then a layer of foil, and hide for at least a week.

12. Serve sliced thinly with butter, which leaves more for yourself to have in secret, cut into thick chunks.

Advent calendars and lots of vowels

One of the most amazing ingredients I discovered in my journey to create lovely tasting gluten free and dairy free cakes and bakes is polenta. This was something I'd never even heard of, but thought I'd give it a go anyway and sent my personal shopper (Mr M!) out to buy some. Neither of us really knew what it was or where it would be found in the supermarket. Mr M never lets me down, though, and he arrived back proudly announcing that he had managed to get some.

I looked at this packet, which seemed pretty much like dough to me, or a bit like soft marzipan. Hmmm, I thought. I looked at the polenta and looked at my recipe. 'Stir in the polenta,' said the recipe. There was no way on this earth that I was going to be able to stir in that lump of polenta. If I'd done some research earlier, I'd have discovered there are different types of polenta. Experts would say that polenta is not an ingredient but that it's a dish made from coarse cornmeal (a bit like porridge).

Just to confuse you even more, there's coarse polenta or fine polenta, but often this is called cornmeal or maize flour. The packet that my personal shopper had purchased with pride was ready-made polenta! Once I realised which form I needed, I began using coarse polenta, which produced a lovely tasting cake but was a bit gritty. Then I discovered fine polenta (cornmeal/maize flour) which I now use when making pastry, cakes, and biscuits. One of the nicest cakes I put this in has to be the simple polenta cake. It's not a fancy-looking cake, but it's just lovely to have with a cup of tea or as a pudding served with hot custard. When people ask me what polenta cake is, I tell them that it is a bit like a madeira cake but not as dry.

It took me a little while to decide which customer I was going to name this after, but really the answer was jumping out at me all the time. It just has to be Treasa's Polenta Cake, as she always choses this – mostly with custard – and has been known to take it away with a pot of custard for later when the children are sleeping!

Treasa first came into the tearoom, after we'd been open for only a few months, telling us that she was nearly jumping with joy when she saw our sign in large white and purple letters saying Mother Murphy's Tearoom. She told us how she hoped we'd serve real home-made scones with home-made jam and proper tea. I do believe that we met all her hopes that day.

Along with Treasa came her lovely husband, Glenn, and their little boy, Caolan. Caolan was a lovely boy, and he was very comfortable sitting in one of our brand-new highchairs. Treasa, Glenn, and Caolan soon became regulars in the tearoom. We laugh that sometimes Glenn is called Greg, though, as Mr M called him Greg for months without anyone correcting him! We also laugh that Treasa's idea of a two-course meal is a scone with jam to start with, followed by cake and custard. Sounds perfectly fine to me!

As we approached our first Christmas in the tearoom, we introduced our Christmas Advent Calendar which I had hand-stitched and quilted so that it could be used year after year (and it is now a tearoom tradition). In each pocket we put an envelope with a little token inside, with prizes ranging from a free hot drink, a free piece of cake, and a hand-made bauble. But somewhere hidden in the pockets was Afternoon Tea for Two. Who do you think picked out this fabulous prize from our first Advent Calendar? That's right, young Caolan. I think it took half an hour for Treasa to stop jumping around the tearoom with joy at winning this.

Over the next year or two, we watched Caolan grow until he no longer needed the highchair. Then one day, a very green-looking Treasa came into the tearoom. 'Well, that'll be you pregnant then,' I laughed! Anyway, a few months down the line, along came little Aoife.

I think she was only a couple of days old when she was introduced to the tearoom. If I remember, I taught her to crochet on her first visit, and have photographic evidence somewhere! We have watched these two little children grow, and I can say without a doubt that the customers also just love it when these two come along. At the time of writing this, we had just had another visit from them, and I couldn't believe how grown up they both were. Little Caolan was playing dominoes with Dashing Tom, and Aoife was telling me how lovely her ham sandwich was. This really is what our tearoom is all about, with lovely people making our tearoom family as special as it is. I still joke with Treasa, though, that she chose her children's names with as many vowels as possible just to confuse me.

Treasa and Aoife

Treasa and Caolan

Treasa and Greg (Glenn!)

Treasa's Polenta Cake

Makes a 9" round cake

Ingredients

For the Cake

200g stork block

200g caster sugar

4 free range eggs, lightly beaten

200g ground almonds

100g fine polenta

2 teaspoons baking powder

2 tablespoons lemon juice

2 tablespoons almond milk

For the Icing

50g icing sugar

1 tablespoon lemon juice

Equipment

9" round deep loose-bottomed cake tin

Method

For the Cake

1   Preheat oven to 180°c/160°c fan oven.

2   Grease and line a 9" round cake tin with parchment paper.

3   Put the stork and sugar into a free-standing mixer (or use a hand-held whisk) and beat until light and fluffy.

4   Add the beaten eggs, a little at a time, beating well between each addition.

5   Mix the ground almonds, polenta, and baking powder together in a bowl and then add to the mixer. Mix on a low speed until well blended.

6   Stir in the lemon juice, then the almond milk.

7   Pour the mixture into the prepared cake tin and bake in the pre-heated oven for 40 minutes (a cake tester inserted into the centre of the cake should come out clean).

8   Remove from the oven and leave to cool in the tin for ten minutes.

9   After ten minutes, remove from the cake tin, remove the parchment paper, and leave to cool completely on a wire rack.

For the Icing

10   Mix the icing sugar with the lemon juice until you have a runny icing. If it is a little thick, add a few drops of water. If it is too runny, add a little more icing sugar.

11   Put the icing into a piping bag, cut off the end of the bag (no nozzle needed), drizzle the icing over the cooled cake, and leave to set.

Plain and simple doesn't have to be boring

The humble Victoria Sponge (or Victoria Sandwich Cake) was named after Queen Victoria, who was known to enjoy a sponge cake with her afternoon tea. You may think that the Victoria Sponge is just a plain cake and something people make when they only know how to make basic cakes. How wrong you are, though. I've tasted many, many Victoria Sponges and found them to be dry and boring. Don't get me wrong, I've tasted many more that have been heaven on a plate. If the sponge is light and moist, the jam home-made, and any extra ingredients top quality, the resulting cake can be a showstopper.

Different versions of the Victoria Sponge cake can be made using this recipe, by changing the jam, adding some frosting and bits and pieces, or making a simple two-layer sponge with home-made raspberry jam in the middle and a good dusting of icing sugar over the top for a simple but classic version. For a more spectacular cake, add butter cream in the middle and on the top of the cake, add some rosewater extract, cover with ground pistachio nuts, and you have a magnificent looking Rosewater and Pistachio Cake.

I've used this recipe to make birthday cakes that have then been covered in fondant icing, and nobody has known that it's been gluten and dairy free.

My first Victoria Sponges, as with many of my cakes and bakes, were not gluten free and dairy free and I was worried about trying to change something that customers found so tasty. I tried a few different gluten free and dairy free recipes, but found them to be heavy, dry, and they only kept one day – which is not a good thing in the tearoom. Fortunately, there are lots of different groups on Facebook where they talk about different recipes, and I saw that many people were saying they just adapted a standard recipe. I remembered that I had once made a fabulous Victoria Sponge cake using the Hairy Bikers' recipe, so I dug this back out. Then I changed the ingredients to be gluten free and dairy free, and added a vital touch of xanthan gum.

The first time I made this tweaked version, I knew before it even went into the oven that it was going to be a good cake. Once you've made a few cakes you do get to recognise a good cake batter. This can often be a bit of a life-saver, because you can then tell that you've made a mistake putting the ingredients together. I remember once making a cake and using the all-in method (where you just put everything in the mixer and mix). It was only when I'd mixed everything together and noticed it was not blending as it should that I realised I'd omitted the sugar!

If you've never made a Victoria Sponge before, I'd suggest that you make the two-layer version first; simply sandwich together with home-made raspberry jam, and a good sprinkling of icing sugar on top. That way, you get to taste the cake in its naked form before starting to add your own touches of different extracts, flavourings, nuts, chocolate, and butter cream. However you make yours, make sure that you always sit down, relax, and enjoy a large slice of your masterpiece with a steaming cup of tea. For quality assurance purposes only, of course!

Traditional Victoria Sponge

Makes a two layer 9" round cake

Ingredients

250g soft stork block

250g caster sugar

4 free range eggs, lightly beaten

1 teaspoon vanilla extract

250g gluten free self-raising flour (I use Dove's)

1 teaspoon gluten free baking powder

½ teaspoon xanthan gum

A good dollop of home-made raspberry jam

Equipment

2 x 9" loose-bottomed sandwich tins

Method

1   Preheat oven to 180°c/160°c fan oven.

2   Grease and line two 9" round sandwich tins with parchment paper.

3   Put the flour, baking powder, and xanthan gum in a bowl and mix well.

3   Place the sugar and stork block into a free-standing mixer (or use a hand-held whisk) and beat together until light and fluffy. This will take a good few minutes. Stop the mixer and use a spatula to scrape the mixture from the sides of the bowls a couple of times to make sure it all gets blended.

4   With the mixer still running, add the eggs a little at a time, beating well between each addition until all combined and the mixture is smooth.

5   Lower the speed of the mixer and gradually add the flour mix, one tablespoon at a time, until it has all been added.

6   Add the vanilla extract and mix until just blended.

7   Divide the cake mixture equally between the prepared tins and level the tops with a palette knife.

8   Bake in a pre-heated oven for 25-30 minutes until risen, golden brown, and a cake tester comes out clean.

9   Remove from the oven and leave to cool for 10 minutes in the tins.

10   Remove from the tins, removing the parchment paper, and place on a wire rack to cool completely.

11   Place one of your sponges on the serving plate, flat-side down, and spread the top of it with a good dollop of raspberry jam.

12   Carefully place the other sponge on top of this, flat-side down.

13   Sprinkle with icing sugar for decoration.

14   Make yourself a pot of steaming tea, take a big slice from your Victoria Sponge, and enjoy.

Adapting the traditional Victoria sponge

Once you've mastered the traditional Victoria Sponge (and carried out lots of quality assurance, of course), you can start to make your Victoria Sponge into a showstopper. Try adding different flavours and colours to the sponge, and butter icing to make things look really stunning. Use melted chocolate, coconut, ground nuts or sugar sprinkles to decorate the cake, or even try some fancy piping. Don't worry if your piping isn't perfect, as nobody will notice because they'll be too busy enjoying eating the cake.

Just a few suggestions:
Blackcurrant and Cinnamon
Coconut and Raspberry
Rosewater and Pistachio
Orange, Lemon, and Gooseberry

The choices are up to you and what you like. Experiment with flavours and colours, and you will start to get an idea of what goes together and what you like.

Blackcurrant And Cinnamon Victoria Sponge

Makes a two or three layer 9" round cake

Ingredients

For a 2-layer Cake

250g stork block

250g caster sugar

4 free range eggs, lightly beaten

1 teaspoon vanilla extract

250g gluten free self-raising flour (I use Dove's)

1 teaspoon gluten free baking powder

½ teaspoon xanthan gum

Home-made blackcurrant jelly-jam

For a 3-layer Cake

375g stork block

375g caster sugar

6 free range eggs, lightly beaten

1.5 teaspoon vanilla extract

375g gluten free self-raising flour (I use Dove's)

1.5 teaspoon gluten free baking powder

1 teaspoon xanthan gum

Home-made blackcurrant jelly-jam

For the Butter Cream

250g icing sugar

125g stork block

2 teaspoons hot water

1 teaspoon ground cinnamon

For the Butter Cream

375g icing sugar

190g stork block

3 teaspoons hot water

1.5 teaspoons ground cinnamon

Equipment

2 or 3 x 9" loose-bottomed sandwich tins

Method

For the sponge

1   Preheat oven to 180°c/160°c fan oven.

2   Grease and line two or three 9" round sandwich tins with parchment paper.

3   Put the flour, baking powder, and xanthan gum in a bowl and mix well.

4   Place the sugar and stork block into a free-standing mixer (or use a hand-held whisk) and beat together until light and fluffy. This will take a good few minutes. Stop the mixer and use a spatula to scrape the mixture from the sides of the bowls a couple of times to make sure it all gets blended.

5   With the mixer still running, add the eggs a little at a time, beating well between each addition until all combined and the mixture is smooth.

6   Lower the speed of the mixer and gradually add the flour mix, one tablespoon at a time, until it has all been added.

7   Add the vanilla extract and mix until just blended.

8   Divide the cake mixture equally between the prepared tins and level the tops with a palette knife.

9   Bake in pre-heated oven for 25-30 minutes until risen and golden brown.

10 Remove from the oven and leave to cool for 10 minutes in the tins, then remove from the tins, remove the parchment paper, and place on a wire rack to cool completely.

For the Butter Cream

11 Put the stork, icing sugar, cinnamon, and hot water into the free-standing mixer (or use a hand-held whisk) and beat until light, smooth, and spreadable.

12 Place one of your sponges on the serving plate flat-side down and spread with some of the butter icing. (Use half of the butter cream if making a two-layer cake and a third of the butter cream if making a three-layer cake.)

13 Spread a good dollop of jam on the flat side of the other sponge and carefully place this sponge, jam-side down, on top of the first one. (Repeat with the third sponge if you are making a three-layer cake.)

14 Spread the remaining butter cream on the top cake. Use a cocktail stick or cake tester to swirl a little extra blackcurrant jelly into the icing to give a swirl effect.

When fruit salad no longer cuts the mustard

Growing up in a household where there was not an abundance of money, any cakes or bakes that appeared were a real treat and never lasted long. I can still remember how excited I was if I spied one of the neat pink boxes containing Mr Kipling's cakes. To me, it didn't matter which of his cakes were inside the box, it was just so exciting to be having one of his amazing cakes and that was the treat.

My favourite, without a doubt, was the Battenberg with its bright pink and yellow sponge covered in soft marzipan. This was followed closely by the French Fancies, all shiny in their coloured icing, and filled with soft sponge and a secret dollop of cream. Let's not forget the Viennese Whirls with their short, crumbly biscuit filled with sweet jam. Sometimes we had the luxury ones with an extra filling of cream and drizzled or dipped in chocolate. Oh, the memories!

Over the years I've tried (and often failed) to replicate some of these cakes. From the days when Mr M and I did have a television, I watched the Hairy Bikers make with ease their Viennese Whirls, followed their recipe, and hey-presto had my own wonderful Viennese Whirls.

As Mother Murphy's developed and we continued to expand our range of gluten free and dairy free goodies, I set about making a Viennese Whirl for our 'Delicious Without' range.

The first gluten free and dairy free version contained some xanthan gum and some dairy free milk to hold them together and stop them being too dry. The smell from the oven was terrible and the resulting biscuit something on the lines of dried-out cement. So, back to the drawing board it was.

Eventually, after many tweaks, I was able to make lovely gluten free and dairy free Viennese Whirls that smell nice in the oven, look great, don't collapse when you look at them and, more importantly, taste like a real Viennese Whirl. These are a

Danielle

favourite in the tearoom, and I vary them with the different jams or jellies we have available at the time, and either drizzle them or dip them in plain, milk, or white chocolate.

At the time of writing this, I had just finished making a batch of these beauties and filled them with our blackcurrant jelly-jam. As I was baking them, I posted photos on our Facebook and Instagram pages, asking if anyone was drooling at them. The response was hilarious.

Sue, my old boss in France, commented that her fruit salad was not really cutting the mustard after seeing my photos. Danielle, from Aikman Carpets next door to the tearoom, was literally drooling in her response and couldn't wait to get into the tearoom the following day to get one for herself.

Seeing Danielle practically running into the tearoom and eating her Viennese Whirl before she ate her sandwich, I thought what better name to give these delights than Danielle's Viennese Whirls. Of course, you can also read about Danielle in Gina's Gingernuts. She no longer helps herself to our cakes, of course.

Danielle's Viennese Whirls

Makes about 24 biscuits or 12 Viennese Whirls

Ingredients

For the Biscuit

250g very soft stork block

50g icing sugar

115 g gluten free plain flour (I use Dove's)

115g ground almonds

50g cornflour

For the Filling

100g very soft stork block

200g icing sugar

1 teaspoon vanilla extract

Home-made jam

100g gluten and dairy free chocolate

Method

For the Biscuit

1   *Preheat oven to 190°c/170°c fan oven.*

2   *Line two baking trays with parchment paper.*

3   *Draw circles on the parchment paper using a 4cm cutter. Turn the parchment paper over once you have drawn on it, so that you do not get pen on your biscuits!*

4   *Put all the biscuit ingredients in a free-standing mixer or food processor, and beat until light and fluffy.*

5   *Put a large star icing nozzle into a piping bag and spoon the mixture into it.*

6   *Pipe about 24 rosettes with the mixture onto your circles.*

7   *Bake in the pre-heated oven for 10 minutes or until just lightly golden brown.*

8   *Remove from the oven and allow to cool completely on a wire rack.*

For the Filling

9   *Put the stork, icing sugar, and vanilla extract into the mixer and beat until very light and smooth.*

10 *Turn all the biscuits upside down and put half of them on one rack, and half on another.*

11 *Spoon a little jam of your choice onto half of the biscuits.*

12 *Put a large star icing nozzle into a piping bag and spoon the filling into it.*

13 *Pipe a rosette of filling on the other half of the biscuits.*

14 *Sandwich the two halves together.*

15 *Put the chocolate in a glass bowl and melt in the microwave, 30 seconds at a time, until smooth and glossy.*

16 *You can now either drizzle the melted chocolate over the Viennese Whirls or dip each one and half coat them in chocolate.*

17 *Allow the chocolate to set completely, and sprinkle with icing sugar just before serving.*

My favourite food actually is chocolate cake. I need to have a slice of chocolate cake every single day, without fail.

Sona Ali Khan (Actress)

Dressing up for cake

There is only one thing better than chocolate fudge cake, and that's white chocolate fudge cake. Oh, hang on, though. What about chocolate fudge cake served warm with ice cream, cream, or hot custard? Admit it, chocolate fudge cake in any form is just perfect. Home-made, of course, is not the sickly, over-sweet cake you find in lots of places. Just try making this and then you'll realise why I'm often disappointed with cakes that are commercially bought.

Dave and Louise

Remember, too, it doesn't matter how you put the topping on. You can simply plonk it on, spread it smoothly, or try some delicate piping. Sprinkle a bit of cocoa power on to finish and this will look and taste just amazing.

We've had our chocolate fudge cake and mint chocolate fudge cake in the tearoom since we opened, but I thought I'd try this with white choc-olate. Now, I have a little confession to make here about white chocolate. My son, Benjamin, was born on 10th March, 1986, and that year Easter came along not long afterwards. Naturally, I had to buy him a white chocolate Easter egg or two, because white chocolate is good for children, isn't it? Of course, he was a little too young to eat the Easter eggs and, being the perfect new mum, I ate them for him. It's rumoured I only had children just to give me an excuse to buy in more white chocolate! Do you remember the Milky Bar advert and can still sing all the words?

However, making our cakes and bakes dairy free meant I could no longer use white chocolate, until I discovered the amazing gluten free and dairy free chocolates at Plamil Foods. Who'd have thought that dairy free chocolate could taste this good? I have to admit to trying to come up with all sorts of recipes to put this white chocolate in now that I've found it.

The first time I made this White Chocolate Fudge Cake, the customers simply couldn't get enough of it. Danielle from Aikmen's Carpets next door to us was almost banging on the door when she saw my Facebook post and the picture of this. However, it just has to be Dave's White Chocolate Fudge Cake, because it's not every day that somebody makes a special trip to your tearoom on his way to a wedding, dressed in a posh suit, just to have a piece of White Chocolate Fudge Cake.

Dave's White Chocolate Fudge Cake

Makes a two-layer, 9" round cake
(or 24 mini cakes)

Ingredients

For Cake

75g cocoa powder

100ml boiling water

½ teaspoon xanthan gum

263g gluten free self-raising flour

1.5 teaspoons gluten free baking powder

413g caster sugar

150g stork block softened

75ml almond milk

5 free range eggs, lightly beaten

For the Chocolate Fudge

200g gluten and dairy free white chocolate

175g stork block

70ml almond milk

1½ teaspoons vanilla extract

600g icing sugar

Cocoa powder for dusting

Equipment

2 x 9" deep loose-bottomed cake tins or

2 x 12-hole mini Victoria sponge tins

Method

For the Cake

1   Preheat oven to 180°c/160°c fan oven.

2   Grease and line two 9" round cake tins, or grease with parchment paper, or grease two 12-hole mini sandwich tins.

3   Dissolve the cocoa powder in the boiling water.

4   Put the xanthan gum, flour, baking powder, and sugar into a free-standing mixer (or use a hand-held mixer) and mix until combined and there are no lumps left.

5   Add the cocoa mix, beaten eggs, almond milk, and stork to the flour mix. Beat until you have a well-blended smooth mixture.

6   Divide the mixture between the two prepared cake tins and smooth the surface.

7   Bake in the pre-heated oven for 30 minutes or until a cake tester/knife inserted into the centre of the cakes comes out clean.

8   Remove from the oven, but leave the cakes for 20 minutes before removing them from the tins and placing on a wire rack to cool completely. If you are making individual cakes, slice the cold cakes in half horizontally.

For the White Chocolate Fudge Filling and Coating

9   Melt the white chocolate in a bowl over a pan of gently simmering water. Once the chocolate has started to melt, remove from the heat and stir gently until all the chocolate has melted.

10   Put the icing sugar, stork, almond milk, and vanilla extract in the free-standing mixer and mix on low speed until combined.

11   Add the melted white chocolate, then turn the mixer onto high and beat for a few minutes until the mixture is light and smooth. If the mixture seems a little soft, add some more icing sugar.

12   Place one of the cooled sponges bottom-side down on a cake stand/plate and spread with a layer of the frosting.

13   Carefully place the second sponge, bottom-side down, on top of this and spread the remaining icing over the top and sides of the cake, smoothing with a palate knife. You can reserve some of the frosting and use this to pipe on top of the cake in your own design, but simply covering the cake is just as effective.

14   Finish with a sprinkling of cocoa powder over the cake.

15   To make this extra special, serve slightly warm with a good dollop of fresh cream or ice cream. You don't need a big piece, as it is very rich.

Covid-19 live chats

All those years ago, when I was still running our training company and starting to dabble in a home baking business, this chocolate fudge cake was one of the very first gluten free and dairy free things I made. I was very naive about this gluten free thing, and there were many, many disasters. The first chocolate fudge cake looked absolutely amazing, until I tried to cut into it; it just crumbled as the knife touched it. The mess on the plate was delicious, but a cake it was not, and certainly not something I'd be happy to ask people to pay for.

Fast forward a few months, and I had a cake that really was a Chocolate Fudge Cake. I'd used a combination of recipes, using the sponge from one book and the frosting from another. It was lovely and everyone enjoyed it, and when we opened the tearoom, this quickly became a firm favourite with the customers.

My concern, though, was that the recipe used so much sugar that you could almost hear the sugar police sirens sounding when this cake was served in the tearoom. I set about trying to change this while still having a sticky, chocolatey fudge cake,

A very old photo of Debra, baby Bethany and Karen

but needed something more than just a sponge cake. It had to have that rich chocolate taste, and the frosting needed to be sticky and able to cope with being warmed slightly in the microwave to serve as hot chocolate fudge cake.

Each time I tweaked the cake, it tasted lovely, but finally, many cakes down the line, I finally had my own Chocolate Fudge Cake that was delicious, chocolatey, scrummy, gluten free, dairy free and, most importantly, it had much less sugar than my original version. The final test was what the customers thought of it, but they all agreed that even though the previous ones had been delicious, this version was far superior.

Oddly enough, though, this cake didn't seem to have a customer's name to it, perhaps because it could have had a million and one customer's names against it. As I've mentioned already, the tearoom was forced to close in March 2020 as part of the lockdown across the country for the battle against the Covid-19 virus. In an attempt to keep everyone's spirits up during this difficult time (including mine and Mr M's), we tried to have daily live chats on Facebook, talking about anything and everything. Hopefully, everyone enjoyed these as much as we did. During these daily live chats, I offered a few of the remaining cakes up for customer names, and one night we announced we were looking for a name for the Chocolate Fudge Cake.

Lots of people gave reasons why they should have the cake named after them, but my oldest friend, Karen, won hands down. Karen said that we never see each other enough and if I named it after her, I'd be reminded of her every time I served it. Just in case this wasn't enough, she reminded me that many years ago I had been the one to introduce her daughter Bethany to chocolate! So, Karen's Chocolate Fudge Cake it became.

We just need the tearoom to re-open for customers to see the Chocolate Fudge Cake with its new name in pride of place.

Just who is this Karen then? I met Karen when we were pupils at Princess Mary Girls' Grammar School in Halifax. Karen came late to the school, at the beginning of the 5th year, by which time I was already established in the school, though quite a loner. I remember sitting daydreaming out of the form room window and seeing this new person running up and down the hockey pitch, and knowing right then that this girl was the friend I'd been waiting for.

Over the last 40 years, we have been firm friends despite a geographical distance. We played hockey together, swam together, and had a holiday in Scotland together to celebrate finishing our

O' Levels. I spent time with Karen's amazing mum, Barbara, and her equally fabulous Grandma and Grandad. You know when you need somewhere safe to go? Well, my safe place was to visit Karen and her family. Did they know my life was a bit of a mess? Probably. Did they ever criticise or belittle me? Never. Did they always welcome me with open arms? Always!

Bethany, Marcus, Debra, Karen and Adrian

One of my best moments in the tearoom was when Karen, her lovely husband Adrian, and her children Bethany and Marcus, turned up unannounced. No mean feat when the tearoom is in Falkirk, Central Scotland, and Karen lives in North Yorkshire!

As I write, we are waiting for Karen to build an extension to her house so we can have a Tearoom Road Trip to Yorkshire, and to visit the Wensleydale Creamery in Hawes. Currently there are about 20 people going on this road trip. Maybe that will be a second book – Mother Murphy's Tearoom After Lockdown.

Karen's Chocolate Fudge Cake

Makes a two-layer, 9" round cake
(or 24 mini cakes)

Ingredients

For the Cake

75g cocoa powder

100ml boiling water

½ teaspoon xanthan gum

263g gluten free self-rising flour

1.5 teaspoons gluten free baking powder

413g caster sugar

150g stork block softened

75ml almond milk

5 free range eggs, lightly beaten

For the Chocolate Fudge

250ml cold water

100g cocoa powder

300g golden syrup

200g gluten and dairy free plain chocolate

50g stork block

200g icing sugar

Equipment

2 x 9" deep loose-bottomed cake tins or

2 x 12-hole mini Victoria sponge tins

Method

For the Cake

1   Preheat oven to 180°c/160°c fan oven.

2   Grease and line two 9" round cake tins with parchment paper, or grease two 12-hole mini sandwich tins.

3   Dissolve the cocoa powder in the boiling water.

4   Put the xanthan gum, flour, baking powder, and sugar into a free-standing mixer (or use a hand-held mixer) and mix until combined and there are no lumps left.

5   Add the cocoa mix, beaten eggs, almond milk, and stork to the flour mix. Beat until you have a well-blended smooth mixture.

6   Divide the mixture between the two prepared cake tins and smooth the surface.

7   Bake in the pre-heated oven for 30 minutes, or until a cake tester/knife inserted into the centre of the cakes comes out clean.

8   Remove from the oven, but leave the cakes in the tins for 20 minutes before removing them from the tins and placing on a wire rack to cool completely. If you are making individual cakes, slice the cold cakes horizontally.

Chocolate Fudge Filling and Coating

9   Put the water, cocoa, and golden syrup into a pan and bring to the boil, whisking continually.

10   Simmer for 4 minutes, stirring gently.

11   Remove from the heat and beat in the chocolate and stork.

12   Leave the mixture to cool then beat in the icing sugar.

13   Allow the frosting to settle for a few minutes. If it is still too runny, keep adding more icing sugar until it is thick enough to spread. Remember, though, that it will go firmer once it sets.

14   Place one of the cooled sponges bottom-side down on a cake stand/plate, and spread with a layer of the frosting.

15   Carefully place the second sponge, bottom-side down, on top of this and spread the remaining icing over the top and sides of the cake, smoothing with a palate knife.

16   Finish with a light sprinkling of icing sugar over the cake.

17   To make this extra special, you could serve a piece of this slightly warm with a good dollop of fresh cream or ice cream. You don't need a big piece as it is very rich.

Popeye, spinach, and a surprisingly good chocolate cake

I'm one of these strange people who has never spent hours and hours glued to the TV, and Mr M and I have not had a TV at home for about five years now. It's been a godsend during the Covid-19 outbreak, because we've not been subjected to the ongoing doom and gloom of the constant news bulletins.

As a youngster, we had a TV at home, but obviously didn't have the hundreds of TV channels that youngsters today do. There was plenty of choice, though, and I did like to watch the various cartoons on offer, especially Popeye. Remember him? The one-eyed sailor who eats spinach, has a girlfriend called Olive Oyl, and is always battling with Bluto the Terrible.

When my children were youngsters, we had a holiday on the lovely island of Malta, visiting the film set where the Popeye film starring the late Robin Williams was made in the early 1980s. I remember the set then being a bit run-down and the kids didn't really know who Popeye was, but nowadays it's all been re-vamped and is a big tourist attraction for Malta.

In the tearoom, I was always looking at different recipes and trying new ways to make cakes tasty and different, when I came across a magazine from Australia. I was instantly drawn to this one because of the delicious looking chocolate cake on its front page, only to be disappointed to find that this amazing looking creation was called Chocolate, Zucchini, and Spinach Cake with Avocado Chocolate Frosting. The magazine was talking about boosting your bakes with a good dose of vegetables to get a step closer to having your recommended five servings a day.

Now, we all know that me and vegetables are not the best of friends. Could I even imagine trying to make a cake with all these vegetables in it? There was only one way to find out. I set about converting the recipe quantities from cups to grams, and turning the ingredients into gluten free and dairy free ones.

One of the first steps in making the cake was to put the unpeeled courgettes (zucchini) into a blender with the milk. What a mess this looked. Surely I wasn't going to serve this to people? But I persevered. Next, the spinach and cocoa were added to this mess. Well, now I was totally convinced I'd soon be throwing away this dark green mixture.

However, by the time I'd finished making the cake batter, I was feeling a little better about it and thought it might be ok for a trial. So, the batter went into the oven. I waited to make the chocolate frosting, still convinced the cake wouldn't turn out. A little while later, though, the most amazing looking chocolate cake was sitting on my cooling trays, waiting for its chocolate frosting.

Still unsure whether the customers would go for this cake, and certainly thinking there could be no confessing about all the strange ingredients in one cake, I pondered what to call it. I hit upon the name of Popeye's Surprisingly Good Chocolate Cake.

Customers were tempted by the cake but were not told what was in it until they'd tried it. Of course, I had to do some quality assurance on the cake, too. If I hadn't made it myself, I wouldn't have believed what ingredients were used in it. It was amazing.

Even Mr M, who tells everyone – to my horror – that he doesn't like cake, had some and said it was lovely! Now, let me introduce my Popeye's Surprisingly Good Chocolate Cake.

Popeye's Surprisingly Good Chocolate Cake

Makes a two-layer, 9" round cake

Ingredients

For the Cake

400g (about 2) courgettes, unpeeled but chopped

237ml almond milk

60g spinach leaves

100g cocoa powder

250g stork block

400g light brown sugar

6 free range eggs

240g gluten free plain flour (I use Dove's)

1 teaspoon xanthan gum

1 teaspoon bicarbonate of soda

½ teaspoon gluten free baking powder

For the Chocolate Frosting

2 avocados, halved and stoned

100g cocoa powder

125g icing sugar

1.5 teaspoons vanilla extract

Equipment

2 x 9" deep loose-bottomed cake tins

Method

For the Cake

1   *Preheat oven to 180°c/160°c fan oven.*

2   *Grease and line two 9" round cake tins with parchment paper.*

3   *Put the flour, xanthan gum, bicarbonate of soda, and baking powder into a bowl, mix to combine, and put to one side.*

4   *Put the courgettes and almond milk in a blender and blitz until smooth. Add in the spinach and cocoa powder and blitz again.*

5   *Place the melted stork and sugar into a free-standing mixer (or use a hand-held whisk) and mix until combined.*

6   *Add the courgette mix into the mixer and beat until smooth.*

7   *Next add the flour mixture and beat on a slow setting until well combined.*

8   *Divide the mixture between the two prepared baking tins and bake in the preheated oven for 50 minutes or until a cake test pressed into the centre of the cake comes out clean.*

9   *Leave the cakes to cool in the tins for 15 minutes before removing from the tins and leaving to cool completely on a wire rack.*

Chocolate Frosting

10   *Put all the frosting ingredients into a food processor and process until you get a smooth paste, adding a little almond milk if you feel it is too thick to spread.*

11   *Put one of the cooled cakes on a serving plate, smooth side down, and spread with half of the frosting.*

12   *Place the other cake on top of this, smooth down, and spread the rest of your frosting over the top of this.*

13   *You could finish this with fresh fruit on the top or just leave it as it is.*

14   *As an extra treat, serve warm with some cream or ice cream.*

Pudding is my favourite part of any meal and I always have one if I can manage it.

Fiona Bruce

Learning to be brave when ordering from a menu

In my teens, I'd only had the pleasure of eating out at restaurants on a handful of times, and was really too scared to order anything from the menu I didn't know and recognise. During one meal out with a group of people in the fabulous Zeffirelli's restaurant at Ambleside, I was busy telling one of my friends how much I hated garlic. 'Really?' he said with a raised eyebrow. 'That pâté you're piling onto your toast is oozing with garlic!'

On another occasion, in Bowness-on-Windermere, I wanted to try the Lake District speciality of Sticky Toffee Pudding, but read on the menu it was made with dates. I wasn't really sure I wanted to try a pudding with strange fruit in it, but plucked up the courage and ordered it. I was expecting to be presented with a dish full of big chunks of fruit, but what I received was heaven on a plate. It was a dark, sticky, sweet, light sponge with the most amazing toffee sauce poured over it.

My fondant Mrs Tiggy-Winkle and Langdale Pikes for our Lake District themes cake in the tearoom

I soon learned that sticky toffee pudding, served warm with lashings of hot custard or ice cream, is one of life's comforts – especially if it's cold outside. It's said that this amazing pudding was created in the 1970s by the late John Tovey, of the Miller Howe Hotel in Windermere, in the beautiful Lake District. You all know how much I love both the Lake District and puddings, so to have them connected is just perfect for me.

For one of our birthdays at the tearoom, we had a Lake District theme. I made a cake decorated with the iconic Langdale Pikes and Mrs Tiggy-Winkle, Borrowdale Tea Loaf, Kendal Mint Cake, and of course, Sticky Toffee Pudding. And the customers just loved it.

As we developed our gluten free and dairy free delights, I thought about trying to convert this, wondering if a dairy free sticky toffee sauce would be just as good as the one I'd first tasted. Well, I could have eaten the whole batch of sauce with a large spoon, straight from the pan! Nowadays, I make my sticky toffee puddings as individual cakes that are just the perfect size.

Sticky Toffee Pudding

Makes a 9" round cake or 12 individual loaves

Ingredients

For the Cake

150g dried dates, chopped into small pieces

220ml boiling water

80g stork block

130g light brown sugar

2 free range eggs, lightly beaten

1 teaspoon vanilla extract

50g golden syrup

2 teaspoons bicarbonate of soda

200g gluten free plain flour (I use Dove's)

¼ teaspoon xanthan gum

For the Sticky Toffee Sauce

125ml soya cream

200g dark brown sugar

100g stork block

½ teaspoon vanilla extract

Pinch of salt

Equipment

9" deep loose-bottomed cake tin or

12 disposable mini loaf cases

Method

For the Cake

1   Preheat oven to 180°c/160°c fan oven.

2   Grease and line a 9" round cake tin with parchment paper, or put 12 disposable mini loaf cases on to baking trays.

3   Mix the flour and xanthan gum together in a bowl and put to one side.

4   Place the dates in a bowl with the boiling water and leave for a few minutes.

5   Put the stork and sugar into a free-standing mixer (or use a hand-held whisk) and beat until fluffy and light in colour.

6   Add the eggs a little at a time, beating well until well mixed and light and fluffy.

7   Add the vanilla extract and the golden syrup, and beat again until blended.

8   Mix the bicarbonate of soda with the date mixture then add this, with the flour mix, to your sugar mixture in the mixer. Beat briefly to get a smooth but runny batter.

9   Pour the mixture into the prepared tins and bake in the preheated oven for 35 minutes until well risen and browned.

10   Remove from the tin (but leave in the disposable loaf cases, if using) and leave to cool on a wire rack.

Making the Sticky Toffee Sauce

11   Put all the sauce ingredients in a pan on a low heat and allow to melt slowly, then simmer for 5 minutes, stirring all the time.

12   Pour over your cakes while they are still warm, and leave to soak in.

Sometimes you just want a biscuit

Let's take a moment to ponder the wonder of the humble biscuit. What is there to say about biscuits? Where should I start? As you probably know by now, I have the world's greatest sweet tooth and can think of nothing better than sitting down with a hot cup of tea and a slab of home-made cake. Sometimes, though, it's a biscuit that's needed and not a cake.

Who am I kidding?! It has to be a plate of biscuits. I don't know about you, but I find a whole packet of Jaffa cakes can disappear in the time it takes to boil the kettle! I read a saying once that quoted, 'if you feel there is something missing in your life it is almost always a biscuit'. Because of this, I thought I'd start this section with a clip from the daily postings I made on our Facebook page during my experimental gluten free month:

1 May, 2016 - first Sunday opening and Debra's gluten free month - Day 1

We were a little unsure whether we'd have any customers today as it was our first week of opening on a Sunday. How wrong were we! If today is anything to go by, Mother Murphy's will continue to open on a Sunday.

Day 1 of my gluten free month to get a better understanding of how well our menu meets customers' needs in the tearoom for gluten free requirements. Here goes.

I swapped my usual Scots Porridge Oats to Tesco's free from oats, and then had my usual banana and yoghurt for breakfast. Lunch at the tearoom was easy enough – Jim's lentil soup with one of our new 'Delicious Without' bread rolls, followed by a 'Delicious Without' treacle scone and our home-made raspberry jam. My extra treat in the afternoon was a piece of orange polenta slice.

What did I miss in the tearoom on my first gluten free day? Yes, it was a simple digestive biscuit. We usually have shortbread available, but this isn't part of our 'Delicious Without' range. I do believe I've seen a recipe for gluten free digestive biscuits, so you might well find 'Delicious Without' Digestives on our menu soon.

Creating our own digestive biscuits

If I had a tearoom full of cakes but was craving a simple biscuit, how many more people would be the same? Scouring the internet for recipes for digestive biscuits, I came up with one that seemed ok, then changed the butter to stork block and the milk to almond milk to make them dairy free as well as gluten free. For the flour, I used Dove Farm's plain flour. Eventually I was happy that the biscuits were indeed yummy.

Obviously, lots of taste testing had to be carried out before we could serve them in the tearoom. Could I call them Digestives, or would people be disappointed because they didn't taste exactly like the digestives we all know? What could I call them? Unable to think of a name, I called them 'Biscuit with No Name'. The customers loved these biscuits – and loved the name.

Sweet, but not too sweet, was the verdict; better than the bought versions, was another comment. They became the Biscuit with No Name, but a few weeks later a new customer came in and asked why they didn't have a name. He tried one of these and declared they should be called Wannabes, because they want to be a digestive. Perfect!

Developing these further, I made a Wannabe Chocolate Cream and these just flew out of the tearoom. I asked what other flavours of cream the customers would like, and the general opinion was that it didn't really matter what the cream was, as long as the biscuit was the same. The Wannabe Cream Biscuit recipe is, therefore, only limited by your imagination for flavour.

These biscuits are incredibly versatile. Try them plain with a cup of tea or coffee, or I love them with a slice of Wensleydale cheese on them. And simply add a cream filling and they become just a dream biscuit.

When I get tired, I start eating things that I wouldn't normally crave, like biscuits, because they'll give me a bit of energy to keep going.

Carol Vorderman

A barking dog, a helicopter rescue, and lemon wannabes

Our humble Wannabe biscuit was a bit of life-saver for me, too, when I was hospitalised after my dramatic helicopter rescue from the Scottish mountains. Now that I follow a gluten free diet for my joints (it really does make a difference), I was limited at snack time by the hospital's choices. Fortunately I had some Lemon Wannabes in my rucksack, left over from my uneaten lunch, and Mr M was able to bring me further supplies of more Lemon Wannabes and plain Wannabes, so I could nibble away on these biscuits when I felt well enough to eat.

When the hospital was not able to provide me with gluten free toast at breakfast or supper time, I was able to have a plain Wannabe with jam. Oh my! How the other patients looked on in envy. Did I share my Wannabes? Not a chance. These were like gold dust to me during my two-week stay in hospital. Of course, this tale just had to be included in the book for you. Read on…

I guess Tuesday, 13th August, 2019, will stick in my mind for a long time (and is probably etched on Mr M's mind forever). As is usual on my day off from the tearoom, I was heading out onto the hills with my walking pal, Beatrix the Collie. No Mr M this time, as his knees no longer allow him to tackle the high Munro peaks.

The two of us set off with my rucksack packed with plenty of warm clothes, a picnic for me, a picnic for Beatrix (yes, Mr M packs a picnic for the dog!), a flask of tea, and a drink of juice. Of course, there was Chocolate Covered Kendal Mint Cake, too.

Those of you who've read my previous tales of heading out towards the remote Glen Lyon will already know that the drive itself is a bit of an adventure up from the village of Killin on the single-track road. It's not just as scary when there's no snow or ice about (or when you don't have a back-seat driver).

Anyway, arriving at the car park on the Ben Lawers Reserve, the views were already great. There were a few ominous black clouds but also a fair old wind, so they'd be blown away, hopefully to give a day of sunshine and showers. It was decidedly chilly for the time of year and I'd already put my long trousers and jacket on before I set off.

Ben Lawers is probably one of my favourite climbs (and remains so even after this latest adventure). Sitting high above Killin in Perthshire, it's the highest mountain in the southern part of the Scottish Highlands, and is the tenth highest Munro in Scotland. Is that why I love to climb it? Not really. I love this range of mountains because of the remoteness you feel, even though in reality you're only a short distance away from civilisation.

My preferred route takes you first up the smaller Munro of Beinn Ghlas. The route twists and winds its way up the first mountain, and with every turn

Enjoying some Kendal Mint Cake

281

you're blessed with views that seem to open up even more, revealing mountain after mountain. The route is a mixture of a bit of scrambling at times but also a feeling of strolling along a grassy path, with the extra bonus of a short ridge to descend before the final ascent to the goal of Ben Lawers at 1,214m (3,984ft). To put it into perspective, Ben Nevis, Britain's highest mountain, is 1,345 (4412ft).

Shortly after leaving the car park, I found myself surrounded by the biggest, juiciest bilberries (or blaeberries) I've seen for many years. I worked out that by the time me and Beatrix had eaten our picnics on route, our sandwich bags would be empty, and I'd be able to amaze Mr M with a huge batch of bilberries for turning into our lovely wild berry jelly-jam. Usually you have to spend all day picking these tiny berries to gather enough for even a small batch, but today would be different. I made a plan to gather these lovely bilberries on my way back down to the car. Best laid plans of mice and men, eh?!

Before long, the heat of the sun and the shelter of the mountains brought out the dreaded midges en masse. I stopped and smothered my midge spray over my face and hands, even rubbing it into my hair, as I could feel the beasties munching on my scalp. As I'm one for taking a bit of reaction to midge bites, I'm always armed with my spray.

However, I was soon laughing at the midges when, before too long, the previously mentioned ominous black clouds opened and my waterproofs were swiftly put on. The rain was soon blown away, but I left my waterproofs on to be ready for the next downpour (a move that proved very helpful as I later lay on the ground).

We progressed up the twisting path of Beinn Ghlas, and Beatrix found her stone for the day and encouraged everyone she met to throw it for her. Trust me, Collies have a way of letting everyone know exactly what they want you to do. I was having a fabulous time chatting to lots of different people, including a lovely lady and her son (who would soon become my heroes) who spent time throwing stones for Beatrix.

It was turning into a glorious day. The views were, as always, just stunning, the sun was shining, and I was feeling great. As you near the top of Beinn Ghlas, there's a little respite where you almost feel to be walking along a grassy field. The steep, twisting climb has been conquered, and there's a good long section of level walking before the next final haul to complete the first Munro of the day. With the wind at this point starting to pick up as you gain height and exit the shelter of the lower mountains, my trusty woolly hat was now on (again another good move for later).

Once over the final ascent to Beinn Glas, you get your first view of the summit of Ben Lawers, and the route now descends gradually over a shoulder ridge. I always put Beatrix on her lead at this point, as the ridge has some steep drops. It's funny to watch her because she always waits at for me here, as though she knows the lead will be coming out. Maybe she's glad of the security of the lead over this bit (or maybe she thinks I need her help over this section!). Anyway, as we descended, we had a bit of a chat (yes, I chat to my dog!). Beatrix got a couple of her biscuits, while I had my Kendal Mint Cake and take lots of photos.

Approaching the final section of Ben Lawers, we stopped to have a chat to a couple of other walkers who also had a Collie. Beatrix and the other dog had a bit of a run about together and I chatted to the walkers for a good ten minutes. We parted company, and they descended the mountain as I set off to finish

Ben Lawers. That's when totally out of the blue my head started swimming and I felt like I was spinning around. Sit down a minute, Debra, I told myself. I sat on a rock and watched the world literally go round and round. I must be a bit dehydrated, I told myself, and sat a little longer and ate my apple. Looking up at Ben Lawers, I suddenly lost all inclination to climb to the summit.

Just at the point where I was resting is where you can join an old deer stalker's path around Beinn Ghlas that eventually takes you back to join the path to descend to the car park. I decided the best thing would be to take the easier track to gather myself on the walk down, find a good spot for lunch, and then pick the bilberries on the way back to the car.

Standing up felt a little strange, and I was certainly still light-headed. Undeterred, though, I started down the track. Now, going along a track on a slight descent, you'd imagine would be an easy task. But suddenly I felt like I was carrying an elephant on my chest, I had pins and needles down both arms and across my face, and breathing was, well, a bit difficult.

Just putting one foot in front of the other was proving very difficult, but I managed to get myself to a flat-looking rock and plonked myself down. A little voice inside my head told me, 'Debra, get your lunch out, have a sandwich and a cup of tea.' So, I tried this, but not very successfully. The little voice laughed at me now and said, 'You're trained in first aid, Debra. You know what's happening, really.'

Lots of things started going through my mind. I was fit, healthy, and not even out of breath at the top of the mountain, so why would I be having a heart attack? Seriously? What to do? Laugh as you will, but I got out my iPhone and took a selfie of myself to see how I really looked. Well, that scared me even more than how I felt. Yep, I was having a heart attack! Right, let's phone 999 and summon help.

It's at that point that I realised walking down the track that little way had in fact taken me away from the phone signal you get at the top of the mountain. Oh flip! I know, I thought. That WhatsApp thing Benjamin told me about is good when you don't have a signal. Not wanting to alarm Mr M at this point, I sent a message to my trusty pal, Crafty Sal. I told her how I felt, where I was, and that I had no signal to call 999. Oh flip, and more flip! I could see that the message didn't go.

It was at this point that I really started to have a bit of a panic. I looked back up the hill and saw the lady and her son I'd been talking to earlier. Right, Debra, calm down, try to relax, and wait for them to get to you. Beatrix, by this point, was starting to have a bit of her own panic as she realised all was not good with her walking pal, and she was barking away to tell the whole world. This barking seemed to be echoing around the whole of Glen Lyon.

As they approached me, I told the lady I didn't feel too well, though I guess she could probably tell this. I remember having a discussion with her about what to do, and she said that she'd go back up to the top of the mountain and summon help.

So, I waited, moving myself down onto the ground. To be fair, there was not much I could do by then because my whole body felt like it was getting buried in cement. My arms wouldn't move. It's funny the things that cross your mind at times like this. I thought how sad it was that now I couldn't manage to send a message to Mr M. What if I died of this and he then found out I had sent a message to Salena and not him? What about Ben and Chloe, though?

The amazing people who helped me on the hill and the fantastic helicopter crew who landed a helicopter on the side of a mountain

From there, things get a bit blurry. I remember hearing Beatrix barking and barking like she has never done before. She was licking my face and bringing more stones for me (stones make everything ok in Beatrix's eyes). I was aware that more people came and told me everything was going to be ok. They wrapped me up in my spare jackets and I told them I had emergency blankets in my rucksack – emergency blankets that I've carried around with me for over thirty years and never needed to use! It's at times like this that the closeness of a stranger's face, the feeling of somebody holding your hand and a reassuring voice, is everything to you.

Amidst my confusion, shock, and nausea, I was aware that somebody said the helicopter was on its way and that someone had spoken to Jim. I was conscious enough to worry then that Beatrix would be afraid of the helicopter and would be even more afraid that I was getting lifted into it without her. It was also at this point I found out just how strong the downdraught of a helicopter is!

I remember bits of the helicopter ride and being given aspirin to chew. To be honest, by the time I was Ninewells Hospital, the heart pain had diminished a little and I was just exhausted. I no longer felt that the worst was imminent, and even told myself that I'd been exaggerating how I felt.

Fast forward a few hours: Salena by now had received my message and was phoning me to tell me to calm down and to phone 999. Can I just tell you that twice now I've needed Salena's help on the mountains, and twice she's not answered my call, so her friendship membership was well and truly cancelled. (We have laughed about this since, though, and I reinstated her friendship membership yet again.)

What followed was a blur of blood tests, drugs, more tests, more drugs, and a tired Mr M eventually finding his way up to me after hours of worrying and driving. Knowing that I'd suffered a heart attack and was being airlifted to Dundee, he had the tough task of getting one of our lovely neighbours, Chris, to drive up to his least favourite Glen Lyon, collect Beatrix and my car, drive all the way to Kirkintilloch, then drive all the way up to Dundee, finally arriving at my bedside around 11pm. We laugh now, though, that I still thought it was only about 3pm.

Anyway, over the next couple of weeks, I was fastened to a heart monitor, had blood tests, echograms, an angiogram, more blood tests, was discharged, re-admitted to hospital in Glasgow, more echoes, more blood tests, and an MRI.

All the results showed that, yes, I had suffered a heart attack, and my heart had suffered a little muscle damage. However, my angiogram and MRI showed that all my arteries are perfectly fine. Although there had been a heart attack, the cause was most likely to have been an infection of some sort attacking my heart, rather than my heart being in poor shape.

Tests were carried out for Lyme's Disease, and I was pumped full of antibiotics after I told them of an infected bite on my ankle a few weeks earlier. But the consultant told me to get back to my usual self as quickly as possible, to rest when I want to rest, and before long I would be back making scones and climbing Munros as normal. I am at no greater risk of suffering another heart attack than any other person, I was told, and this could have happened to me at any time and was not caused by climbing the Munro.

Now I needed to recover. I was tired, sore, and certainly a bit emotional. But I'm Debra, and those of you who know me well will know that I was determined to be back in action before long. I was on a bucketload of drugs that lowered my already low blood pressure and lowered my already low pulse, making me a little unsteady on my feet and constantly feeling lightheaded. My body would adjust to this soon. though. My right arm was still sore from the angiogram, my veins looked like every one of them had been punctured, and I was bruised everywhere – but that's all.

I'm incredibly grateful for the amazing people who helped me, both on the mountain, in the helicopter, in Ninewells Hospital, and at Glasgow Royal Infirmary. A bit of public investigation has told me that it was lovely Sarah and her son who originally found me and ran back up and down the mountain to get in touch with the emergency services and Jim. Judith and Colin were the young couple who helped get me covered in jackets and my emergency blankets. Caroline was the lovely lady who sat alongside me, kept me calm, warm, and held my hand. And Niall and his brother were amongst those on the hill helping to keep me warm and safe, and who took the most amazing video of my helicopter rescue. There were many people whose names I have not found out.

Beatrix did what she thought best and barked the whole world to my rescue. Dogs really are man's best friend.

The comments I received on Facebook were overwhelming, and really did keep me going over those first dark few weeks for me. You are all amazing. Thank you.

Of course, I am blessed to have the magnificent Mr M at my side. I will always be eternally grateful for this and for the fact that he loves and knows me enough not to have said those words, 'You will never go on the hills alone again.' He is, however, getting me a new GPS device that will allow me to contact emergency services when I'm out of phone signal!

So, where do the Lemon Wannabes come in? Well, fortunately I had a stash of these with me on the hill and at home, and these biscuits kept me going in the hospital when I just needed some of my home baking.

Of course, the song for my blog that week had to be How Long Have I Been Sleeping? by Jackson Browne.

Wannabe Digestive Biscuits

Makes about 60 single biscuits (30 if made into cream biscuits)

These Wannabe Digestives are lovely by themselves. I have them just as they come, with cheese, or with jam. They are just such a versatile biscuit. Sometimes I dip the smooth side in some melted chocolate to make chocolate digestives. Of course, making a lovely filling and sandwiching two together makes for an exceedingly scrummy treat.

Ingredients

For the Biscuit

160g gluten free oats

60g pumpkin seeds

60g sunflower seeds

620g gluten free plain flour

200g dark brown sugar

200g stork block (cut into cubes)

1 teaspoon salt

4 tablespoons gluten free baking powder

200 ml almond milk

Chocolate Cream Filling

200g very soft stork block

500g icing sugar

100g custard powder

1 teaspoon vanilla extract

2 tablespoons almond milk

50g gluten and dairy free chocolate

Lemon Cream Filling

200g very soft stork block

600g icing sugar

1 teaspoon lemon extract

1 tablespoon lemon juice

2 tablespoons almond milk

Yellow food colouring

Method

For the Biscuit

1   Preheat oven to 200°c/180°c fan oven.

2   Line several baking trays with parchment paper.

3   Put the oats, sunflower seeds, and pumpkin seeds in a food processor and blitz until fine.

4   Put the oat mixture, flour, baking powder, stork and sugar into a free-standing mixer and mix until well mixed.

5   Add the almond milk and mix until you get a stiff dough.

5   Dust the work surface with a little gluten free flour, and gently knead the dough until smooth then cut the dough in two halves (this makes it easier to roll out).

6   Roll the dough out to about 5mm thick and cut with a 3-inch round cutter dipped in flour to stop it sticking.

7   Re-roll the dough left and cut more biscuits until all the dough has been used. You should get about 60 biscuits.

8   Use a fish-slice or palette knife to lift the cut dough onto the prepared baking trays.

9   Bake for 15 minutes until golden and just firm to touch (they'll become crisper once cold).

10   Remove from the oven, leave on the baking tray for 10 minutes, then transfer to a wire rack to cool completely.

For the Filling

12   Put all the cream ingredients in the free-standing mixer (or use an electric whisk) and beat until light, soft and smooth.

13   Turn half of the biscuits over and pipe a good dollop of icing onto each biscuit.

14   Cover with the remaining biscuits (fancy side up) and press down gently.

Love them or hate them

The Bourbon biscuit is another nostalgic biscuit from the old family favourite selection. Who didn't have these as a child, pulling the two biscuits apart to scrape the chocolate filling off with your teeth? What a surprise it was to discover in the tearoom that the Bourbon biscuit is a bit like marmite – either loved or hated. One lady even described the Bourbon as being the spawn of the devil!

The only Bourbon creams I've ever made have been gluten free and dairy free, but eating these takes me right back to my childhood. As an extra bonus, ours are larger than the commercially made ones.

The humble Bourbon came to my rescue at the Scottish Specialist Food Show in January 2020. We'd been invited to this by our tea supplier, Edinburgh Tea & Coffee Company, and were incredibly excited to try out new products, find new suppliers, and to buy products to add to our growing gift section in the tearoom. As always, Mr M made us a lovely packed lunch and flask of tea, adding in a couple of my Bourbon Creams just in case.

As lunchtime approached, we found ourselves a seat in the packed eating area. Feeling slightly guilty at sitting with my own food and not buying from the other providers, Mr M was instructed to go on the hunt for gluten free goodies to add to our lunch. Alas, he came back empty-handed, so munching away on Mother Murphy's gluten free Bourbon Creams became a guilt-free experience.

Who knows, maybe in time, Mother Murphy's will be supplying our own family favourite selection across the country? I can see it now: Bourbon Creams, Custard Creams, Nice Coconut Creams, Jammy Dodgers, and Wannabe Digestive Biscuits, all gluten free and dairy free, coming to a shop near you…

My Bourbon Cream was another biscuit offered up for grabs at our daily live Facebook chats during Covid-19. It wasn't just a case of being able to shout the loudest or fastest to get the biscuit named after you; people had to justify their request. During the chat that night, Chloe was watching along with little Minnie, and tugging away at my heartstrings by saying that Neill, Minnie's Daddy, should get the biscuit named after him.

'We are struggling down here in Halifax during lockdown without seeing you. Also, Neill has given you Minnie, your gorgeous granddaughter, and now there's another baby on the way,' I was told. Well, this won hands up.

So, there it is, in public and for the world to hear. Not only is there the amazing Minnie Violet, but we are now awaiting baby number 2 (or Peter, as I am currently calling him) to arrive in autumn 2020. If ever we needed something to look forward to in this troubled time of the virus and lockdown, a new baby is giving us just that. Because of this, Neill, the bourbons are yours.

This photo has to be my favourite one of Neill and Minnie – the things a Daddy will do to protect his baby.

Neill and Minnie

Neill's Bourbon Cream Biscuits

Makes about 20 biscuits

Ingredients

For the Biscuit
220g stork block
180g dark brown sugar
100g golden syrup
Pinch of salt
1 teaspoon bicarbonate of soda
200g rice flour
160g cornflour
120g cocoa powder

Chocolate Cream Filling
260g icing sugar
2 teaspoon cornflour
50g cocoa powder
150g stork block
1 teaspoon vanilla extract
2 teaspoons boiling water

Method

For Biscuit

1   Preheat oven to 180°c/160°c fan oven.

2   Line several baking trays with parchment paper.

3   In a bowl, mix together the flour, cornflour, and cocoa powder, and put to one side.

3   Put the stork, brown sugar, salt, golden syrup and bicarbonate of soda into a free-standing mixer (or use a hand-held whisk) and beat until smooth and pale in colour.

4   Add the flour mixture and beat until you have a smooth, soft dough.

5   Remove from the mixer and knead on a floured worktop until completely smooth.

6   Cut the dough in half (makes it easier to roll out later), wrap in clingfilm, and put into the fridge for about an hour until firm enough to roll.

7   Take the chilled dough from the fridge and remove the clingfilm.

8   Roll out on a well-floured worktop. Don't roll it out too thin or the biscuits will burn quickly in the oven, but don't have it too thick – remember you will be putting two together with a chocolate filling. You can make these any shape or size you want. The traditional bourbon biscuit is an oblong. I like to make mine 5cm x 7cm. You can use a cookie cutter for these if you like. I don't have a specific cutter for these, but use my accordion cutter to make sure they are all the same size. Re-roll the dough left, and cut more biscuits until all the dough has been used.

9   Use a fish-slice or palette knife to lift the cut dough onto the prepared baking trays.

10 To produce the classic design for the bourbon, make two rows of holes with a cake tester or cocktail stick.

11 Bake for 10 minutes until just firm to touch (they will become crisper once cold). Be careful, because they burn easily.

12 Remove from the oven, leave on the baking tray for 10 minutes, then transfer to a wire rack to cool completely.

For the Filling

13 Put all the cream ingredients in the free-standing mixer (or use an electric whisk) and beat until light, soft, and smooth.

14 Turn half of the biscuits over and pipe a good dollop of icing onto each biscuit.

15 Cover with the remaining biscuits (fancy side up) and press down gently.

A man called Tom

As I've mentioned many times in this book, I loved the family favourite biscuits when I was growing up, with the humble custard cream being at the top of the biscuit leader board.

After our visit to the Free From Allergy Show and tasting some of the gluten free custard creams on offer, I decided that it must be possible to make a nice tasting gluten free and dairy free biscuit.

A few trials down the road, I came up with a lovely tasting biscuit that, in my opinion, was streets ahead of the manufactured versions. What would the customers think, though? Would my gluten free and dairy free version match the lovely original custard creams we all remember from childhood?

Dashing Tom

Mother Murphy's Custard Creams fly out of the tearoom like hotcakes, and another biscuit has been added to my collection in my aim to recreate the family favourite selection in a gluten free and dairy free version.

One customer who loves these is the adorable Dashing Tom. As he was enjoying one of these, I sent a photo to his daughter, and she joked that the biscuit was nearly as big as her Dad. Tom just couldn't praise these biscuits enough and they very quickly became Dashing Tom's Custard Creams. But just who is Dashing Tom?

Shortly after I'd met Bev (of Bev's Carrot Cake), she brought along her dad, Tom, to the tearoom. In walked this very dapper looking gentleman, dressed in his three-piece suit, wearing one of his lovely smiles. 'I'm Tom. I've come to show you my book folding.' And as quick as that, Tom became part of our tearoom family. We chatted, laughed, and discussed crafts, book folding, and everything else we could, as if we'd known each other for years.

It wasn't long before Tom became Dashing Tom, because he's always well dressed and always, always wears a shirt and tie. Everyone loves Dashing Tom, and Dashing Tom loves everyone. Tom has taught us how to do the art of book folding. He's also joined us for card making, chatting, cake eating, dominoes with Mr M, but mainly just to be part of the tearoom community. He's taken Murphy the Tearoom Mouse on a couple of holidays, including a cruise to Gibraltar. We still don't know everything they got up to on that holiday!

We've seen Tom have his own battles, too. On his way to the tearoom one day, Tom took a tumble, breaking his hip. But everyone was amazed at how quickly Tom bounced back, and I like to think that returning to the tearoom helped him with his recovery.

So, when you try these Custard Creams, think of Dashing Tom in his three-piece suit, being everything a gentleman should be.

Dashing Tom's Custard Creams

Makes about 48 single biscuits (24 doubled up)

Ingredients

For the Biscuit

300g very soft stork block

300g caster sugar

300g fine polenta

300g rice flour

200g custard powder

2 free range eggs

2 teaspoons vanilla extract

For the Cream Filling

200g very soft stork block

500g icing sugar

100g custard powder

2 teaspoons vanilla extract

100g gluten and dairy free white chocolate (I use Plamil's)

Method

For Biscuit

1. *Preheat oven to 170°c/150°c fan oven.*
2. *Line several baking trays with parchment paper.*
3. *Put the sugar, polenta, rice flour, and custard powder in a free-standing mixer and whizz to mix.*
4. *Add the stork, and whizz until there are no large lumps of stork left.*
5. *Add the egg and vanilla extract and whizz again until the mixture forms a stiff dough.*
6. *Dust the work surface with a little plain flour (remember to use gluten free flour) and knead the dough until smooth, then cut the dough in two halves (this makes it easier to roll out later).*
7. *Roll the dough out to about 5mm thick and cut with a cutter dipped in flour to stop it sticking. (I use a 3-inch square cutter, but you can decide on the size and shape of your biscuits.)*
8. *Re-roll the dough left and cut more biscuits until all the dough has been used.*
9. *Use a fish-slice or palette knife to lift the cut dough onto the prepared baking trays.*
10. *Use a fork or stamp to put a design of your choice on your biscuits.*
11. *Bake for 20 minutes until golden and just firm to touch (they will become crisper once cold).*
12. *Remove from the oven, leave on the baking tray for 10 minutes, then transfer to a wire rack to cool completely.*

For the Filling

13. *Place the chocolate in a bowl over a pan of simmering water and stir gently until melted. Remove from the heat and put to one side.*
14. *Put the stork, icing sugar, custard powder, and vanilla extract in the free-standing mixer and beat until smooth (start slowly or you will have icing sugar all over!).*
26. *Add the melted chocolate and beat again until smooth.*
16. *Turn half of the biscuits over and pipe a good dollop of icing onto each biscuit.*
17. *Cover with the remaining biscuits (fancy side up) and press down gently.*
18. *Make yourself a cup of steaming hot tea and take time to enjoy one of these with a good book.*

Is it a shortcake, German, or empire biscuit?

Empire Biscuits were a new delight for me when I moved up to Scotland from Yorkshire, although sometimes the shop-bought Empires were way too big and hard, putting me off making them. However, an old colleague of mine from my training days, Lorraine, kindly gave me a no-fail recipe for her Empires. I tried these and I've been hooked ever since.

Mine are slightly smaller than those you can usually buy in the shops, but they literally do just melt in your mouth. Nobody complains about them being smaller, which just proves that a hand-made biscuit, made with quality ingredients, can be smaller but far superior to a large, hard, mass-produced one.

There is always a discussion in the tearoom as to what should go on top of the Empire Biscuit. Should it be a cherry or a jelly tot? On one of my stay-at-home days after my heart attack, I was feeling well enough to do some baking and decided to make Empires. You know things are bad and cabin fever is taking over when you find yourself having a heated discussion with yourself about what to put on top of the biscuits.

Well, 'we' decided to consult t'internet. You wouldn't believe how much information there is about these little biscuits! Is it an Empire Biscuit, is it a German Biscuit, or is it just a shortcake biscuit? My extensive research revealed that posh Empire Biscuits have a cherry on top, but the good people in Scotland apparently prefer a jelly tot, whilst the people in Ireland like a coconut topping. As 'we' didn't have a third person to make the decision, or indeed even a second person, I decided to go with all three. Generally, though, I go between jelly tots and cherries, but change them, adding hearts, iced flowers, or iced holly, depending on any themes in the tearoom at the time.

I did wonder about the merits of trying to adapt my now fail-safe Empire Biscuit recipe to try to make it gluten free and dairy free. It took me a long time and many attempts before I was happy that my gluten free and dairy free version matched the original version, and yes, I did consider giving up on several occasions. But the stress and disasters were worth it, and I'm very proud of my gluten free and dairy free version, and believe they beat many a standard Empire Biscuit I've tasted in my time!

Why Kirsten's Empires, though? In 2017, we had a Baby Hat Challenge at the tearoom to knit or crochet baby hats for the local Neo-Natal Department. In June 2017, we delivered over 300 hats to Forth Valley Hospital, and we then set ourselves another challenge to complete a further 500 hats from 1 July to 31 December, 2017. And this time we achieved 1138 hats, plus some extra blankets, bootees, and cardigans!

These fabulous hats and extras were made by our lovely customers, who were only too pleased to work on this project. We also had people from all over the UK sending us contributions for the challenge. Hats were sent from as far away as Cambridge, Birmingham, and North Yorkshire. People who had never done any knitting or crochet before were proud to produce one hat; we had one amazing lady, Linda in Birmingham, who produced one hat for every day of the challenge, and ladies at the High Flats in Falkirk worked on this project for us, producing over 200 hats.

I am amazed by everyone who took part in this challenge, from those doing the knitting or crochet to those who donated wool, and I'm sure that each and every hat has been made with love for all the little babies. My own dear daughter, Chloe, who has her own Angel Babies, was very touched that we choose this as our tearoom challenge.

The following year, the tearoom challenge was to make 100 baby blankets for the hospital by 31st December, 2018. Once again, people from all over the country joined the challenge. Some people made a whole host of blankets, other people made just one square for a blanket, but each contribution was greatly appreciated. We blasted our target, and Forth Valley Hospital was in awe at the mountain of blankets we delivered.

Kirsten

It just seems to me that the tearoom attracts the most amazing people! Thank you to everyone again.

So, it was a wonderful coincidence that one of our new customers who came in hunt of the new gluten free and dairy free Empire Biscuits was a nurse from the Neo-Natal ward, where our knitted and crocheted hats and blankets had been delivered. It just had to be then that our Empire Biscuits became Kirsten's Empire Biscuits.

I've shown the recipe for both the original and gluten free and dairy free versions, though we now only make Kirsten's Empire Biscuits in the tearoom to avoid confusion and disappointment to our gluten free and dairy free customers.

Lorraine's Empire Biscuits - Original Recipe

Makes around 20 single biscuits (10 doubled up)

Ingredients

For the Biscuit
200g plain flour
200g butter cut into small cubes
50g icing sugar
50g cornflour

For the Icing
200g icing sugar
About 1 tablespoon lemon juice
Jelly Tots

Method

For Biscuit

1   *Preheat oven to 200°c/180°c fan oven.*

2   *Line several baking trays with parchment paper.*

3   *Put all the biscuit ingredients in a free-standing mixer or food processor, and beat/whizz until the mixture comes together as a soft dough.*

4   *Dust the worktop with flour, roll the dough out to about the thickness of a pound coin, and cut with a cutter dipped in flour to stop it sticking. (I use a 3-inch round cutter, but you can decide on the size and shape of your biscuits.)*

5   *Re-roll the dough left and cut more biscuits until all the dough has been used.*

6   *Use a fish-slice or palette knife to lift the cut dough onto the prepared baking trays.*

7   *Bake for 10 minutes (you don't want them to brown).*

8   *Remove from the oven and transfer to a wire rack to cool completely.*

For Icing

9   *Put the icing sugar in a bowl.*

10 *Warm the lemon juice gently in a pan or microwave, add to the icing sugar, and mix until smooth. Add cold water if required, until you get an icing that is thick enough to spread with a knife.*

11 *Turn half of the biscuits over and put a good dollop of your chosen jam on each one.*

12 *Spread the other half of the biscuits with the icing, and put an iced biscuit on each of the jammed biscuits.*

13 *Place a jelly tot on each one before the icing sets, and leave to set completely.*

Kirsten's Empire Biscuits - Gluten-free Version

Makes around 20 single biscuits (10 doubled up)

Ingredients

For the Biscuit
150g gluten free plain flour

50g ground almonds

200g stork block cut into small cubes

50g icing sugar

50g cornflour

For the Icing
250 g icing sugar

About 1 tablespoon lemon juice

Jelly Tots

Method

For Biscuit

1   Preheat oven to 200°c/180°c fan oven.

2   Line several baking trays with parchment paper.

3   Put all the biscuit ingredients in a free-standing mixer or food processor, and beat/whizz until the mixture comes together as a soft dough.

4   Dust the worktop with gluten free flour, roll the dough out to about the thickness of a pound coin, and cut with a cutter dipped in flour to stop it sticking. (I use a 3-inch round cutter, but you can decide on the size and shape of your biscuits.)

5   Re-roll the dough left and cut more biscuits until all the dough has been used.

6   Use a fish-slice or palette knife to lift the cut dough onto the prepared baking trays.

7   Bake for 15 minutes (you do not want them to brown).

8   Remove from the oven. Leave on the baking trays for 10 minutes, and then transfer to a wire rack to cool completely.

For Icing

9   Put the icing sugar in a bowl.

10   Warm the lemon juice gently in a pan or microwave, add to the icing sugar and mix until smooth. Add cold water if required, until you get an icing that is thick enough to spread with a knife.

11   Turn half of the biscuits over and put a good dollop of your chosen jam on each one.

12   Spread the other half of the biscuits with the icing and put an iced biscuit on each of the jammed biscuits.

13   Place a jelly tot on each one before the icing sets, and leave to set completely.

But I did them before the Great British Bake Off

I keep saying that home-made biscuits and cakes are vastly superior to the commercially made versions. Dare I say it, though, Fig Rolls for me are lovely whether they're home-made or shop-bought, and I can eat a packet of these delights whilst the kettle's boiling. Shop-bought fig rolls have a pastry that's a little harder than home-made versions, though I've still yet to see or taste a commercially made gluten free fig roll.

I made fig rolls years ago and loved them. Although not a big fan of figs by themselves, in a fig roll I can't get enough of them, and they are just what the doctor ordered. Until the late 19th century, it was believed that most illnesses were linked to digestive problems, with many physicians recommending a daily intake of biscuits and fruit. The fig roll was a perfect solution to this. Fancy being told by the doctor you need to eat biscuits!

Some recipes for fig rolls have different ingredients in the filling – apricots, dates, and honey being some of them. I like my fig rolls to have the simple ingredients of figs, dates, sugar, and mixed spice. Some recipes don't include cooking the filling first, but again, I like to cook mine before adding it to the pastry dough.

Once I'd started to create my own Mother Murphy's gluten free biscuit selection, I knew the fig roll had to be included. As with other biscuits, it took me a few attempts to create a recipe that tasted

as good as the well-known fig rolls. So I was gutted when I decided to make these again for the tearoom at the same time as the Great British Bake Off had contestants baking them. It made it appear as though I was following the trend, but I like to believe the GBBO was following in the footsteps of Mother Murphy's!

There are couple of tips I've learned in my times making these delights. Firstly, when you've cooked your fig filling, allow it to cool completely before adding it to the pastry dough. If this is still even slightly warm, it starts to melt the fat in the pastry before you have chance to mould it and get it in the oven.

Secondly, don't be tempted to over-fill the pastry dough or the rolls will explode in the oven. The first time I made fig rolls, I decided that the recipe had nowhere near enough filling, so doubled it up. It took me ages to clean up the oven.

Finally, it's lovely to have all the fig rolls the same size and have the fancy lines across the top to make them look like the traditional ones, but if yours are different sizes and the pastry has cracked, it doesn't matter. They'll still taste delightful, and you'll have no problems getting people to share these with you.

My recipe makes 48 biscuits, and they freeze perfectly. If you don't want to make that many, just half or quarter the recipe. I think if you're going to go to the effort of making these, why would you only want 12 fig rolls? These will be eaten as quality assurance and you'll not have any left for others to share!

Fig Rolls

Makes 48 biscuits

Ingredients

For the Biscuit

700g gluten free plain flour

½ teaspoon salt

1 teaspoon gluten free baking powder

2 teaspoons xanthan gum

200g stork block, cut into small pieces

160g light brown sugar

4 free range eggs, lightly beaten

2 teaspoons vanilla extract

For the Filling

450g soft dried figs, roughly chopped

150g chopped dried dates

75g light brown sugar

3 teaspoons mixed spice

3 balls stem ginger, drained, and grated with a zester

Method

For Biscuit

1   Mix together the flour, salt, baking powder, and xanthan gum in a large bowl and put to one side.

2   Put the stork and sugar in a free-standing mixer (or use a hand-held whisk) and beat until pale and creamy.

3   Add the egg with the vanilla extract a little at a time, beating between each addition.

4   Gradually add the flour to the mixture with the mixer on slow, and beat until all combined and you have a soft dough.

5   Empty the mixture onto a floured worktop and cut into 4 pieces. Wrap each piece in clingfilm and place in the fridge to chill whilst you make the filling.

For the Filling

6   Put the figs and sugar into a pan with enough cold water to just cover the figs.

7   Bring the mixture to the boil on the hob, then reduce the heat and simmer for about 10 minutes until the figs are soft and the mixture has thickened.

8   Put the fig mix in a food processor and blitz until you have a paste. Add the mixed spice and ginger, and blitz again to combine.

9   Empty the mixture out into a large bowl and pop into the fridge to chill and firm up.

10   Preheat oven to 190°c/170°c fan oven, and line 4 baking trays with parchment paper.

11   Take the chilled biscuit dough from the fridge and remove the clingfilm.

12   Knead each piece slightly on a well-floured piece of parchment paper until smooth, and roll out to a rectangle, 25cm x 24cm. Cut the rectangle in half to give you two pieces, 25cm x 12cm. You should now have 8 rectangles of dough.

13   Take the cooled filling from the fridge and spoon into a large piping bag (no nozzle required). Cut off the end of the piping bag and squeeze a thick line of the filling lengthways down the centre of each piece of biscuit dough.

14   Brush the long edge of the biscuit dough with water, and lift and roll the dough over the fig mixture, using the parchment paper to help. The dough should overlap and seal in the filling. Repeat this until you have eight giant fig rolls.

15   Carefully transfer the fig rolls to your prepared baking trays, seam side down, and cut each giant roll into six equal pieces.

16   Press a fork along the top of each roll to flatten slightly and give the distinctive fig roll decoration.

17   Bake in the pre-heated oven for 20 minutes until lightly browned.

18   Remove from the oven and cool on a wire rack.

Baking is both an art and a science.

Sherry Yard (Chef)

A tale of misunderstanding

Gingerbread men, for me, are one of those treats that should be served at Bonfire Night, along with Yorkshire Parkin and Flapjacks, although I'm quite partial to a Christmas gingerbread man, too.

Gingerbread men originate from away back in the 1600s when they were sold in London streets. And I'm sure you all remember the tale of the Gingerbread Boy – the biscuit made by a childless woman, desperate for a child of her own, but the boy runs away once taken out of the oven.

Both my children loved gingerbread men when they were growing up. So, when preparing a few treats to take to my granddaughter Minnie's first birthday party, I decided to make some small gingerbread men for her. At the time I was making these, my son Ben was visiting us and asked to help with some baking. He was quite proud of himself for helping to make the gingerbread men for his niece's birthday party, but I think he did quite a bit of taste testing, too!

Ben leaving the train at Duruinsh

Ben doesn't get as much of a mention on Mother Murphy's Facebook page as Chloe does, because he doesn't use this particular social media. But many customers in the tearoom now know Ben, as he visits as often as he can from Halifax, and likes to while away a few hours in the tearoom, enjoying nothing better than to have a big breakfast made by Mr M, followed by some strong Americanos, cappuccinos, or lattes (or all of them!). He's joined in with some crafting, and isn't afraid to pop on an apron to do some serving and clearing up for us, though in truth he's much happier to sit with the customers chatting and eating cake.

The tearoom family certainly seem to have taken Ben to their hearts, just as they have with Chloe. Some of them even decided that they trusted him to such an extent that when he made a suggestion for our book club, they jumped at the chance to pick his choice. They have since declared that Ben's choice of books cannot be trusted ever again, as nobody enjoyed the book! (It wouldn't be fair for me to name the book here, though.)

Mr M and Ben taking in the view

If I was to pick a cake or biscuit to name after Ben, I'd pick the humble custard cream, but this is now Dashing Tom's, so I thought I'd tell you a little tale about Ben, custard creams, and a case of misunderstanding.

In 2011, Mr M and I were undertaking another one of our summer cycle tours around Scotland.

Ben giving a helping hand to Mr M -
long before the misunderstanding

Ben asked if he could come along to meet us at some point, to do some more cycling in Scotland with us – he'd joined us the previous year, cycling from Pitlochry to Aviemore with us, and had been blown away with the scenery.

On our tour this time, we were again travelling to different places each night, but had booked to stay five nights in a remote log cabin at Duirinish, just outside Plockton, North West Scotland, to allow Ben to join us.

To reach us, he had to make the long, long train journey from England, up to Inverness, and then across country, to get off at the tiny request stop station of Duirinish – just before the train reaches Kyle of Lochalsh – even managing to carry a birthday cake for Jim in his cycle panniers all the way!

We had a great few days, including a cycle over the Skye Bridge to let Ben do some cycling on the Isle of Skye. One of Ben's favourite books and films is Ring of Bright Water by Gavin Maxwell, so I planned a route that took in the area from the book, down to the Glenachulish Ferry at Kylerhea, back up the steep, steep hill, to eventually return to Duirinish – a round trip of just about thirty miles. But thirty hilly miles!

In the morning, as always, Jim made up packed lunches for us. He asked Ben, who can eat for Britain, how many sandwiches he'd like. 'Just two, please,' replied Ben.

Paniers full of packed lunches and flasks of tea, off we cycled down the sweeping single-track road from Duirinish to the Kyle of Lochalsh and over the Skye Bridge. We couldn't have planned a better day. The sun was shining and the views were amazing.

After cycling a while, we had a little stop and Ben pulled out his secret stash of custard creams from his rucksack and started gobbling these up. Always being Mum, I warned him to save some for later when he might be needing them. 'No need. Jim's made us lots of butties for later,' laughed Ben.

After more cycling on the quiet, but hilly single track A87 towards Kylerhea, it was fast approaching lunchtime, so we found a suitable spot in the glorious sunshine to eat our well- earned packed lunched amidst the beautiful scenery.

I could see Ben's eyes lighting up at the thought of the two great big butties Jim had made for him. But to Ben's despair, he soon realised that his idea of two sandwiches was very different to Jim's idea of two sandwiches. Ben was anticipating two sandwiches, each made from two slices of bread, but to his horror Jim had made him two butties made from two slices of bread cut in half! My strapping, 6ft tall son suddenly looked like a little boy who'd just had his sweeties stolen from him. Fortunately for Ben, I always carry extra goodies and biscuits on cycle rides, just in case of emergencies.

On the way back, we stopped at Kyleakin to visit the Ring of Bright Water museum, calling in at a little café there, where we all had chip butties. These were the best chip butties I've ever tasted, and Ben ate every single bit of his. Ben has since forgiven Jim for this misunderstanding, even seeing the funny side of it. But now, whenever Jim asks him how many sandwiches he wants, Ben always tells him how many slices of bread he would like!

Going back to the gingerbread men then… as Ben helped with the Gingerbread Men for Minnie's birthday, I decided Ben's Gingerbread Men they would be.

Ben's Gingerbread Men

Makes around 24 biscuits

Ingredients

For the Biscuit

1100g gluten free plain flour

1 teaspoon xanthan gum

2 teaspoons bicarbonate of soda

6 teaspoons ground ginger

300g stork block cut into cubes

500g dark brown sugar

4 free range eggs, lightly beaten

240g golden syrup

For the Icing

250 g icing sugar

About 1 tablespoon cold water

Jelly Tots or sweets of your choice

Method

For the Biscuit

1   Preheat oven to 170°c/150°c fan oven.

2   Line several baking trays with parchment paper.

3   Place the flour, ginger, xanthan gum, and bicarbonate of soda in a large bowl, mix to combine, and set aside.

3   Put the stork and brown sugar in a free-standing mixer (or use a hand-held whisk) and beat until the mixture is light and fluffy.

4   Add the eggs a little at a time, beating between each addition.

5   Add the golden syrup to the mixture and whisk until all combined.

Ben

6   Next add the flour mixture into your mixer and beat slowly until well combined.

7   Empty the mixture onto a well-floured worktop and knead gently until smooth.

8   Cut the dough into two (this makes it easier to roll out later), wrap in clingfilm, and place in the fridge for about an hour until firm enough to roll.

9   Take the chilled dough from the fridge and remove the clingfilm.

10   Dust the worktop with gluten free flour, roll the dough out to about the thickness of a pound coin, and cut with a cutter dipped in flour to stop it sticking. (I use a large gingerbread man cutter, but you can decide on the size and shape of your biscuits.)

11   Re-roll the dough left, and cut more biscuits until all the dough has been used.

12   Use a fish-slice or palette knife to lift the cut dough onto the prepared baking trays.

13   Bake for 15 minutes.

14   Remove from the oven and carefully transfer to a wire rack to cool completely.

For Icing

15   Put the icing sugar in a bowl and mix with the cold water, adding more water if required, until you get an icing that is thick enough pipe.

17   Pipe faces and any other decorations you want on your biscuits.

18   Before the icing sets, add any sweets to finish off your decorations.

Ginger Cream Biscuits

Makes about 46 single biscuits (23 doubled up)

Ingredients

For the Biscuit

300g very soft stork block

300g caster sugar

300g fine polenta

300g rice flour

200g cornflour

2 free range eggs

3 teaspoons ground ginger

3 teaspoons mixed spice

3 teaspoons ground cinnamon

2 teaspoons ginger syrup

For the Ginger Cream

200g very soft stork block

500g icing sugar

100g gluten and dairy free white chocolate

4 teaspoons ginger extract

Method

For the Biscuit

1. Preheat oven to 170°c/150°c fan oven.

2. Line several baking trays with parchment paper.

3. Put the sugar, polenta, rice flour, cornflour, and spices in a free-standing mixer (or use a hand-held whisk) and whizz to mix.

4. Add the stork, and mix until there are no large lumps of stork left.

5. Add the egg and ginger extract and beat again until mixture forms a stiff dough.

6. Dust the work surface with a little plain flour (remember to use gluten free flour) and knead the dough until smooth, then cut the dough in two halves (this makes it easier to roll out later).

7. If you have time, wrap the dough in clingfilm and pop into the fridge for about 30 minutes before rolling out.

8. Take the dough from the fridge and remove the clingfilm. Roll the dough out on your floured worktop to about 5mm thick, and cut with a cutter dipped in flour to stop it sticking. (I use a 3-inch square cutter, but you can decide on the size and shape of your biscuits.)

9. Re-roll the dough left, and cut more biscuits until all the dough has been used.

10. Use a fish-slice or palette knife to lift the cut dough onto the prepared baking trays.

11. Use a fork or stamp to put a design of your choice on your biscuits.

12. Bake for 20 minutes until golden and just firm to touch (they will become crisper once cold).

13. Remove from the oven, leave on the baking tray for 10 minutes, then transfer to a wire rack to cool completely.

For the Filling

14. Put the stork in the free-standing mixer (or use an electric whisk) and beat until soft and smooth.

15. Add the icing sugar, cornflour, and ginger extract, and beat until smooth (start slowly or you will have icing sugar all over!).

16. Turn half of the biscuits over, and pipe a good dollop of icing onto each biscuit.

17. Cover with the remaining biscuits (fancy side up) and press down gently.

You need to learn to say please and thank you

If you're looking for a perfect dunking biscuit to accompany your cup of tea, then the good old-fashioned ginger nut is just right. My favourite ginger nuts, growing up, were the ones made by McVities. These were simply the best; just the right size, crispy enough to hold their own when being dunked, and they didn't faint into the tea. I could easily go through a packet with one cup of tea, and never thought I'd be able to match them when making my own. However, one day I set about making my own and couldn't believe how easy it was to make these biscuits, or how amazing they tasted. I can count on one hand the number of times I've bought a ginger nut since.

When we opened the tearoom, these lovely biscuits had to be on the menu straight away for those who like just a biscuit and not a cake. They quickly became a customer favourite, and you can generally find a jar of these in the tearoom.

Remember Bev of the Puppy Dog Eyes? Well, she was desperate to be able to have our ginger nuts, but needed them to be gluten free and dairy free. A few tweaks here and there, and I soon had a gluten free and dairy free ginger nut that I was very pleased with. Of course, they then quickly became Bev's Ginger Nuts.

During one of our Craft, Chat, and Cake sessions, we were chatting about all the different cakes and who they were named after, when we realised with horror that one of our regular crafters, Gina, didn't have a cake named after her. When Gina arrives at the tearoom, the first thing she does (even before saying hello!) is to check the cake display and look for the ginger nuts. What was I to do? The ginger nuts already had a name, but really these were Gina's favourites.

Our crafting gang are a share-and-share-alike kind of gang, and Bev kindly offered to hand over the ginger nuts to Gina if she could have the Carrot Cake, because, in her words, 'It's the nicest carrot cake I have ever eaten.' Deal done! So, now our ginger nuts are not only gluten free and dairy free, but are also Gina's!

But why ginger nuts and manners, I hear you ask. Well, in the tearoom we have a sign on the wall, advising people not to help themselves to the cakes. I've tried to do this in a funny way, with a photo of the lovely Minnie saying, 'Do not touch Grandma's cakes'. Now, I feel I need to point out here that I'm not in the habit of telling customers what they can and can't do, and indeed, didn't even want to have 'Do Not' signs at all. However, there were two things that people regularly did in the tearoom that just had to be stopped.

The first was to try to eat and drink things they had not bought in Mother Murphy's Tearoom. It's just a quirk of running a business that we need people to buy things from us, and not just bring in their own food and drink. The second is people helping themselves to cakes from the display. One of my pet hates when I go out to a tearoom or café is when the cakes are not covered over, so I make sure that every single cake in our tearoom is covered over in a glass cake stand and, if possible, individually wrapped in clingfilm. This makes sure that there's no contamination from gluten to non-gluten things, but more importantly, prevents germs from sticky fingers, sneezes, coughs, flies, dust, and the likes.

Yet even with the signs on the wall, I still have to remind people of our little rules. Of course, I am not quite as polite when they try to pick up the cakes! The regular customers know our rules and fully understand them, even acting as my cake protectors. There are shrieks, cries, and gasps when people try to handle the cakes.

One hilarious example of this was with Gina's three-year grandson, Ruaridh. He is one of those little boys you can have brilliant conversations with, and you just feel much better for the chat. One afternoon, a customer came into the tearoom and just couldn't wait to get her hands on a piece of our caramel slice. When she helped herself to it, the tearoom customers all gasped with horror. Ruaridh calmly got up from his chair, went over to the customer, and said in his very stern little voice, 'You need to learn to say please and thank you.' Out of the mouths of babes indeed!

Danielle has never helped herself again, and we still laugh at this.

Gina

Gina's Gingernuts

Makes around 60 biscuits

Ingredients

> 250g stork block
> 150g golden syrup
> 700g gluten free self-raising flour
> 2 pinches of salt
> 1 teaspoon xanthan gum
> 400g caster sugar
> 4 tablespoons ground ginger
> 2 teaspoons bicarbonate of soda
> 2 free range eggs, lightly beaten

Method

1. Put the stork and golden syrup in a pan and gently melt on a low heat on the hob. Allow to cool slightly.

2. Put the flour, xanthan gum, salt, sugar, bicarbonate of soda, and ginger into a large bowl and mix until well combined.

3. Add the slightly cooled golden syrup mixture and the beaten eggs. Mix until you have a soft dough.

4. Empty the dough onto your worktop and divide into four equal portions (around 400g each).

5. Shape each portion into a roll about 15cm long, and wrap in clingfilm. Pop the dough rolls into the freezer for about half an hour to firm up.

6. Preheat oven to 180°c/160°c fan oven and line several baking trays with parchment paper.

7. Take the dough from the freezer and remove the clingfilm.

8. Slice each roll into 1cm portions and place on the baking trays, pressing down gently. Remember to leave space between them, as they will grow in the oven.

9. Bake in the pre-heated oven for 15 minutes for a chewy biscuit, or 20 minutes for a crunchy biscuit.

10. Remove from the oven and transfer carefully to a wire rack to cool completely.

11. Take a seat, relax, and enjoy one or two of these with a steaming cup of tea.

Licking the plate clean

Many a stressful hour is spent working out the best way to make lovely gluten free and dairy free goodies, sometimes even wondering if it's all really worth it. Then into the tearoom comes a little person who can't usually get treats because she needs a dairy free diet, and shows us that it absolutely is all worth it.

Sasha licking the plate clean

In my quest to re-create the old family favourite biscuits, I set about tackling the Lemon Puff biscuit. The original Lemon Puffs were made from two sticky, caramelised square, crumbly biscuits, sandwiched together with a lemon cream, and they were just perfect. My Lemon Cream biscuits don't have the puff pastry, but do have that light-as-a-feather texture, with a filling that actually tastes of lemon. When these were introduced to the tearoom, they flew off the counter as quickly as I could make them. Customers were buying them to eat in the tearoom and to take home with them.

One Saturday, I had my eye on the last lemon cream biscuit to enjoy during our Craft, Chat, and Cake Session, when to my dismay one of our other crafters, Shona, ordered the last one. She did say through gritted teeth that she'd have something else if I really wanted it, but Mr M told me I couldn't deprive the customers of the biscuits, so I had to go without. I've still not forgotten this, Shona!

The first week we had these biscuits out, into the tearoom came a little girl, Sasha, with her sister Isla and her mum. Sasha has to have her food dairy free, and after eating her dairy free bacon butty, she opted for one of our new lemon creams and clearly loved it. She was actually licking the plate clean!

Licking the plate isn't something we usually encourage in the tearoom, but I couldn't help but laugh and take a photo. Being new to the tearoom, the biscuits didn't yet have a customer name, so of course, they just had to become Sasha's Lemon Creams. Sasha was very happy to pose for the photos, but little sister Isla had to have her photo taken, too.

Sasha   *Isla*

Sasha's Lemon Cream Biscuits

Makes about 46 single biscuits (23 doubled up)

Ingredients

For the Biscuit

300g very soft stork block

300g caster sugar

300g fine polenta

300g rice flour

200g cornflour

2 free range eggs

Grated zest of two lemons

1 teaspoon vanilla extract

For the Lemon Cream

200g very soft stork block

500g icing sugar

100g gluten and dairy free white chocolate

2 tablespoons lemon juice

1 teaspoon lemon extract

Method

For the Biscuit

1   Preheat oven to 170°c/150°c fan oven.

2   Line several baking trays with parchment paper.

3   Put the sugar, polenta, rice flour, cornflour, and spices in a free-standing mixer (or use a hand-held whisk) and whizz to mix.

4   Add the stork, and whizz until there are no large lumps of stork left.

5   Add the egg, lemon zest, and vanilla extract, then whizz again until mixture forms a stiff dough.

6   Dust the work surface with a little plain flour (remember to use gluten free flour) and knead the dough until smooth, then cut the dough in two halves (this makes it easier to roll out later).

7   If you have time, wrap the dough in clingfilm and pop into the fridge for about 30 minutes before rolling out.

8   Take the dough from the fridge and remove the clingfilm. Roll the dough out on your floured worktop to about 5mm thick, and cut with a cutter dipped in flour to stop it sticking. (I use a 3-inch square cutter, but you can decide on the size and shape of your biscuits.)

8   Re-roll the dough left and cut more biscuits until all the dough has been used.

9   Use a fish-slice or palette knife to lift the cut dough onto the prepared baking trays.

10 Use a fork or stamp to put a design of your choice on your biscuits.

11 Bake for 20 minutes until golden and just firm to touch (they will become crisper once cold).

12 Remove from the oven, leave on the baking tray for 10 minutes, then transfer to a wire rack to cool completely.

For the Filling

13 Put the stork in the free-standing mixer (or use an electric whisk) and beat until soft and smooth.

14 Add the icing sugar, white chocolate, lemon juice, and lemon extract, then beat until smooth (start slowly or you will have icing sugar all over!).

15 Turn half of the biscuits over, and pipe a good dollop of icing onto each biscuit.

16 Cover with the remaining biscuits (fancy side up) and press down gently.

Pocket-money comics

Growing up, I loved being at school and learning. I even enjoyed homework! Away from the schoolbooks, one of my treats with my pocket money was to buy the Beano or Dandy comic. Did you know that the Jammie Dodger was named after a character in the Beano comic, Rodger the Dodger? The dodger in his name was because Rodger was always trying to think of ways to dodge his homework, much to the despair of his father.

The Jammie Dodger biscuit was one of the family favourite biscuits I enjoyed growing up, and as I started to create our own gluten free and dairy free family favourite selection, it was one that had to be tackled. Sometimes I sprinkle the top of the biscuit with icing sugar; other times I bake sugar into the top biscuit to give that crunch. The jam must be home-made and the biscuit has to have a bit of crunch, but not be too hard.

"I'm going to need a SWAT team ready to mobilize, street-level maps covering all of Florida, a pot of coffee, twelve jammie dodgers and a fez."

The Doctor (Doctor Who - The Impossible Astronaut)

Jammie Dodgers

Makes about 50 single biscuits (25 doubled up)

Ingredients

For the biscuits

500g gluten free self-raising flour (I use Dove's)

120g cornflour

80g ground almonds

200g caster sugar

300g stork block, cut into cubes

125g golden syrup

4 teaspoons vanilla extract

For the filling

2 small jars raspberry jam

2 tablespoons cold water

Extra caster sugar and icing sugar for sprinkling

Method

1 Pre-heat the oven to 170°c/150°c and line four baking trays with parchment paper.

2 Put the flour, cornflour, ground almonds, and sugar into a free-standing mixer or into a large bowl, and mix until blended.

3 Add the stork, and mix until it starts to form a breadcrumb-like texture (or rub in with your fingers).

4 Next, add the vanilla extract and golden syrup and continue to mix until you have a soft dough.

5 Cut the dough into two equal pieces, wrap in clingfilm and chill in the fridge for 30 minutes.

6 Take the dough from the fridge and remove the clingfilm. Dust the worktop with gluten free flour, roll the dough out to about the thickness of a pound coin, and cut with a cutter dipped in flour to stop it sticking. (I use a 3 inch round fluted cutter, but you can decide on the size and shape of your biscuits.)

7 Re-roll the dough left, and cut more biscuits until all the dough has been used.

8 Use a fish-slice or palette knife to lift the cut dough onto the prepared baking trays.

9 Once the biscuits are on the tray, cut holes in the centre of half the biscuits using a smaller cutter.

10 Bake for 8 minutes and remove them from the oven. (Skip this bit if you want your finished biscuits sprinkled with icing sugar, and bake your biscuits for 12 minutes.)

11 Sprinkle caster sugar over the biscuits with holes, pop them back in the oven, and bake for a further 4 minutes until golden brown – but don't let them burn. They will seem a bit soft but will firm up once they cool down.

12 Leave the biscuits on the tray to cool for 5 minutes, then transfer to a wire rack to finish cooling. (You can sprinkle the biscuits with holes with a little icing sugar now. if you wish.)

13 Take your chosen jam (I prefer to use home-made raspberry jam for these) and mix it in a bowl. If it seems a little stiff, add a little cold water to make it easier to spread.

14 Spread a good dollop of your jam over the biscuits with no hole.

15 Gently press the biscuits with holes on top of the jammed biscuits so that jam peeks through the hole.

16 Make yourself a nice cup of tea, grab yourself an old Beano annual, and enjoy the antics of Rodger the Dodger and his pals as you savour the simplicity of the humble Jammie Dodger.

When Mother Murphy became Grandma

I first told this story shortly after the birth of my amazing granddaughter, Minnie Violet. It's a heart-warming and heart-breaking tale about my daughter Chloe and the long journey she had to endure before the arrival of her beautiful daughter Minnie, but it is also a tale of love, hope, and determination. It's important for me to include this in the book, as the story and Minnie herself have helped so many people both in and out of the tearoom. Chloe would also like this to be read by everyone, because in her words, 'What if, by telling my story, it gives hope to just one person and gives them the strength to continue their journey.' So, here goes…

Let's take a little trip back to 2007. A short conversation from my 16-year-old daughter, Chloe, was to change my whole outlook on life, when she announced she was pregnant. Not the news I was looking forward to hearing from my young daughter, but pregnant she was. Concern at Chloe's young age was soon replaced with excitement about becoming Grandma. Unfortunately, this wasn't going to be as smooth a journey as I'd have hoped for my daughter, sadly ending in an early miscarriage, which was soon followed by another miscarriage.

In 2009, Chloe became pregnant again. This time, she passed all the usual milestones and, flying past the usual twelve week worrying time, we thought this was her time. Two days after my birthday, 20 October, 2009, Chloe went into premature labour and suffered the unbearable pain of her first stillborn baby, Michael.

I can't explain the pain of seeing your daughter going through such terrible heartache whilst being unable to do anything to help. No words, no actions, no money, nothing I could do would make this easier for Chloe. Behind this heartache of Chloe's, my own heart was breaking for the grandchildren that were not to be. How could it be fair that one person should have to endure such pain? How could one person deal with such pain?

The next few years passed and more miscarriages followed. Tests were carried out, therapy given, but still the miscarriages happened.

2012 seemed to start well, though, and soon Chloe was pregnant again, sharing this news with me almost from day one. Every day I spoke to Chloe, and every day we chatted about the pregnancy. Six weeks passed, then twelve weeks approached for the first scan. Everything was perfect. We took the pregnancy day by day, and eventually the date for the twenty-week scan arrived, showing that this little baby was going to be girl. Oh my! This was going to be Chloe's time. Every day we talked about things to look forward to, and the things Chloe would be doing with her daughter. My heart was bursting with pride when Chloe told me she'd chosen the name Nieve Debra Olive for her baby.

The 1st November found me at home making smiley face biscuits for our Bonfire Night supper up here in Scotland, when I received a phone call that was to change my life forever. It was Chloe, and just as though she was saying hello, she simply said, 'The baby has died.' I heard a noise and realised that I was wailing. Jim, standing next to me, picked me up off the floor. 'Will you come down, please?' asked Chloe.

What followed is still a bit of a blur. A long, dark, cold, icy journey down to Halifax from Kirkintilloch; stopping at Tebay services on the M6; trying to eat something but feeling sick at the very thought. I needed to be in Halifax and with Chloe.

On Saturday, 3rd November, 2012, two days after learning that her baby had died, my incredibly brave and amazing daughter endured – with no complaining, no tears, no words – the unbearable labour of her angel baby Nieve. My granddaughter! It's no exaggeration to say that every day since then, I've seen my daughter's face as she held her stillborn baby. The shock, the pain, the heartache, but somehow I could see the acceptance. I held my granddaughter, my perfect little granddaughter, who had somehow just fallen asleep for ever.

What followed was just a nightmare. A funeral. A small white coffin. Holding my daughter up whilst we buried her daughter. How on earth was Chloe going to get through this? How could I help her through this? It was my job – no, my aim in life, to make everything ok for my children. How could I have let this happen? How could I have stopped this from happening? How could anyone have stopped this happening? How could anyone help Chloe now?

Over the coming months, I shed tears by the bucketful. Every time I closed my eyes, I saw my daughter's haunted face; I saw my perfect, but sleeping granddaughter, and my heart was breaking. How on earth was Chloe going to get through this pain and heartache?

However, get through this Chloe did. She got through it day by day. What I could see, though, was a girl who was sad from the core. There was no happiness in her. My beautiful daughter was completely broken. I was broken.

Meanwhile, Mother Murphy's Tearoom opened, and Chloe found the strength to come and be with us for the open day. She came to celebrate our 1st birthday at the tearoom. But still she was broken, with her heart aching for her lost babies and to be a mum.

Over the next few years, there followed more miscarriages, with more pain, more heartache, and more tears. Then in 2018, Chloe told me she thought she was pregnant. Only a few days. Pregnancy tests followed. Yes, it was true, Chloe was pregnant, but my only thought was that I couldn't bear any more heartache for my daughter.

With her history, Chloe was going to be closely monitored during this pregnancy, but there was nothing extra that could be done, because there were no known medical reasons for the previous losses. Day by day, we held our breaths as the pregnancy developed. Six weeks, twelve weeks. First scan, second scan. Everything looked perfect. Chloe had the most awful morning sickness, which everyone told her was a good sign. Regular scans followed, along with heartbeat monitoring. Twenty weeks, and the scan showed that the baby was another girl. A small baby on the scan, but the pregnancy was going perfectly, otherwise.

I probably stopped breathing at this point. I couldn't concentrate. I ate chocolate. I ate cake. I ate more chocolate. I ate more cake. I couldn't sleep. I couldn't craft. But the tearoom still had to be run.

I was under strict instructions from Chloe that I couldn't tell anyone she was pregnant. I did wonder how she was going to hide the growing bump, but understood her concerns. Of course, there were a few people I told in the tearoom. Ok, I told lots of people. Chloe had a bit of a laugh at the idea that I'd not told anyone, but I didn't, of course, tell anyone on the wide, wide world of Facebook so really, I'd not told anyone.

Over the next few months, the tearoom was my haven. I had to bake, to organise crafts, to talk to people, to listen to people's concerns, to be a shoulder to cry on when they needed it, and I had to laugh with people. Inside, I was a mess. I cried many, many times, because I was scared my daughter would have to go through terrible heartache again. I remember my friend Salena taking me to the Cup and Saucer Tearoom for a birthday afternoon tea, and me crying over the sandwiches. Salena just listened. Thank you, Salena.

Eventually, a date was set for induction at thirty-eight weeks. Everything was perfect except for baby being a bit small, so scans were carried out every two weeks. As the time progressed and baby stayed small, the induction date was brought forward to 13th December – just about thirty-six weeks.

Wednesday, 12th December, I travelled down to Halifax. The train journey was a bit of a blur with my mind running in overdrive. Over the months, Jim had long since stopped expecting any common sense from me, and was just amazing dealing with my anxiety, holding me and ignoring my tantrums, wiping my tears, and doing everything he could to reassure me. There was only one thing was going to reassure me, though.

On 13th December, we took Chloe into the Calderdale Royal Hospital. Induction medication was given in the manner it is given (!), and I started to crochet a blanket as I waited with Chloe. I was going nowhere until this labour was over. Not usually one for praying, I can tell you that I prayed hard that night. I'm sure that everyone in the tearoom was praying and waiting.

Jim was holding the fort and passing on my regular updates. The blanket was growing, but that was the only thing progressing.

Twenty-four hours later, Chloe's waters were broken. The labour room was full of every piece of equipment you could imagine. The consultant was not expecting anything to go wrong but, as she put it, 'we're prepared for everything'. Suddenly things progressed, and the nurse standing next to me pressed the emergency button. The room was quickly filled with about 100 people (or so it seemed). 'One more push and she'll be here.'

Then she was here. No suction, no help needed, no respirator required. This perfect, perfect, pink, tiny, breathing baby was in her mother's arms. Yes, I cried. But this time, with tears of joy, relief, and love.

I have the most amazing photo of Chloe holding her newborn baby, and the love in her eyes is amazing. Minnie Violet is just perfect. Chloe is just perfect.

That night, I slept like a baby.

This is a tale of love, sadness, heartache, and tears. Most of all, though, it is a tale of one girl's determination, strength, and endurance to become a mother. I have no doubt that Chloe will be the most amazing mother, and if little Minnie Violet loves me half as much as I loved my Grandma, then all will be great.

It is also a tale of support, warmth, thoughts, and concern that a whole group of people who had never even met Chloe gave us. I keep saying that we created our tearoom to be a place in the community where everyone could come along, feel safe, feel loved, and feel needed. But I didn't fully realise until then that the tearoom and our wonderful customers have also provided that love and support to me. Thank you.

Behind this story, of course, there is a tale of hope, with Chloe never once giving up hope of becoming a mother.

Now we have our miracle Minnie, we can start to build new memories. The grief for the lost babies will never go. But with tiny steps, one day at a time, Minnie will help Chloe to smile again. And one day in the near future, I hope to see my daughter laugh like she used to laugh – something I've not seen for a long, long time.

Going back to November 2012 when I was making smiley face biscuits, I vowed never to make those biscuits again until there was a baby to celebrate with. In the tearoom when we open again in January, there will be smiley face biscuits. I am sure there'll be tears when I make them, but tears of both joy and sadness

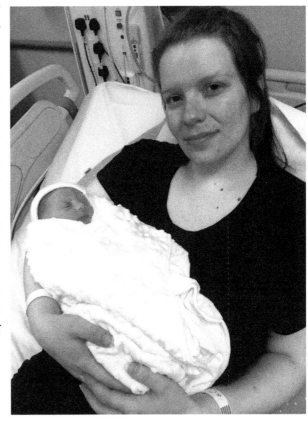

My amazing Daughter Chloe and Miracle Minnie just after she was born

Minnie's Smiley Faces

Makes about 60 single biscuits (30 doubled up)

To make the Smiley Face biscuits, I use a 5cm cutter for half of the biscuits and a 5cm matching smiley face cutter for the other half of the biscuits, using a set from Lakeland. I've also made these in the tearoom with a mint filling, and drizzled chocolate over them rather than icing. However you make them, they will most certainly make you smile when you see them on the plate.

Ingredients

For the biscuits
500g gluten free self-raising flour
120g cornflour
80g rice flour
200g caster sugar
300g stork block
125g golden syrup
4 teaspoons vanilla extract
For the filling
2 small jars raspberry jam
2 teaspoons cold water
Icing sugar for dusting

Method

1. Preheat oven to 170°c/150°c fan oven.

2. Line several baking trays with parchment paper.

3. Put the flour, cornflour, rice flour, and sugar into free-standing mixer (or use a hand-held whisk) and whizz to mix.

4. Add the stork, and whizz until there are no large lumps of stork left.

5. Add the golden syrup and vanilla extract then whizz again until mixture forms a stiff dough.

6. Dust the work surface with a little plain flour (remember to use gluten free flour) and knead the dough until smooth, then cut the dough in two halves, wrap in clingfilm, and pop in the fridge for 30 minutes. This makes it easier to roll out later.

7. Roll the one half of the dough out to about 5mm thick, and cut with the plain round cutter dipped in flour to stop it sticking.

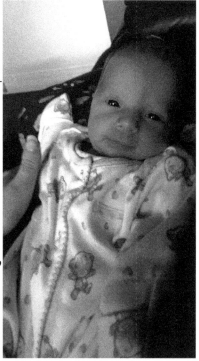

The Look of Love

8. Re-roll the dough left, and cut more biscuits until all the dough has been used.

9. Use a fish-slice or palette knife to lift the cut dough onto the prepared baking trays.

10. Repeat with the second half of the dough, but use the smiley face cutter this time.

11. Bake for 20 minutes until golden and just firm to touch (they will become crisper once cold).

12. Remove from the oven, leave on the baking tray for 10 minutes, then transfer to a wire rack to cool completely.

13. Mix the jam in a bowl to soften it (adding a couple of teaspoons of cold water if it is very thick) and pop into a piping bag (no nozzle needed).

14. Turn the plain circles over, and pipe a good dollop of the jam onto each one.

15. Sprinkle a dusting of icing sugar (or drizzle icing or melted chocolate) over the smiley face biscuits, and press one on top of each of the jammy plain biscuits.

16. Sit down with a pile of these with a large pot of steaming tea, and think of Minnie's smiley face and the joy she is giving to everyone she meets.

My first published recipe

I grew up with traditional biscuits and the family favourite selection of Nice Coconut Creams, Bourbons, Custard Creams, Jammie Dodgers and Digestives. These were often seen as cheap biscuits, but I just loved them – and still do. Customers in the tearoom also love the simple cakes and biscuits they recognise. One biscuit I recreated was the Nice Coconut Cream, but also made it gluten free and dairy free, and customers said they reminded them of their childhood. Result!

One day, flicking through one of the gluten free magazine online sites, I found a little section encouraging you to submit your own recipes. Could I do that? I wondered. Should I do that? Were my biscuits even good enough? I consulted with my pal Salena the coeliac. 'Of course you should,' was her reply.

To make sure my entry was well written and could be followed by others, I sent a copy of my Nice Coconut Cream recipe for her to try out. I'm sure Salena won't mind me telling you she was the perfect person to try out my recipe, because she's a good cook but doesn't do much baking. She followed my recipe exactly, but forgot to read the notes telling you how many biscuits it made.

Before long, Salena had a massive batch of Nice Coconut Cream biscuits to share out at her craft club in Ayrshire. The verdict from everyone was that they were great, giving me the final confidence to submit my recipe to the Gluten Free Heaven magazine. I couldn't quite believe it when they emailed me and asked for more photos, as they wanted to print the recipe.

Each month I bought the magazine, but each month there was no Nice Coconut Cream recipe. Oh well, I thought, at least they considered printing it.

Then out of the blue, one day my phone bleeped with a message from Salena, telling me to look in the magazine that month. I couldn't find the magazine anywhere. I caught the train over to Kilmarnock to go to the Craft Meeting with Salena. We popped into WHSmith, and there on the shelf was the October 2017 Gluten Free Heaven magazine with my very own recipe and photo looking back at me. I was beside myself as I went to pay for the magazine, and beamed with pride as I thrust the open magazine at the bemused shop assistant, telling him, 'That's my recipe. Right there.'

For a couple of years, the recipe stayed the same. Then in 2019, with all the hype about Brexit, I started to worry about whether I'd able to continue to source guaranteed gluten free ground almonds and, if so, would I even be able to afford to use them. So, I started to tweak some of my recipes, and finally I plucked up the courage to adapt my now famous Nice Coconut Cream recipe. Well, the biscuits went from being to scrummy to being even more delicious, with my Nice Coconut Cream Biscuits now being gluten free, dairy free, and nut free.

Nice Coconut Cream Biscuits

Makes about 46 single biscuits (23 doubled up)

Ingredients

For the Biscuit
300g very soft stork block

300g caster sugar

300g fine polenta

300g rice flour

200 g cornflour

100g desiccated coconut

2 free range eggs

2 teaspoons vanilla extract

For the Coconut Cream
200g very soft stork block

550g icing sugar

50g desiccated coconut

100g gluten and dairy free white chocolate (I use Plamil's)

2 teaspoon vanilla extract

Method

For the Biscuit

1   *Preheat oven to 170°c/150°c fan oven.*

2   *Line several baking trays with parchment paper.*

3   *Put the sugar, polenta, rice flour, cornflour and coconut in a free-standing mixer and whizz to mix.*

4   *Add the stork, and whizz until there are no large lumps of stork left.*

5   *Add the egg and vanilla extract, and whizz again until mixture forms a stiff dough.*

6   *Dust the work surface with a little plain flour (remember to use gluten free flour) and knead the dough until smooth, then cut the dough in two halves (this makes it easier to roll out later).*

7   *Roll the dough out to about 5mm thick and cut with a cutter dipped in flour to stop it sticking. (I use a 3-inch square cutter, but you can decide on the size and shape of your biscuits.)*

8   *Re-roll the dough left, and cut more biscuits until all the dough has been used.*

9   *Use a fish-slice or palette knife to lift the cut dough onto the prepared baking trays.*

10 *Use a fork or stamp to put a design of your choice on your biscuits.*

11 *Bake for 20 minutes until golden and just firm to touch (they will become crisper once cold).*

12 *Remove from the oven, leave on the baking tray for 10 minutes, then transfer to a wire rack to cool completely.*

For the Filling

13 *Place the chocolate in a bowl over a pan of simmering water and stir gently until melted. Remove from the heat and put to one side.*

14 *Put the stork, icing sugar, coconut, and vanilla extract in the free-standing mixer and beat until smooth (start slowly or you will have icing sugar all over!).*

15 *Add the melted chocolate and beat again until smooth.*

16 *Turn half of the biscuits over, and pipe a good dollop of icing onto each biscuit.*

17 *Cover with the remaining biscuits (fancy side up) and press down gently.*

18 *Invite a couple of friends over, make a big pot of steaming hot tea, and enjoy reminiscing about old-fashioned biscuits.*

The humble oatcake

The humble oatcake. What could be more comforting than a tasty oatcake smothered in butter and topped with a slice of Wensleydale cheese? Well, ok, how about an oatcake with lashings of cream cheese topped with home-made strawberry jam. Of course, if an oatcake is the real deal, then it can be enjoyed just on its own.

Oatcakes have been around for centuries and may even go back long before Roman times. Whether they're gluten free or not, they're made with simple, natural, and wholesome ingredients. If you want the technical stuff, they're supposed to have a high mineral content – good for maintaining energy levels. They have a low glycaemic index – good for managing blood sugars. Of course, being full of oats, they're reported to help lower cholesterol, too. Who would have believed that such a little cake could be this healthy?!

They are very versatile, too: perhaps something to have with soup, to replace bread; served with a ploughman's lunch; with pate; as a snack with cheese; or just something to nibble on with a cup of tea.

Sandra, Georgie and Mr M

When making these, I make a huge batch, freeze them, take them out of the freezer when needed, and pop them on the griddle for a minute or two. They are just yummy warm. One customer especially likes the oatcakes toasted and is a little like me, being able to eat them just as they come. Who might this customer be? The lovely Sandra, of course.

But who is Sandra? Well, Sandra and her lovely wife, Georgie, first appeared in the tearoom not long after we opened. They confessed to not being tearoom or café people, but that the new tearoom on their street had seemed to draw them in. Over the years, Sandra and Georgie have become members of our tearoom family, like long-lost friends. Two nicer people you'll struggle to find.

Sandra is a very crafty person, too. And as I write this section during the Coronavirus lockdown, Sandra has once again shown her kind soul by creating a rainbow for the outside of the closed tearoom. The rainbow has become a symbol of hope for everyone during the lockdown period, and has appeared in windows all over the world and across social media.

Sandra's Oatcakes

Makes about 60 small oatcakes

Once you've made these oatcakes, you'll never again think of oatcakes being a boring biscuit to have when the cupboards are void of all other treats. How thick you like these is your choice, as is the size. I like mine to be thin and slightly larger than bite-sized. Just remember that if you roll these out very thin, the baked oatcake will be crisper and harder than a thicker one, but don't be tempted to make them too thick or they will not be enjoyable to eat and will be more like a dry flapjack!

Ingredients

> 500g gluten free porridge oats
> 50g stork block
> 1 teaspoon bicarbonate of soda
> 20g brown sugar
> 2 teaspoons salt
> 300ml hot water

Method

1. *Preheat oven to 180°c/160°c fan oven.*

2. *Line several baking trays with parchment paper.*

3. *Put the oats into a food processor and blitz until there are no large oats left.*

4. *Place the bicarbonate of soda, salt, and sugar into a large bowl, add the grounds oats and stir to combine.*

5. *Add the melted stork and stir with a wooden spoon.*

6. *Add most of the hot water and stir again.*

7. *Now knead the mixture with your hands to bring everything together. Add more hot water if it is too dry to form a stiff dough.*

8. *Empty the dough onto a floured worktop and cut into two (this makes it easier to roll out).*

9. *Roll out the dough to the thickness you like your oatcakes (remember they will not rise or spread in the oven), and cut out to the size you prefer.*

10. *Use a fish-slice to place the oatcakes on the prepared baking trays.*

11. *Re-roll the dough, and repeat until all the dough has been made.*

12. *Bake in the pre-heated oven for 10 minutes.*

13. *Remove from the oven, use a fish-slice to turn the oatcakes over, return to the oven, and bake for a further 5 minutes.*

14. *Take from the oven and transfer the oatcakes to a wire rack to cool complete.*

15. *Now take a handful of these, spread with your favourite topping, and enjoy with a cup of steaming hot tea.*

Strawberry Creams

Makes about 46 single biscuits (23 doubled up)

Ingredients

For the Biscuit
300 g very soft stork block

300 g caster sugar

300 g fine polenta

300 g rice flour

200g cornflour

2 free range eggs

1 teaspoon vanilla extract

For the Strawberry Cream
200 g very soft stork block

500 g icing sugar

100g strawberry Nesquik

1 teaspoon vanilla extra

Pink food colouring

Method

For Biscuit

1 Preheat oven to 170oc/150oc fan oven.

2 Line several baking trays with parchment paper.

3 Put the sugar, polenta, and rice flour in a free-standing mixer (or use a hand-held whisk) and whizz to mix.

4 Add the stork, and whizz until there are no large lumps of stork left.

5 Add the egg and vanilla extract, and whizz again until mixture forms a stiff dough.

6 Dust the work surface with a little plain flour (remember to use gluten free flour) and knead the dough until smooth, then cut the dough in two halves (this makes it easier to roll out later).

7 If you have time, wrap the dough in clingfilm and pop into the fridge for about 30 minutes before rolling out.

8 Take the dough from the fridge and remove the clingfilm. Roll the dough out on your floured worktop to about 5mm thick, and cut with a cutter dipped in flour to stop it sticking. (I use a 3-inch square cutter, but you can decide on the size and shape of your biscuits.)

9 Re-roll the dough left, and cut more biscuits until all the dough has been used.

10 Use a fish-slice or palette knife to lift the cut dough onto the prepared baking trays.

11 Use a fork or stamp to put a design of your choice on your biscuits.

12 Bake for 20 minutes until golden and just firm to touch (they will become crisper once cold).

13 Remove from the oven, leave on the baking tray for 10 minutes, then transfer to a wire rack to cool completely.

For the Filling

14 Put the stork in the free-standing mixer (or use an electric whisk) and beat until soft and smooth.

15 Add the icing sugar, Nesquik, vanilla extract, and food colouring, and beat until smooth (start slowly or you will have icing sugar all over!).

16 Turn half of the biscuits over, and pipe a good dollop of icing onto each biscuit.

17 Cover with the remaining biscuits (fancy side up) and press down gently.

Christmas baking at the tearoom

During my childhood, I wasn't all that keen on the rich Christmas treats such as mince pies or Christmas cake, but this all changed with my 'O' Level Domestic Science lessons at school. I enjoyed the practical side of the course but wasn't all that keen on the theory, not quite getting my head around why I needed to know the structure of an egg when all I wanted to know was whether the recipe asked for a yolk, white, or whole egg!

Domestic Science was made even more enjoyable for me as my best friend, Karen, was also doing this course, so we had many great hours chatting, laughing, and cooking or baking together. I remember, though, with horror that during one lesson we had to make soused herring. This was the first time in my life I'd needed to cut the head off a fish. Actually, it was probably the first time I'd handled a real dead fish!

I made the mistake of putting the knife down gently on the fish and feeling the knife going through the flesh, only to find that I couldn't go through with it. Karen, being my best pal, quickly took over and did the dastardly deed before the teacher could come along and force me do it myself. That's why Karen will always be my best friend!

Karen and Debra

Apart from the fish episode, we did some great cooking and baking, and I look back on these lessons with great affection. We had a brilliant teacher, who just wanted everyone to enjoy baking and cooking.

It was during these two years of domestic science lessons that I made my first Christmas cake. Over a period of eight weeks, we prepared the fruit, let it soak in alcohol, made the cakes, let them mature, then made the marzipan and icing. I think this must be one of the best experiences of my school life, and I remember it every year now when making my Christmas cakes. It was making my own fruit cake, filled with only the best ingredients, along with the love and support of Karen and our teacher, that encouraged me to try this again once I'd left home. And I can probably count on one hand the number of times I've bought a Christmas cake since, rather than making my own.

I like to believe that my children benefited from my home baking and Christmas treats. Sometimes, though, you can just have too much. Usually, children find Christmas cake too rich for their young tastebuds, but my son Benjamin was (and still is!) unique. As a five-year-old, he just loved Christmas cake, mince pies, and Christmas pudding. We still laugh together remembering the year I made what soon became my signature Christmas cake – a large, round fruit cake, decorated with marzipan, and royal icing to look like snow. To make it easier to cut pieces, I first cut out a quarter of the large cake which I planned to cut into smaller pieces. I can still see Ben's eyes almost popping out of his head and his little voice saying, 'Oh Mummy, I can't eat that big piece.'

Of course, once I had the taste for real Christmas cake, my tastebuds seemed to click into the fruit flavours, and now I could eat Christmas cake and mince pies all year around.

Talking of mince pies, these were another of the Christmas treats I disliked growing up. They were too sweet, too spicy, tasted of alcohol, and the pastry was disgusting. The first mince pies I started to make were made with bought mincemeat, to which I added apple and brandy, but made my own pastry. Even then, these were far superior to the ones I remember growing up.

Jim   Beatrix   Debra

Over the years, my mince pies improved, becoming very popular with friends and family. Eventually, I started to make my own mincemeat, and couldn't believe how easy it was and how it totally changed the mince pies.

With this success in mind, once the tearoom opened, I assumed my mince pies would sell by the hundreds. Over the autumn, I made my mincemeat and then made enough mince pies to feed the whole of Scotland. Thank goodness for commercial freezers! December came, and my mince pieces were displayed for sale every day. Surprisingly, though, these delights were overlooked by the customers, with only a few selling over the whole of the festive season! Needless to say, Mr M and I were eating mince pies at home for the next six months (which was not too much of a hardship).

The following year, I tweaked my mincemeat further to make it gluten free and dairy free. Who even knew that you could make mincemeat without suet and it could taste just as good? As long as you put in a good selection of the traditional Christmas dried fruits, plenty good quality brown sugar, and a good helping of alcohol, the mincemeat can't fail to be good. It's so easy to make and just gets better the longer you leave it.

The important thing to remember when preparing for Christmas is that it should be a fun time. Don't put yourself under so much pressure that you don't enjoy the baking. Prepare things in advance and freeze as many things as you have room for. Mince pies, Baileys Mini Chocolate Logs, and the Nearly There Cake are just some of the things you can make in advance, freeze, and defrost, to provide you with magical treats to share with family and friends over the festive period.

The deer destroyer

Over the time that the tearoom has been open, the customers have taken Mr M into their hearts and probably love him nearly as much as I do. My posts with photos of Mr M on social media are the ones that create the most reaction. When I sneak away for a few days down to Halifax to visit my children, I used to worry about how Mr M would cope in the tearoom by himself. But there was no need at all, as there was always somebody happy to help, take the orders, make the drinks, and clear the tables. It really is a magical tearoom family indeed.

Now, Mr M is indeed very special, but sometimes he's done or said things that have led to him being given different names – some that can't be repeated in this book. So, let's take a look at the naming of Mr M. It all started with him being named James Daniel by his parents (not very different to his younger brother, who is called Daniel James!). His father was also James, but known to everyone as Jim. To avoid confusion, Mr M was known as Jimmy by his friends and family. Even now, I think I'm the only one who calls him Jim, meaning the tearoom family got to know James as Jim. In time, this soon became Mr M, and this is the name most people use now when talking to him or referring to him.

Of course, there was the time Mr M became known as The Fat Controller. Now, Mr M can in no way be mistaken as the Fat Controller, as he is one of those very lucky people who can eat all day long and not see his waistline grow. In my case, I just need to look at a cake and can see the scales laughing at me!

Anyway, in one of our random discussions at the tearoom, I asked Mr M if I reminded him of a ballerina. Mr M thought for a few minutes and replied, 'Ballerina? More like Thomas the Tank Engine.' The customers in the tearoom at the time gasped in horror, ducked for cover, and waited for my response, but one customer simply said, 'That must make him The Fat Controller.' I found this hilarious, and the name stuck for a while.

Then there was the Christmas I was making the Bailey's Mini Chocolate Logs. Preparing the decorations in advance, a good few hours were spent rolling out the fondant icing, cutting out hundreds of deer, and decorating each one with eyes and a red nose, which were then left on the worktop in the kitchen to dry out. After a long walk with Beatrix, I came back to find the worktop empty, with Mr M telling me, 'Oh, I thought they were just scraps and I threw them away.' Oh, how I laughed at his joke… until I realised he was not joking! Because of this, Mr M became known for a while as The Deer Destroyer.

These Baileys Mini Chocolate Logs have now become one of our customers' favourite bakes during the Christmas season. Sometimes it feels like the whole of December is spent making these delights, as people enjoy them so much in the tearoom, take them home with them, or order them for their Christmas tables at home. My daughter even asked for these to be on the menu for Christmas Day at our house.

Initially, I made them simply following a recipe which had them made with butter, wheat flour, and the original Bailey's Irish Cream. But there were so many requests that first year to make them gluten free and dairy free, that the next year I set out to try to make this possible. Converting the recipe to gluten free was not a problem, but making it dairy free was proving a little difficult because of the Bailey's Irish Cream. Then, lo and behold, did Baileys not bring out a dairy free version of this drink in the form of Baileys

Almande Dairy Free Almond Drink. This was a little difficult to source the first year, but now it's readily available in December from most large supermarkets, and it allows me to make gluten free and dairy free Baileys Mini Chocolate Yule Logs which are just as delicious as the original ones.

For those who can have dairy, I have a stash of Cadbury's Flakes that I crumble on top of them when they're served. To date, I've not managed to source a dairy free version of anything that matches the scrummy Cadbury's flakes. Let me know if you have any suggestions.

I've said before that I wanted to make our tearoom a place where everyone feels welcome, safe, and included. In 2019, the tearoom glowed brightly and led the way for a special customer to find us and become part of the tearoom family.

Teresa first came into the tearoom with her support worker Susan (of Susan's Home-Cooked Ham). We're proud to say it was not long before we'd made Teresa feel safe and secure enough to come along by herself. Teresa is a pleasure to have in the tearoom and readily chats to everyone who comes in, giving cuddles and hugs to all. You may not know you need a hug, but Teresa seems to know, and everyone gets a cuddle when she arrives or leaves the tearoom.

Teresa has tried numerous new crafts in the tearoom, too, including quilting, sewing, card making, crochet, knitting, and candle making. The smile on her face when she tries a new craft and sees what she's really capable of, is fabulous to see.

The tearoom family have taken Teresa under their wings, even organising to take her to other cafes when we were closed for a while during holidays and my illness. Our tearoom family members are just fabulous.

It was a bit of a surprise to find out a few months after Teresa's first visit that she has coeliac disease, but we are pleased we can now help Teresa with her diet restrictions and make sure that everything she gets in the tearoom is gluten free and safe for her to eat. Teresa just loves our cakes, and I guess we could name every cake after her. However, the choice for which cake to name after Teresa was not difficult.

In December 2019, she tried Bailey's Mini Chocolate Yule Logs, and probably had one of these delights every time she came into the tearoom. So, Teresa's Bailey's Mini Chocolate Yule Logs they became.

Teresa

Teresa's Bailey's Mini Chocolate Yule Logs

Makes 24 mini loaves

Ingredients

For Cake

2 teaspoons instant coffee granules

250ml boiling water

200g stork block

550g caster sugar

4 free range eggs

400g gluten free self-raising flour

1 teaspoon xanthan gum

1 teaspoon gluten free baking powder

150g cocoa powder

250ml Baileys Almande Dairy Free Almond Drink (or other Irish Cream drink)

For the Frosting

250g stork block

700g icing sugar

150ml Baileys Almande Dairy Free Almond Drink (or other Irish Cream drink)

Cocoa powder to sprinkle

8 Flake bars (optional, if you don't need yours to stay dairy free)

Extra decorations made from roll-out icing, such as holly leaves or reindeer.

Method

For the Cake

1   Preheat oven to 180oc/160oc fan oven.

2   Put 24 mini loaf cases on two baking trays. I use disposable ones so no need to grease or line with parchment paper.

3   Dissolve the coffee in the boiling water and set aside to cool.

4   Cream together the stork and sugar in a free-standing mixer (or use an electric hand whisk) until light and fluffy.

5   Add the lightly beaten eggs a little at a time, beating well until all combined.

6   Put the flour, cocoa, baking powder, and xanthan gum into a bowl and stir well to combine.

7   Add the cooled coffee to the Baileys.

8   With the mixer running on low speed, add a tablespoon at a time of the flour mix and some of the Baileys mix until everything is all combined and smooth.

8   Divide the mixture out between the mini loaf cases (I use a small ice cream scoop) and smooth the tops with a teaspoon.

9   Bake in the pre-heated oven for 15-20 minutes until the sponge is firm to touch.

10 Remove from the oven and leave to cool on a wire rack.

For the Frosting

11 Put the stork block, icing sugar, and Baileys in the free-standing whisk on a low speed, and mix until combined. Turn the whisk up and beat for a few minutes until the mixture is light, smooth, creamy, and a nice light cream colour.

12 Put the frosting into a piping bag with a fluted nozzle, and pipe onto the cooled cakes.

13 Decorate with your chosen decorations and finish with a light dusting of cocoa powder.

14 Lock the door, put on a suitable film such as Miracle on 34th Street, and enjoy a couple of hours of heaven with your Baileys Mini Chocolate Yule Logs, a pot of tea, and some Christmas cheer.

Boozy Bakewell Tart

Makes a 9" round tart

If, for some strange reason, you find yourself with some of your home-made Christmas mincemeat left over, why not try putting it in a Bakewell Tart instead of your usual home-made jam? Quite a few people say they don't like Christmas mincemeat, but it's probably because they've never tasted home-made mincemeat. The same people in the tearoom who swore they didn't like Christmas mincemeat couldn't get enough of my Boozy Bakewell Tart.

I know that you can read Annie's Gooseberry Bakewell Tart earlier in the book, but the whole recipe is repeated here for you as Boozy Bakewell so that you don't need to keep flicking back.

Just like the other Bakewell Tarts, serve this with a good helping of hot, steaming custard and you've just turned a teatime delight into heaven!

Ingredients

For the Pastry Base
100g stork block
50g caster sugar
1 free range egg lightly beaten
100g gluten free plain flour
100g fine polenta
Enough home-made Christmas mincemeat to cover the base of the tart

For the Icing
200g icing sugar
1 tablespoon warm water
50g gluten and dairy free chocolate

For the Filling
100 g stork block
100g caster sugar
2 free range eggs lightly beaten
75g ground almonds
25g gluten free plain flour
1 teaspoon almond extract

Equipment

9" round loose-bottomed flan tin

Method

For the Pastry

1   *Preheat oven to 190oc/170oc fan oven.*

2   *Grease a 9" round loose-bottom flan tin.*

3   *Put the polenta, flour, and caster sugar in a free-standing mixer and mix for a minute to blend. Add the stork, and mix slowly until you have something that looks like breadcrumbs. Add the egg and continue to mix until the mixture forms a soft pastry.*

4   *Empty the pastry onto a well-floured worktop (gluten free flour, of course), knead gently until smooth, then wrap in clingfilm and pop in the fridge for 30 minutes.*

5   *Remove the clingfilm and roll out the chilled pastry on a well-floured worktop until it is large enough to cover the base and sides of the flan tin (or cut out with a pastry cutter).*

6   *Using a rolling pin, carefully transfer the pastry to the prepared tin(s). Smooth out any cracks and trim the pastry to be level with the top of the tin.*

7   *Line the pastry case with parchment paper, fill with baking beans, and blind bake for 10 minutes.*

8   *Once baked, remove from the oven, and take out the baking beans and parchment paper, but leave the pastry in the tin. Be careful, as the baking beans will be very hot.*

9   *Spread home-made Christmas mincemeat over the base of the pastry. Be generous but not too lavish here, or your chosen mincemeat will ooze out of the tart once you add the filling.*

For the Filling

10   *Cream together the caster sugar and stork until light and fluffy.*

11   *Add the eggs slowly, a little at a time, beating with each addition.*

12   *Stir in the ground almonds, flour, and almond extract.*

13   *Spread over the jam in pastry case and bake for 25-30 minutes until golden brown and the filling feels firm to touch.*

14   *Leave to cool completely in the tin, then carefully remove from the tin and place on a serving plate*

For the Icing

15   *In a large bowl, mix the icing sugar with warm water to make an icing just thick enough to spread.*

16   *Put the chocolate in another bowl over a pan of simmering water, then pour and put this into a piping bag.*

17   *Snip off the very end of the piping bag and pipe thin lines of chocolate across the icing.*

18   *Quickly, before the icing and chocolate set, run a sharp knife through the lines one way then the other to create a feathered effect and leave to set before serving.*

Soda Bread

Makes two loaves

Christmas baking and cooking can be time consuming and fiddly, with lots of strange ingredients you won't use for the rest of the year. The food is often rich, sweet, and probably very plentiful! That's why it's nice to bake something that involves very few ingredients and takes a ridiculously short amount of time to make. The main meal on Christmas Day must have all the traditional foods for me – turkey with all the trimmings, and must, just must, include Yorkshire puddings. Then there has to be Christmas pudding, Christmas cake, mince pies, truffles, and cheese and biscuits. Phew!

On Christmas Eve, we like to have an easy day without too much effort going into the food. My favourite Christmas Eve tea is to have our honey glazed ham with some of Mr M's fabulous roast potatoes, Heinz baked beans, and home-made soda bread. At supper that night, we finish off any remaining soda bread toast and some home-made jam. This soda bread has a lovely taste, a crunchy crust, and is a simple treat rather than just the usual bread. It is Christmas, after all!

Soda bread doesn't keep very well and is best eaten on the day it is made, especially when making it gluten free. I like to make two loaves (if you're going to have the oven on, no point baking only one loaf!). Once cooled, slice one of the loaves and freeze it, ready to take out a couple of slices when you need it. If you just want to make one loaf, simply half the ingredients.

Just a note here. I did try to make this both gluten free and dairy free, but found that without the buttermilk it just didn't have the real soda bread taste to it, so this version is gluten free but not dairy free.

Ingredients

700g gluten free plain flour
100g gluten free porridge oats
2 teaspoons bicarbonate of soda
3 teaspoons salt
1 teaspoon caster sugar
2 free range eggs
2 x 284 cartons buttermilk
Milk to glaze
Extra porridge oats for the topping

Method

1 Preheat oven to 190oc/170oc fan oven.

2 Line two baking trays with parchment paper.

3 Put the porridge oats in the food processer and blitz for a couple of minutes until fine. (You have now made your own gluten free oatmeal.)

4 Put the flour, ground oats, salt, bicarbonate of soda, and sugar into a large bowl and stir to combine.

5 Put the buttermilk and eggs into a separate bowl and whisk for a minute to combine.

6 Add the buttermilk mix to the flour mix and stir with a large wooden spoon until the mixture starts to come together as a dough. Finish bringing it together into a smooth dough with your hands.

7 Empty the dough onto a lightly floured worktop and cut into two pieces, shape the two pieces into rough oval shapes, and place onto the prepared baking trays.

9 Brush each loaf with some milk and sprinkle with some extra oats.

10 Score the loaves diagonally with a knife and bake in the preheated oven for 50 minutes.

11 Remove from the oven, take off the baking tray, and allow to cool on a wire rack.

12 Enjoy this simple bread just as it comes, with lashings of butter.

Christmas truffles

Most of the recipes included in this book are things I've made and served in the tearoom, but these delicious Christmas Truffles are one of the exceptions. I first made these over 20 years ago when my son and daughter, Ben and Chloe, were just small children. Chloe just loves these and begs me to make them all the time for her, but I only make these in December for Christmas, because if we had them all the year round they'd stop being such a fabulous treat, much to her disappointment.

Although I've not made these for sale in the tearoom, I did make them as little gifts for those who came to our first Christmas Afternoon Tea for 16 in 2015, and they went down a storm. These truffles make great Christmas presents, especially if you find or make a nice box to put them in with some Christmassy tissue paper. Just remember to put a note on the box telling the recipient to keep the truffles in the fridge until they are eaten. They'll keep for two weeks in the fridge.

One year I even froze mine, as I'd made them to take to Chloe for her Christmas present, but the winter weather in Scotland got the better of my travel plans and I had to stay at home. Chloe's truffles were popped in the freezer and were perfect once defrosted, with Chloe getting her Christmas Truffles in February that year!

Chloe and her truffles

Sometimes truffles can be a little too sweet and sickly, but these are balanced out nicely with the addition of sponge and ground almonds. For the sponge, you can use Madeira cake or some plain Victoria sponge. Rather than making a separate bake just for the sponge, I use the mix for my three-tier Victoria sponge but put one layer of the sponge to one side to use for the truffles. One 9" round layer of my Victoria sponge cake will be enough to make a huge batch of truffles, giving you about 120 truffles!

This does, of course, ensure that your truffles are gluten free. You could use a ready-made Madeira cake or plain sponge, but home-made is just the best, and you know exactly what's in the sponge.

You can make all the truffles the same, but using different coatings turns them into something special. You're limited only by your imagination and personal choice. Some people like just chocolate coated truffles, some like chopped nuts, some like cocoa powder, and some absolutely hate cocoa powder. If you make a large selection, people have lots to choose from – just make sure to keep some of your favourite ones stashed away for yourself to eat.

I love to serve a large plate of my truffles later on Christmas Day when everyone's ready for a little treat with their tea or coffee. Make the truffles quite small so people can enjoy one or two of these delights without being overwhelmed by them.

Chloe's Christmas Truffles

Makes about 120 truffles

This might sound like an extraordinary large number of truffles, but let me reassure you that once you make these you will want to give them out as presents and share them with friends and family. So, they will soon disappear!

To make my truffles, I make one batch of truffle mix using dark chocolate and one batch using white chocolate.

When I'm coating the truffles, I like to do milk, dark, and white chocolate coatings. Firstly, I melt the milk chocolate, coat as many truffles as I can with this, then repeat the process for dark and for white chocolate. Once I have my chocolate coated truffles, I can see how many truffles I have left, then choose a selection of other coatings and make a pretty selection.

Ingredients

For the Sponge
(You could use the recipe for my 3-layer Victoria Sponge and use one of the layers for the truffles, or follow the recipe below to make just enough sponge for the truffles)
125 g soft stork block
125 g caster sugar
2 free range eggs, lightly beaten
½ teaspoon vanilla extract
125 g gluten free self-rising flour (I use Dove's)
½ teaspoon gluten free baking powder
¼ teaspoon xanthan gum

For the Truffle Mix

Plain Chocolate Truffles	White Chocolate Truffles
250g plain chocolate	*250g white chocolate*
150g plain gluten free sponge	*150g gluten free plain sponge*
150g icing sugar	*150g icing sugar*
150g ground almonds	*150g ground almonds*
60ml brandy/rum	*60ml brandy/rum*
120ml fresh double cream	*120ml fresh double cream*
or a dairy alternative	*or a dairy alternative*

For the Truffle Coatings

200g milk chocolate

200g dark chocolate

200g white chocolate

Plus, 50g of your chosen coatings, such as:

Icing sugar	*Coloured sugar strands (hundreds and thousands)*
Cocoa powder	*Coloured sugar*
Chopped mixed nuts	*Desiccated coconut*
Chocolate Sprinkles	

Method

For the Sponge

1   *Preheat oven to 180oc/160oc fan oven.*

2   *Grease and line a 9" round sandwich tin with parchment paper.*

3   *Put the flour, baking powder, and xanthan gum in a bowl and mix well.*

3   *Place the sugar and stork block into a free-standing mixer (or use a hand-held whisk) and beat together until light and fluffy. This will take a good few minutes. Stop the mixer and use a spatula to scrape the mixture from the sides of the bowls a couple of times to make sure it all gets blended.*

4   *With the mixer still running, add the eggs a little at a time, beating well between each addition, until all combined and the mixture is smooth.*

5   *Lower the speed of the mixer and gradually add the flour mix, one tablespoon at a time, until it has all been added.*

6   *Add the vanilla extract and mix until just blended.*

7   *Spoon the cake mixture into the prepared tin and level the top with a palette knife.*

8   Bake in pre-heated oven for 25-30 minutes until risen, golden brown, and a cake tester comes out clean.

9   Remove from the oven and leave to cool for 10 minutes in the tin.

10   Remove from the tin, removing the parchment paper, and place on a wire rack to cool completely.

For the Truffle Mix

11   Melt 250g plain chocolate in a bowl over simmering water.

12   Break 150g gluten free sponge into crumbs into a large bowl, and stir in the ground almonds, icing sugar, and brandy/rum.

13   Add the melted chocolate and double cream, and stir until well mixed.

14   Cover the bowl with clingfilm and pop in the fridge for about an hour or until the mixture is firm enough for you to roll into small balls in your hands.

15   Repeat steps 11-14 using 250g white chocolate.

16   Once the mix is firm, take a small amount (about a teaspoon) of the mixture and roll into a ball with your hands. (A good time to get the children involved!) You should get about 60 small balls from each bowl of truffle mixture.

For the Truffle Coatings

17   Melt 200g milk chocolate in a bowl over a pan of simmering water, and remove the bowl from the water.

18   Use two teaspoons to roll a truffle in the chocolate before transferring it carefully to a sweet paper.

19   Repeat with 200g plain chocolate and then 200g white chocolate.

20   See how many truffles you have left to coat, then decide what to coat them in. Put some of your chosen coatings into a small bowls and roll the truffles in them to coat them.

21   Leave the truffles to set then put a selection of them on a pretty plate and enjoy with a nice cup of tea. Just watch how quickly they disappear!

22   Put the remaining truffles in an airtight container between pieces of parchment paper. They will keep for two weeks in the fridge.

*Making your Christmas cake in September is perfect,
as too fresh a cake crumbles when cut.*

Mary Berry

Traditional Christmas cake

I regret that over the years my cookery books from school, including the recipe for the Christmas Cake we made, have been lost. Many different recipes have been tried, but the best recipe by far is by the wonderful Mary Berry.

In the tearoom, I initially made both a Mary Berry version and a gluten free one, but felt the gluten free version was not quite as good as Mary's. The following year, I set about tweaking Mary's version to make it both gluten free and dairy free. The ingredients were very much the same, but I changed the flour to gluten free, added some xanthan gum, changed the egg ratio, and added more black treacle (you can never have too much black treacle, in my opinion).

Throughout December that year, we again had Mary Berry's standard cake in the tearoom along with my adapted version. They did look absolutely the same, so I'd coloured the icing on one of them to make sure there were no mistakes when we served the cakes. We had a taste testing of the two cakes, and many customers couldn't identify which was the gluten free version. Even Mr M got it wrong! Now I only ever make my gluten free and dairy free version in the tearoom and for home.

I used to make the marzipan and the fondant icing for the cakes, too, but nowadays you can get very good quality versions of these, and this also avoids the worry of using raw egg whites in my baking for customers.

Making a Christmas cake isn't a process that can be rushed. I like to have my cakes made by the end of September or October at the very latest. This gives me time to let the cake mature and for me to feed it each week with a good helping of brandy. When you bake the cake, make sure you plan this for a day when you'll not be going anywhere. A large cake can take between four and five hours to bake. Start the cake-making the night before you want to bake it, by soaking the dried fruit in some brandy to allow the fruit to take in all the lovely flavour. It might seem a bit of a hassle, but it really is well worth the effort.

Remember to grease and line the baking tins with a double layer of baking parchment paper, and put two large pieces of baking parchment over the top of the cake, fastened with string around the outside of the tins, to stop the top of the cake drying out and burning during the long bake.

Leave the baked cake to cool completely in the cake tin before removing all the parchment paper. Re-cover the cold cake with a double layer of fresh parchment paper, then a double layer of foil. Put the cake somewhere cool and dark to mature until you decorate it. Each week, peel back the foil and parchment paper, pierce the cake with a cake skewer, and drizzle a couple of tablespoons of brandy over the holes. Allow this to soak in then re-wrap the cake and put away safely again. Do this each week until you decorate the cake.

Marzipan the cake a week or so before you want to eat it. Leave the marzipan-covered cake to dry for a week (unwrapped), then cover with your choice of icing. Finally, leave the icing to dry for a couple of days before serving the cake (if you can resist).

I've listed the ingredients for a 7", 8", and 10" square tin, but the method is the same for all the different sizes.

As for serving the cake, well, it's a bit of a Yorkshire thing, but I like to have Wensleydale cheese with my Christmas cake. We have a saying in Yorkshire: 'Fruit cake without the cheese is like a kiss without the squeeze.' Take a nice thick slice of Christmas cake with an equally thick slice of creamy, crumbly Wensleydale cheese on top of it. The mix of flavours is just amazing.

Every year in the tearoom I like to see how many people I can convince to try this combination. The first year this was introduced to the tearoom, customers thought the cheese was mixed into the Christmas cake. There have certainly been some raised eyebrows when new customers see this, but they soon change their mind once they taste it. At this rate, I'll have the whole of Scotland eating Christmas cake with Wensleydale cheese.

Talking of Wensleydale cheese, I couldn't resist telling you about the Wensleydale Creamery, which is in the lovely market town of Hawes in Wensleydale, right in the heart of my beloved Yorkshire Dales. Even if you don't like cheese, you should visit this area just for the stunning scenery.

You can visit the amazing cheese factory, see cheese being made, and sample hundreds of different cheeses. My favourite has to be plain Wensleydale or Wensleydale with cranberry. Of course, you may know Wensleydale cheese from Wallace and Gromit, but did you know that Gromit is also left-handed?

The fine people at the Wensleydale Creamery kindly sent me some photos to use in my book to continue the quest to get everyone eating Christmas Cake and cheese. During the Covid-19 lockdown, when we were doing daily live Facebook chats, we somehow managed to arrange a Tearoom Road Trip to the Wensleydale Creamery, with everyone planning to stay at my friend Karen's house. It will be interesting to see if this actually happened!

*Photos kindly provided by the Wensleydale Creamery
showing off their lovely cheese*

Traditional Christmas Cake

Makes a 7", 8" or 10" square cake (8", 9", or 11" round)

Ingredients

7" Square Cake or 8" Round Cake

100g glace cherries, chopped

100g dried apricots, chopped

275g currants

175g sultanas

175g raisins

50g mixed peel

5 tablespoons brandy

225g gluten free plain flour

½ teaspoon xanthan gum

1 teaspoon grated nutmeg

1 teaspoon mixed spice

225g stork block

225g dark brown sugar

5 free range eggs

50g mixed chopped nuts

3 tablespoons black treacle

Zest of 1 lemon

Zest of 1 orange

Baking time: 4¼ hours

8" Square Cake or 9" Round Cake

150g glace cherries, chopped

150g dried apricots, chopped

400g currants

225g sultanas

225g raisins

70g mixed peel

7 tablespoons brandy

275g gluten free plain flour

1 teaspoon xanthan gum

1.5 teaspoons grated nutmeg

1.5 teaspoons mixed spice

275g stork block

275g dark brown sugar

6 free range eggs

65g mixed chopped nuts

4 tablespoons black treacle

Zest of 2 lemons

Zest of 2 oranges

Baking time: 4½ hours

10" Square Cake or 11" Round Cake

225g glace cherries, chopped

225g dried apricots, chopped

550g currants

350g sultanas

350g raisins

100g mixed peel

10 tablespoons brandy

450g gluten free plain flour

1.5 teaspoons xanthan gum

2 teaspoons grated nutmeg

2 teaspoons mixed spice

450g stork block

450g dark brown sugar

9 free range eggs

100g mixed chopped nuts

6 tablespoons black treacle

Zest of 3 lemons

Zest of 3 oranges

Baking time: 5 hours

Equipment

7" square loose-bottomed cake tin/ 8" round loose-bottomed cake tin

8" square loose-bottomed cake tin/ 9" round loose-bottomed cake tin

10" square loose-bottomed cake tin/ 11" round loose-bottomed cake tin

Method

Making the Cake

1. Chop the cherries into quarters and rinse them to remove the sticky juice. This helps to stop them sinking to the bottom of the cake (not that it matters if they do!).

2. Put the fruit, cherries, and chopped apricots into a large bowl and mix in the brandy. Cover and leave in a cool place overnight to allow the fruit to soak up the brandy.

3. The next day, preheat the oven to 140°c/120°c fan oven.

4. Grease and line your chosen cake tin with a double layer of parchment paper.

5. Put all the remaining ingredients into another very large bowl and beat well until all combined.

6. Stir the fruit mixture into the flour mixture, and stir well until everything is well mixed.

7. Spoon the mixture into the prepared tin and smooth out the top.

8. Fasten a double layer of parchment paper over the top of the cake and secure around the sides of the tin with string.

9. Bake for between 4¼ and 5 hours, depending on the size of your tin (see ingredients), or until the cake feels firm to touch and a cake tester put into the centre of the cake comes out clean.

10. Leave to cool in the tin, then remove the parchment paper. Wrap in a double layer of fresh parchment paper and then a double layer of foil. Place the cake in a cool, dark place and leave to mature.

11. Roughly every week, take out the cake, pierce all over with a cake tester, and feed with a little brandy then re-wrap and store away safely. This will ensure that your cake is lovely and moist by Christmas.

Covering the Cake in Marzipan

12. About 8 days before you want to serve your cake, you will need to cover it in marzipan.

13. You will need about 1kg of marzipan for a 7" square cake, 1.25kg for an 8" square cake, and 1.75kg for a 10" square cake.

14. Remove all the wrappings and place on a cake board.

15. Heat some apricot jam in the microwave for 10 seconds to make it go runny, and brush this over the top and sides of the cake.

16. *Lightly cover a worktop with icing sugar, then knead and roll out the marzipan to cover the top and sides of the cake. If your cake is round, you could do this in one piece. If your cake is square, it is easier to cover the top and each side separately. Join the edges by gently rubbing together with some icing sugar on your fingers. Don't roll the marzipan too thinly, but don't leave it too thick as you are going to cover the cake in icing, too.*

17. *Leave uncovered for up to one week to allow the marzipan to dry out before icing your cake.*

Covering the Cake in Royal Icing

When it comes to decorating a Christmas Cake, I think that the simplest decorations are the best. My children remember with fond memories the cakes I made as they were growing up when I made Royal Icing to cover the cakes and decorated it to look like snow. Adding a plastic Christmas Tree, Merry Christmas, and Father Christmas, is all that's needed, if you ask me. You can be more adventurous, but I'm just sticking to the basics here from which you then create your own masterpieces. You can cover yours in fondant icing, using the same principles as when covering with marzipan. Snow-effect Royal Icing is just so Christmassy, though (and very forgiving for those not all that confident in fancy icing).

Royal Icing

Ingredients

3 free range egg whites

500g icing sugar

1 teaspoon glycerine (optional)

Method

1. Put the egg whites into the free-standing mixer. Make sure the bowl is totally clean and grease-free.

2. Using the whisk attachment, whisk the eggs slowly for a couple of minutes until frothy.

3. With the mixer on a slow speed, gradually add the icing sugar.

4. Once all the icing sugar has been added, turn the mixer up to high and whisk for about 10 minutes until the icing is brilliant white in colour and stands up in stiff peaks.

5. If you like your icing to stay a little softer rather than too hard, you could stir in the glycerine at this point.

6. Spoon the icing over the cake and spread with a palette knife. Once the whole cake is covered, press gently on the icing with your palette knife and then lift the knife off. This should form snowy peaks over your cake. Before the icing sets, place any decorations you wish to put on the cake.

When is a banana loaf not a banana loaf?

Earlier in this book, you can find my original Banana Loaf recipe. In June 2019, this was one of our treats in the tearoom, when a new customer came along who happily told me she takes the bananas out of her banana loaf and replaces them with Christmas mincemeat. Before I could stop myself, the words, 'Surely that's not a banana loaf then!' fell out of my mouth. We had a laugh about it and I apologised for sounding cheeky, but the customer thankfully saw the funny side.

Anyway, I thought about her suggestion during the day and, remembering that I still had a couple of jars of my home-made Christmas mincemeat left, decided to give it a go. Sometimes when you're only at the mixing stage of making a cake, you know it's going to be good. And that was the case once I had the mix for this in the bowl. The colour and smell were lovely, and I was instantly reminded of Christmas.

My first bake, which used up my remaining mincemeat, I made into a large round cake and it came out of the oven smelling and looking great. There was a problem, though. What should it be called? It was no longer Banana Loaf and, only being June, I couldn't really have any reference to Christmas.

Wendy

With no name jumping out at me, I called it, 'I don't know what to call it', much to the amusement of our regulars. One customer, as she munched her way through her slice, suggested it could be called 'Christmas in June'. I was still not sure, though, as people can be irritated by an early mention of Christmas.

As you know from earlier in the book (Margaret's Lemon Drizzle and Fiona's Stem Ginger Cake), Thursday mornings in the tearoom will almost without fail find Margaret and Fiona whiling away the hours, chatting, laughing, eating and drinking. I love my Thursday mornings, as these are just two of the happiest and friendliest people you could hope to meet.

Now you're just about as likely to find the duo has turned into a trio, with Fiona's daughter, Wendy, often joining the Thursday morning get-together. Wendy is my kind of girl, as tea and cake is always the order of the day. When we had the 'I don't know what to call it' cake on the menu, Wendy couldn't resist it and just had to have a piece. She was in love! She just raved about this cake and said that it should be called 'Halfway There Cake'. Perfect, I thought.

Wendy even suggested that if I made it again, it could be 'A Bit Nearer' or 'Almost There' as we approached Christmas.

'Halfway There' it had to be, and of course, 'Wendy's Halfway There Cake'. Wendy was very disappointed that I'd not be able to make this cake again until December when I had a new batch of my Christmas mincemeat ready for using. Of course, once a new batch of mincemeat was ready, this was made again in December when it became 'Nearly There' and then 'Almost There'. This time, I made the cake as a loaf, which made it easier to serve a thick slice with butter or as a pudding with hot custard.

If you're looking for a way to use up any remaining Christmas mincemeat, I can highly recommend this, and thank you to the lady who suggested this to me all those months ago.

Wendy's Halfway There Loaf

Makes two 2lb loaves

Who would have known that taking the bananas out of your Banana Loaf and replacing them with Christmas mincemeat would produce such a wonderful bake? If you're looking for something that has that taste of Christmas but is not as heavy as Christmas Cake or Christmas Pudding, this is for you. Think of something between a Clootie Dumpling and a traditional fruit loaf, but with the taste of Christmas.

Serve a thick slice of this with a portion of butter, or serve it warm with a good helping of hot steaming custard. You may have guessed that hot steaming custard goes with just about anything in my opinion!

Ingredients

For the Loaf
500g home-made Christmas mincemeat
500g soft brown sugar
5 free range eggs
200g stork block melted
500g gluten free self-raising flour
1 teaspoon gluten free baking powder
¾ teaspoon xanthan gum
For the Honey Topping
2 tablespoons runny honey
2 tablespoons Demerara sugar

Equipment

1 x 2lb loaf tin

Method

For the Loaf

1   Preheat oven to 160oc/140oc fan oven.

2   Line two 2lb loaf tins with parchment paper. (I use a parchment paper liner.)

3   Put the mincemeat and sugar in a free-standing mixer (or use an electric whisk) and mix for a couple of minutes until blended.

4   Add the eggs and beat on medium speed for 5 minutes until well blended and light.

5   Melt the stork block in the microwave and pour into the mincemeat mix slowly, with the mixer running slowly.

6   Put the flour, baking powder, and xanthan gum in a bowl and stir until well combined.

7   Add the flour mix to the mincemeat mix and beat for a couple of minutes until well blended.

8   Pour the mixture into the prepared loaf tins and bake in the pre-heated oven for 50 minutes or until a cake tester/cocktail stick comes out clean.

For the Crunchy Topping

9   Brush the top of the loaves with the honey, and sprinkle with the Demerara sugar.

10 Put back into the oven for 5 minutes.

11 Remove from the oven and allow to cool in the tins.

Christmas Mincemeat

Makes about five 8oz/227g jars small jars

Home-made Christmas mincemeat is so easy to make, and once you've made your own, you'll never buy ready-made again. This mincemeat will keep for at least twelve months if you don't use it all in your Christmas baking.

Traditionally, this is used in Christmas mince pies, but gets added to cakes, Bakewell Tarts, and well, anything I can during the festive season. We even now have Wendy's Halfway There Cake!

Be sure to use good quality dried fruit, good quality sugars, and always buy whole nutmeg to grate as ground nutmeg quickly loses its flavour.

Ingredients

350g currants

350g raisins

350g sultanas

150g chopped dates

200 g mixed peel

100g mixed chopped nuts

2 large cooking apples, peeled, cored, and grated

250 g stork block

450g light brown sugar

1 teaspoon ground nutmeg

2 teaspoons ground allspice

Juice and zest of two oranges

400 g brandy/sherry/rum

Method

1. Put all the ingredients, except for the alcohol, in a large pan.

2. Heat gently on the hob and allow the stork and sugar to melt, stirring occasionally.

3. Once everything is well mixed, gently simmer for 30 minutes.

4. Take off the heat and allow the mincemeat to cool completely before stirring in your chosen alcohol.

5. Spoon into sterilised jars and put in a safe place for at least six weeks to mature before using.

When Christmas mince pies were banned

I love mince pies but try to limit my intake to just December, as I worry that if I have mince pies throughout the year, they'll stop being a Christmas treat to look forward to.

According to historical records, mince pies were originally a main course pie containing minced meat and fruit. As fruits and spices became more readily available and more affordable for all, the fruit spices increased, the meat gradually disappeared, and suet was added.

We all know that sugar and fat police watch everything we eat. Personally, I think a little of what you fancy does you no harm. But if you were eating mince pies with every meal and every cup of tea throughout December… Anyway, let's not talk about my eating habits! The sugar and fat police are not new, though. Do you know that festive treats, including Christmas mince pies and Christmas puddings were banned in England in the 17th century by Oliver Cromwell in an attempt to tackle gluttony?!

One of the debates we often have in the tearoom over a cup of tea and a mince pie is whether the top of the mince pie should be pastry or just icing. I prefer pastry, as I'm quite partial to having a warm mince pie with lashings of hot custard, and I don't think the icing goes well with this. The choice is yours, though.

As you may well imagine, having a Border Collie dog called Beatrix, I'm a big fan of Beatrix Potter. The world really is indebted to this amazing lady for her Peter Rabbit series of stories and for her foresight in protecting the hills and properties in the Lake District. When Beatrix Potter (or Mrs Hellis) died in 1943, she left 4,000 acres of land and countryside to the National Trust, along with 14 farms. This has ensured that the Lake District remains as beautiful for us as when Beatrix Potter knew it.

The Lake District and the Tales of Beatrix Potter go hand-in-hand for me. In fact, I like to believe that I may well have actually been Beatrix Potter, or at least Mrs Tiggy-Winkle! One of my favourite tales by this fantastic lady is The Tailor of Gloucester. My children grew up listening to me reading the tales to them. I did also manage to get a set of DVDs of all the Peter Rabbit Tales (it might actually have been videos to start with!). These were fabulous, and were just about identical to the books. At the start of each animated tale, the actress Niamh Cusack brings Beatrix Potter to life, and is seen writing with the stunning background of the Lake District.

In The Tailor of Gloucester, a Victorian Christmas is depicted, with the servant handing out warm mince pies to Christmas Carol singers calling at Beatrix Potter's home. There is no more comforting Christmas image for me than snow, Christmas mince pies, and carol singers. Add in Beatrix Potter and the Lake District, and you have perfection in my eyes.

Two of my prize possessions at home are a full box set of the Beatrix Potter Peter Rabbit Tales and a special edition coin from the Royal Mint of The Tailor of Gloucester.

Christmas Mince Pies

Makes about 24 mince pies

Ingredients

For the Pastry

300g rice flour

300g fine polenta

½ teaspoon ground mixed spice

150g stork block

60g caster sugar

Grated zest of two oranges

2 free range egg yolks

Extra free-range egg for brushing

Icing sugar to sprinkle

1 extra beaten egg to brush

For the Filling

Two large jars of home-made mincemeat mixed
with 2 tablespoons of brandy

Equipment

2 x 12-hole bun tins

Method

1. Pre-heat the oven to 180oc/160oc fan oven and line 24 bun tins with foil pie tins (or lightly grease the tins).

2. Put the rice flour, polenta, and mixed spice in a free-standing mixer and mix to combine (or do this by hand).

3. Add the stork, and mix until there are no large lumps of stork remaining, then stir in the sugar and orange rind.

4. Next add the egg yolk mix to combine.

5. Add cold water, a couple of tablespoons at a time, and mix until you have a soft pastry.

6. Cut the pastry in half (this makes it easier to roll out) and wrap in clingfilm and pop in the fridge for half an hour.

7. Remove the pastry from the fridge, take off the clingfilm and place on a well-floured worktop.

8. Roll out the pastry thinly and cut out half using a 7.5cm cutter, and half with a slightly smaller cutter, re-rolling to use up all the pastry.

9. Use to line the tins, and fill with a good helping of your home-made mincemeat.

10. Using a pastry brush, lightly brush the edges of the smaller rounds with cold water and place on top of the filled mince pie bottoms, then press around the edge to seal.

11. Brush the tops with beaten egg, and make three small cuts with a knife to allow the steam to escape when cooking.

12. Bake in the pre-heated oven for 20-25 minutes until golden brown.

13. Carefully remove from the tins and cool on a wire rack (but leave in the silver foil cases if you have used them).

14. When cooled, sprinkle generously with icing sugar.

15. Served cold or slightly warmed. Alongside a good helping of hot custard is perfect, too, of course. Get yourself a steaming cup of tea and a copy of The Tailor of Gloucester to indulge in some wonderful Christmas cheer.

Some More Treats

Coconut Ice

Makes a large amount!

Who even knew that coconut ice could taste so lovely? I've had this in the past, but it was always so hard and dry that I never really enjoyed it. But wait until you try this recipe! I make mine pink and white, or green and white, but you can make yours whatever colour you like and add any flavours you like. Be brave and use your imagination, but make sure there's always a plain white layer on your chosen colour and flavour. You could even go that extra mile and dip the pieces in chocolate.

Ok, the sugar police will be chasing you for making this, but you really do only need one piece of this coconut ice. Serve it as a little treat with a cup of tea or coffee.

This keeps very well, too, so you could make a big batch of this, then pop some in bags for presents at Christmas time. Tie the bag with festive ribbon and it will be well received by everyone, I can assure you. At Mother Murphy's, we were especially proud when Hogan's Fine Food Company at Stenhousemuir asked us to supply them with some of this delicious treat.

This is one of the easiest things to make and needs no baking. It is easier to split the ingredients into two bowls and make one bowl white and the other one coloured and flavoured.

It's quite stiff to mix. Just get your hands in and then you can be sure to have it all mixed fully, especially the coloured half.

Ingredients

600g condensed milk

490g icing sugar

490 desiccated coconut

A few drops of red or green food colouring

4 teaspoons peppermint extract (optional)

Equipment

2 x 10" square loose-bottomed cake tins

Method

1   Grease and line two 10" square baking tins with parchment paper.

2   Put half of the icing sugar, half of the desiccated coconut, and half of the condensed milk into a large bowl. Put the other half of the icing sugar, the other half of desiccated coconut, and the other half of condensed milk into another large bowl.

3   Take one of the bowls and mix everything together until well mixed (use your hands to knead it all).

4   Put half of the plain mixture into each of the prepared tins and press down well, making sure you get into all the corners, and level the tops with a palate knife.

5   Take the second bowl and add a few drops of your chosen colour and flavour, and mix in the same way as the plain coconut ice.

6   Put half of this coloured coconut ice over the top of the two plain coconut ice and press down well, again making sure you get into all the corners, and level the tops with a palate knife.

7   Cover with a piece of clingfilm and leave to set in the fridge overnight.

8   Remove from the tins and cut into small squares. Don't be tempted to make the squares too big, as this should really be just a little treat. Lots of little squares look much nicer than a couple of gigantic pieces.

I love being at home and cooking and baking.

Blake Lively (Actress)

Certainly not the cardboard variety!

Meringues are one of the easiest things to make (though not the quickest), and probably the food that to me represents the height of summer. Home-made meringues are a world apart from the cardboard solid ones you can buy in supermarkets that keep for years! At the tearoom, we only make meringues if we can serve them with freshly whipped double cream and Scottish strawberries. I know you can get strawberries from all over the world most of the year round now, but once you've tasted Scottish strawberries, you'll know what I mean.

Now, let's not be silly here. The cream just has to be fresh double cream whipped, allowing it to hold its own between the meringues. None of this squirty stuff from a can! Some people add icing sugar to their cream to sweeten it, but really there's enough sugar in the meringues, and if you use Scottish strawberries at the height of summer, they are the sweetest fruit ever.

Don't just stick to my ideas, though. You can sandwich the meringues together with cream, jam, chocolate sauce, strawberries, raspberries, lemon curd, caramel sauce… anything. They are yours to indulge yourself in.

Meringues should be lightly coloured, crisp on the outside, and chewy on the inside. Using a brown sugar, rather than caster sugar, makes them darker and gives them a slight coffee taste. You can make them a little drier in the middle by leaving the meringues in the oven after you have turned it off, to cool completely.

Make your meringues any size you want, but I like mine bigger than dainty, but not gigantic.

Meringues

Makes 24 meringues (12 sandwiched together)

Ingredients

    6 free range egg whites

    360g caster sugar (or soft brown sugar)

Method

1.   *Pre-heat the oven to 120oc/100oc fan oven, and line several baking trays with parchment paper.*

2.   *Put the egg whites into a large, perfectly clean free-standing mixer (or use a hand-held whisk) and beat until soft peaks form. Do not over-beat at this stage, though.*

3.   *With the mixer still on high speed, add the sugar a tablespoon at a time and beat until the mixture is shiny glossy.*

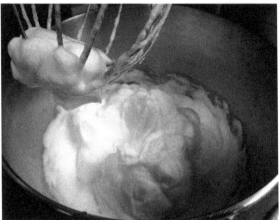

4.   *Use a dessert spoon to place equal dollops of the mixture on the prepared baking trays, a little distance apart. You can alternatively place the mixture into a piping bag and pipe swirls and fancy shapes, but I like my meringues to have a bit of a rustic feel to them.*

5.   *Bake in the pre-heated oven for 75 minutes, until the meringues are slightly darkened. If they are cooked, they should lift easily off the parchment paper.*

6.   *If you like your meringues to be dry and crumbly in the middle, you can turn the oven off, and leave them in the oven until it has cooled down completely. I like mine to be crispy on the outside but a little chewy in the middle.*

7   *Once cooled completely, you can store these for a couple of weeks in an airtight container between pieces of parchment paper.*

8   *Whip up some double cream, add some chopped fresh strawberries, and sandwich two meringues together with a good helping of this cream. Sprinkle generously with icing sugar and serve immediately.*

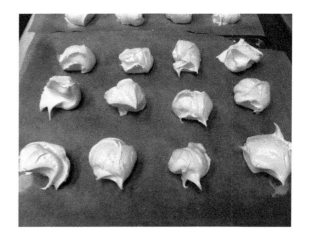

No Yorkshires on Christmas Day!

I may have settled nicely into a life in Scotland, but my heart still beats as a Yorkshire girl, and as such, it's no great surprise that I just love Yorkshire puddings.

Growing up in the heart of the Pennines, one of my first memories of Yorkshire puddings is from a Christmas Day meal, sitting around a huge table in a place called Pudsey – a market town just outside Leeds. (Pudsey Bear from Children in Need was named by one of the BBC designers after her home town of Pudsey.)

At this Christmas meal, there were people I knew, people I didn't know, people I thought I might know, and people I'd never see again. There must have been at least twenty people sitting around this gigantic table, made from lots of little tables all pushed together. Some people had comfy dining chairs, some had less comfy chairs, some had fold-up chairs, and the children had boxes to sit on so we could reach the table. Then came this amazing, golden brown, crispy pudding served in large roasting dishes.

Minnie with Chloe, enjoying her first Yorkshire Pudding

A large square of Yorkshire pudding was placed on my plate and I was offered gravy to go on it. However, at that stage in my young life, I hated gravy. And I mean hated! So, what did I do? I had it dry, with a liberal sprinkling of salt. It was heaven, and I was hooked, wanting Yorkshire puddings at every mealtime. Fortunately, Yorkshires were never in short supply, as everyone seemed to make them. Some people made them large, some small, and some in-between, but home-made Yorkshires are always good.

Made from cheap, simple ingredients, Yorkshire puddings were originally served as a starter to help fill you up before the more expensive meat and vegetables. Nowadays, Yorkshires are more likely to be served with the main meal. I now like gravy to go on the rest of my meal, but still like to have my Yorkshires dry (though I skip the coating of salt these days!). It's not unusual for me to be seen saving my Yorkshires until the end of my meal and eating them with my fingers. For me, it doesn't really matter if the rest of the meal is a disaster, as long are there are home-made Yorkshire puddings.

I moved away from the land of Yorkshire puddings to Scotland, and eventually married Mr M. Not long after meeting him, Sunday dinner was discussed. I was horrified to hear Mr M, the new love of my life and the man I thought was my soul mate, talk about going to the supermarket to buy some Yorkshire puddings for the dinner. Buy Yorkshire puddings?! Who even knew you could buy Yorkshire puddings? Worse than that was to come, though!

Our first Christmas was approaching, and discussions focused on the proposed menu for the Christmas dinner. Now, I know that all Yorkshire folk will share my horror here. Mr M had no intention of having mashed potatoes on the menu or, wait for it, Yorkshire puddings. No Yorkshire puddings on Christmas Day?! That would be worse than finding out that Father Christmas was not real! I'm pleased to report that we still always have Yorkshire puddings on Christmas Day at our house.

My Yorkshire puddings are gluten free, using only cornflour rather than plain wheat flour. When I made them for our Christmas meal for a houseful of Yorkshire folk, praying they'd be acceptable, they rose to the occasion and everyone said they were scrummy. My granddaughter Minnie certainly seemed to like her first tasting of Yorkshire puddings.

Yorkshire Puddings

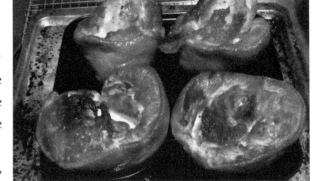

Makes 12 large puddings or 24 small puddings

The secret to a good Yorkshire pudding is to make sure the fat in your baking tins is as hot as you dare get it. That really does mean almost getting it to the smoking stage!

Make your batter about half an hour in advance, then re-whisk it just before pouring it into the tins. I put my prepared batter into a large jug to make it easier to pour into the hot baking tins.

When mixing the batter, I don't use the food mixer or electric whisk, just a simple hand whisk – even just using a fork would be ok.

Remember, these tins with the red-hot fat are boiling! So, make sure you've given yourself a tidy area on your worktop by the oven to allow you to easily take the tins out of the oven (wearing thick oven gloves, of course). When you pour the batter into the tins, the mixture should sizzle when it hits the hot fat. Do this quickly so you can get the tins back into the oven as quickly as possible. Under no circumstances allow anyone to open the oven door until the Yorkshires have been baking for 20 minutes.

I try to time my preparations so that the Yorkshires are just finished baking by the time everything else has been dished out, so that they are still hot and crispy from the oven when I serve them. They're still lovely cold, but will lose their lovely crunch.

Ingredients

> 200g cornflour
> 6 free range eggs
> 300ml semi-skimmed milk
> Salt and pepper to season
> About 6 tablespoons vegetable oil

Method

1   Pre-heat the oven to 220oc/200oc fan oven.

2   Pour in enough vegetable oil to coat the base of each pudding tin.

3   Put the cornflour, salt, and pepper into a large bowl and mix to combine.

4   Put the eggs and milk together in a separate bowl and whisk lightly until combined.

5   Pour the egg and milk mixture into the cornflour and whisk until smooth. There should be no lumps at all, and the batter should be runny.

6   25 minutes before you want to eat, put the prepared pudding tins with the oil into the hot oven for 5 minutes.

7   Carefully take out the pudding tins from the oven and quickly pour the prepared batter into the tins. The mixture should sizzle as you do this if the fat is hot enough.

8   Quickly, but carefully, return the tins to the oven and bake for 20 minutes.

9   Remove from the oven and the puddings should lift easily out of the tins.

10   Place the Yorkshires on a large plate and serve to your guests with pride, making sure you reserve the biggest one for yourself.

Traditional afternoon tea

I couldn't finish my book without a section around the traditional Afternoon Tea. It's not a recipe, but I feel my book wouldn't be complete without a discussion on this wonderful, truly British tradition.

You may have noticed that I refer to my Grandma Lammie a few times in this book. I like to believe that my lovely Grandma lived all her life on tea, jam sandwiches, and cakes. It's probably my memories of this that makes me dream of serving Afternoon Teas, and only Afternoon Teas, all day and every day in the tearoom.

I'd like to think that I created the Afternoon Tea, but sadly this is not the truth. It's believed that Afternoon Tea was first introduced by Anna, the seventh Duchess of Bedford, away back in 1840, when evening meals in the Duchess's household were served at eight o'clock at night. The Duchess was always hungry around four o'clock in the afternoon, and started requesting a little something between meals. This extra meal wasn't intended to be so grand as to replace the evening meal, but enough to fill the long gap between lunch and dinner.

The Duchess would invite a few friends to join her in this 'Afternoon Tea', and before long these friends were holding their own Afternoon Teas at home. Not surprisingly, this became a bit of a fashionable trend, and could soon be found in many hotels and coffee shops around the country.

But what really makes a great Afternoon Tea? An Afternoon Tea should make you giddy at the sight of it. It should be an event. The person serving it to you should do so in a way that makes you, for that moment in time, feel like the most important person in the room. For me, it's also down to the location. It has to be a cosy, relaxed setting, with little or no background music, and with tables far enough apart that I can talk to my companion without shouting or being distracted by the conversations of people at the next tables.

Stevie

Next, how should your Afternoon Tea be presented to you? It must, without exception, be served on a three-tier stand, preferably with a stand for each person. I don't know about you, but I hate having to

have a discussion around the table as to who has had which sandwiches, which scone is yours, or how many cakes you've had. When we were opening the tearoom and collecting all our crockery, I had a bit of a 'discussion' about this with Mr M, as I'd seen silver three-tier stands that held small plates, so each stand would be just for one person.

Mr M said he thought they looked silly and that people wouldn't like them. I'm pleased to say I stuck to my guns with this, and ordered enough of these stands to ensure that even when the tearoom is jam-packed with people having Afternoon

Our first Christmas Afternoon Tea for 16

Teas, each person gets their own three-tier stand. I'm not ashamed to say that I am almost bursting with joy every time I serve our Afternoon Teas, whether it's to just one person or to a packed tearoom of sixteen.

Let's move on to the order of the tiers. In my opinion, it has to be sandwiches on the bottom, scones in the middle, and cakes on the top. Sandwiches must not be able to drop onto the sweet offerings of scones and cakes.

Talking about sandwiches – what fillings should there be? Well, this really is a difficult one and I've now realised that you can't please everybody all of the time. I've had Afternoon Teas served to me where I've really struggled to eat the sandwiches – pretty as they might be – due to the strange, often weird fillings. Others will probably disagree with me on this, but for my Afternoon Tea sandwiches, I like just simple fillings. Who doesn't love an egg mayonnaise sandwich, or tuna, or cheese? Throw in a ham filling (but proper home-cooked ham, and without mustard!) and you have me hands down.

Should the sandwiches be crust-less finger bites? I'm not convinced this is entirely necessary. Being a Yorkshire

Victorian Afternoon Tea

lass, I grew up believing the crusts are the best bit of the loaf, so I'd like the crusts left on, please. Cut them into fingers or triangles, but please don't serve me massive doorstep sandwiches for my Afternoon Tea.

Now, let's take the scones. When I make scones in the tearoom, I don't make gigantic ones that are basically just a lump of dough, but rather light scones that are not too big and certainly not heavy or doughy. For our Afternoon Teas, I make small ones to allow each person to get two scones – one fruit and one plain. I don't need anything fancy in my scone, nothing exotic, just simple sultana or plain, thank you. Even though I have an incredibly sweet tooth, please don't put chocolate in my scones, or cheese and mustard!

There also has to be home-made jam for the scones. In so many places I've been presented with lovely scones, only to have them spoilt by a plastic sachet of commercial jam – and a cheap version at that. Once you've tasted home-made jam, it's difficult to enjoy commercial jam. By the way, if you serve my scone with home-made lemon curd, then I'm in heaven.

Cream, for me, should be simple fresh cream, whipped to be firm. I know some people like clotted cream, but I can't even face serving clotted cream never mind eating it, and can feel my arteries clotting up just thinking about it! Cream and jam are enough for my scone, but we do serve a portion of good quality butter with our scones in the tearoom for those who would like to have butter, cream, and jam, or just to be able to make their own choice. In my opinion, you can spread your jam and cream on your scone in whatever order you please. It's your scone, therefore you get to choose.

Britain at War Afternoon Tea

Finally, let's examine the top tier. The cakes and bakes. This is what an Afternoon Tea is all about, but sadly this tier is often a huge disappointment. The cakes and bakes for me should be dainty, but not so small as to need a magnifying glass to see them. On the other hand, I don't want to be served giant pieces of cake for my Afternoon Tea. Slightly more than bite-sized is just perfect for me.

Cakes should be small enough to pick up with your fingers, and not need a fork to eat them with. At the tearoom, we serve three small cakes or bakes for the top tier – maybe an individual Victoria Sponge, a small Empire Biscuit, and a mini lemon drizzle loaf.

What about the drinks? For me, it has to be leaf tea served in a teapot with a tea strainer, along with china cups and saucers, teaspoons, and sugar lumps. Please don't spoil my lovely Afternoon Tea by giving me a cup of hot water and a teabag on the plate for me to make my own!

Oh, and do not ever bring me my teacup with the milk jug inside it! Please also serve my milk in a pretty milk jug, not a small version of a milk bottle! And never, ever, give me a mug for my tea for my Afternoon Tea!

I do realise that not everyone is partial to tea and we're very happy to serve a drink of your choice for your Afternoon Tea. If you would prefer one of our lovely coffees, or even a cold drink, then that's your choice. It's your Afternoon Tea delight for you to enjoy it as you please. I'll stick to a steaming teapot of Scottish Breakfast tea for mine, though.

While I'm talking about Afternoon Teas, let's just take a minute to think about a gluten free and dairy free option. I've purposely not written a separate section for this, because I feel an Afternoon Tea should still be a fine affair when it's prepared gluten free and dairy free. The only item I've not managed to find yet is a dairy free cream to replace the whipped double fresh cream. But there's no excuse for dry, tasteless sandwiches; scones must not be replaced with fruit; there should be no bought-in Bakewell Tart; and absolutely no chocolate brownies! At the tearoom, it's difficult to tell whether an Afternoon Tea is gluten free and dairy free or not.

We serve Afternoon Tea for one person, or up to sixteen people. Sometimes people just drop in for Afternoon Tea, even at 10am in the morning. Throughout the year, we also have special Afternoon Tea for 16 events. The tearoom's closed for these, and only those lucky enough to have purchased tickets get to attend. These events have turned into some of the most fantastic afternoons in the tearoom, with special ones for Christmas, Mother's Day, and a Victorian Afternoon Tea.

However, I think one of the most outstanding events has to have been the Britain at War Afternoon Tea we held in May 2019. Everyone dressed appropriately for the event, and we had a couple of Land Girls, an Officer, a Gentleman, Amy Johnson, and an Army Medic. We sang wartime-themed songs, including The Music Man, Where Have All the Flowers Gone, Hang Out Your Washing on the Siegfried Line, and I'd Like to Teach the World to Sing. There was a quiz with a prize, with everyone making their own evacuation tags for the deciding question.

I keep saying that I'm the girl living the dream. And that day I really was. My very own tearoom jam-packed with people having Afternoon Tea, chatting, laughing, singing (even crying). We eventually managed to get everyone to leave the tearoom in the early evening, even though the event officially finished at 4pm! If you look on our Facebook page, you can see all the videos from these events. They are certainly ones to watch.

A new chapter for Mother Murphy's

As I was finishing writing my book, the world was dealing with the devastating effects of the Covid-19 virus that was ripping its way across the world. On 1st June, 2020, during one of our Facebook live chats, we announced that we had made what has to be the hardest decision ever. Here's the speech I made:

On 1st April, 2015, my lifelong dream came true, and I opened my very own tearoom with my fabulous husband Jim. It's been everything I hoped for and more. Over the last five years, we've had wonderful customers coming and going. Some came once and never came back. Some came a few times. Some became regular customers, often visiting the tearoom three, four or five times a week. Every single customer has been important to us, and I'm still amazed that people have been willing to hand over their hard-earned cash in our tearoom. Our customers have really become like our very own tearoom family – The Magical Tearoom on the Hill Family. We love you all.

I think one of the magical things for me about running our tearoom has been that we never really knew who would be coming through the door or what would happen that day. We've had so much laughter, tears, chat, gossip, and hugs, hopefully all mixed with our good food and drink. You may have arrived at the tearoom as a stranger, but we hope that by the time you left, you had become a friend.

Over the years, our Craft, Chat, and Cake has grown, and we have loved being able to see people blossom finding new skills they never thought they had. Crafting, chatting, and eating cake really are the best things in life.

Customers (or rather, friends now) have supported us during our own problems and worries. When I needed support during Chloe's pregnancy with Minnie, you were there. When I was a little unwell after my helicopter ride, you were there for both me and Mr M.

Then in March 2020, along came this little virus, Covid-19. Who knew what this would do to the world? Eventually, the government ordered everyone to stay at home, and our tearoom was forced to close.

During this lockdown, we've been trying to have almost daily live chats to help us feel that we are still in contact with our tearoom family and that you are able to still see us.

Every week we watch the news updates, hoping that this virus will vanish as quickly as it appeared. But it keeps growing, and the death toll has been just devastating.

We have been lucky to receive one of the government small business grants, which has been a godsend in allowing us to continue to pay the tearoom rent and other bills that are still appearing, despite us having no customers and no income.

Government reports and timings of the lockdown are starting to become a little clearer (or as clear as mud). As a tearoom, we will most definitely fall in the latter stages of the lifting of restrictions. Even then, given the size of our magical tearoom, we will probably be limited to the number of people we could allow in the tearoom at any one time, perhaps as few as four people.

Over the last five years, the size of our tearoom has allowed us to create a cosy, comfortable, safe place for our customers to come to have a relaxing time, to chat to us, to chat to others, to craft, and to while away the hours. That very thing that was our strength and allowed us to build and create that special place for everyone is the very thing that is now our biggest threat.

Over the last few weeks, we have been trying to plan a new chapter for Mother Murphy's. When we first created Mother Murphy's, we were doing home baking and selling at farmers' markets, Highland Games, and other such events. Our initial plan was to provide a service where we would deliver Afternoon Teas to people's homes, providing everything for you to enjoy a splendid afternoon tea at your home or work.

We feel the time has come for us to revisit that side of the business again, and build up an on-line business for our cakes, bakes, biscuits, and Afternoon Teas. This way, we feel that the government funding we have received will be utilised in a productive way, to allow Mother

Jim and Debra are keeping the tearoom signs safe

Murphy's to continue to trade rather than simply using the whole grant to pay rent and bills on an empty tearoom. Hopefully, over the next few weeks, this will become a reality and you will be able to order your favourite cakes and bakes from us.

It is, therefore, with an unbearably heavy heart we are announcing tonight that Mother Murphy's Tearoom, the Magical Tearoom on the Hill, will not be re-opening. Never say never, though. Who knows? Another year or two down the line, when this virus has been well and truly destroyed and the world is back to normal, there may be another Mother Murphy's Tearoom popping back up again.

Meanwhile, both me and Mr M want to express our thanks and our love to every one of you. My heart is truly broken, but I am trying to see this as a new chapter for Mother Murphy's, rather than an end. A new chapter allows for new adventures, which hopefully you will want to be part of, and we can still somehow keep our Magical Tearoom Family.

Hopefully, by the time you are reading this book, you are now able to order on-line from Mother Murphy's Home Baking and Afternoon Teas. Who knows? If you're reading this a few years down the line, maybe there is another Mother Murphy's Tearoom somewhere, serving the same magic, love, laughter, chat, and of course, tea and cakes.

Acknowledgements

Where do I even start thanking people? How do you let people know how grateful you are for helping you to achieve your lifelong dream? There are many, many people who will not even know they have helped me over the years.

I did all the writing for the book myself, from my thoughts, experiences, and from the tearoom, but producing a book involves so many people.

Never did I imagine that I would be able to find a publisher to take on my project and turn it into a book for me. And never did I imagine that I would have an alfresco meeting with a publisher in my back garden with our tearoom signs around us, as the Covid-19 virus prevented us meeting inside. I can't thank Kim and Sinclair from IndieAuthors enough for their support, skill, and guidance, in helping my book dream become a reality. Thank you for having the belief in me and my tales.

Of course, my writing had to be proofread and edited, which the fantastic Christine did without complaining about all the extra spaces she had to take out of the whole book! Thank you for your great attention to detail and correcting all my errors.

Then, of course, a book wouldn't be a book without a cover. I had in my mind how I wanted my book cover to look, but didn't really know how it was going to happen. Then along came Helen the artist. She listened to my hopes for the book, gathered some of my photos, and produced the most fantastic cover for me. If you look closely, you can even see the backdrop of Langdale Pikes in the distance. Thank you, Helen.

Then there are the people who have helped and supported me throughout my life, giving me the courage to follow my dreams, and never doubting me.

Karen, thank you for being there, always. You are just simply the best.

Sue, thank you for believing in me, supporting me, and guiding me in the right direction to get the help I needed all those years ago, for continuing to believe in me, and of course, interrupting your swimming to proofread my work all the way over in France during lockdown. I truly love you.

To the fantastic Tearoom Family, thank you, every one of you. I hope that you realise how special you all are, whether you came in the tearoom regularly, have only been in once, or have not even been in the tearoom but follow us on social media.

To the amazing strangers who saved my life on Ben Lawers, organised the rescue helicopter, and walked Beatrix back down the mountain. You'll never know how grateful I am to you all.

Salena, thank goodness for you needing gluten free cake, for coming into my life, and staying. I've forgiven you for not answering my call for help twice. Just don't let it happen again!

To my amazing children, Ben and Chloe, who are the most fantastic, beautiful people, despite growing up with a mad mum. Thank you for believing in me and my idea of the book, and for proofreading it for me. I love you both with all my heart.

To Jim, my soul mate and best friend. Thank you for loving me and understanding me enough to allow me to continue my mad, mad adventures, and having enough belief in me to encourage me to follow my dreams. Thank you for reading, re-reading, and reading again my book, to make sure it was perfect. You are the wind beneath my wings. I love the very bones of you.

To Beatrix, where are we going for our next adventure?

To all the readers of my book, I can't thank you enough for buying my book.

To everyone I have not mentioned, thank you, and I love you all.

Debra x

PS – On 8th September, 2020, my fantastic daughter, Chloe, gave birth to Harley Michael. Another treasured grandchild for me. Did I tell you how proud I am?!

Minnie and new baby brother Harley

About the Author

Born in Halifax, West Yorkshire, Debra (or Mother Murphy) learned to deal with the long-term effects of a troubled childhood by escaping into the lovely Yorkshire, Cumbrian and Scottish countryside cycling and walking to find her solace. Work life took Debra from working in a GP surgery as a medical secretary then moving into the training and development world, working for a vocational training company as an Assessor and Internal Verifier. Escaping life even further, Debra packed up her bags and her children to move to Scotland. Work took a bit of a twist when Debra set up her own training company. Finally, in 2015 Debra's life-long dream of running her own tearoom came true in the form of Mother Murphy's Tearoom.

The tearoom quickly developed from Debra's dream to create a tearoom her Grandma would be proud of to becoming an important part of the local community, offering a quiet space; a haven where everyone and anyone is welcome.

Sadly the impact of Coronavirus meant the tearoom closed in 2020. Fear not though you can still enjoy all the delights of the cakes and bakes as Debra took her business online.

Please come and connect with Debra

https://mothermurphys.co.uk/

https://www.facebook.com/MotherMurphys/

https://www.instagram.com/mothermurphystearoom/

Index

a

Afternoon Tea 69, 102, 150, 151, 207, 248, 350, 382, 383, 384, 385
Apple
  Cake 235, 236
  Spiced Jelly-Jam 56
Apricot
  and Ginger Loaf 142, 143
  Charlotte's Fab Slice 171
Avocado 270
  Surprisingly Good Chocolate Cake 270, 271, 272

B

Bakewell Tart
  Boozy 346
  Gooseberry Jelly-Jam 116
Battenberg 33, 34, 35, 60, 118, 119, 120, 121, 122, 154, 258
Biscuits
  Bourbon 288
  Coconut Cream 330
  Custard Creams 14, 288, 292, 293, 294, 330
  Empire 296, 297, 298, 300
  Empire - Gluten-free 300
  Gingerbread men 33, 307, 309
  Ginger Cream 312
  Gingernuts 147, 259, 316
  Lemon Cream 317
  Smiley Faces 328
  Strawberry Cream 338
  Wannabe Digestive 201, 202, 286, 288
Blackcurrant
  And Cinnamon Victoria Sponge 256
  Jelly-jam 50, 256, 258
Blueberries
  Porridge And 80
Bread
  Gluten free 31, 107, 108, 164, 188, 191
  Soda 77, 98, 348
Brussel Sprout Surprise 123, 125

C

Cake
  Battenberg 33, 34, 35, 60, 118, 119, 120, 121, 122, 154, 258
  Carrot 123, 138, 314
  Chocolate Fudge 201, 263, 266, 267, 268
  Chocolate Orange 157, 159
  Coconut 26, 162
  Coffee 84, 165, 166, 188

Lemon Drizzle 119, 147, 188
Mint Chocolate 196
Polenta 248
Popeye's Surprisingly Good Chocolate 271, 272
Spiced Apple 235
Stem Ginger 188, 239, 240, 362
Surprisingly Good Chocolate 270, 271, 272
Traditional Christmas 356, 358
White Chocolate Fudge 201, 263, 264
Candy Road 32, 200, 201, 202, 203, 204
Caramel
  Slice - Gluten Free 134
  Slice - Original 132
Caramel Slice
  - Gluten Free 134
  - Gluten Free And Dairy Free 136
  - Original 132
Carrot
  And Coriander Soup 84
  Cake 123, 138, 314
Carrot cake 123, 138, 314
Certo
  Commercial Pectin (using) 43
Cherry
  Charlotte's Fab Slice 171, 172
  Loaf 147, 148
  Wheat Scones 218
Chocolate
  Fudge Cake 201, 263, 266, 267, 268
  Mint Cake 196
  Orange Cake 157, 159
  (White) Fudge Cake 201, 263, 264
Christmas
  Mincemeat 114, 346, 347, 362, 363, 364, 366
  Mince Pies 366, 368, 369
  Traditional Cake 356, 358
  Truffles 119, 350, 352
Cinder Toffee 20, 22, 23, 24, 32, 201, 202, 204, 244
Cinnamon
  and Blackcurrant Victoria Sponge 256
Coconut 26, 30, 162, 163, 172, 244, 255, 296, 332, 333, 353, 372, 373
  Cake 26, 162
  Charlotte's Fab Slice 171, 172
  Cream Biscuits 330
  Ice 372
Coleslaw 96
Courgettes 138, 162, 270, 272, 273
Curd
  Lemon 60, 61, 62, 63, 72, 106, 114, 115, 117, 155, 211, 375, 384
Currants 152, 153, 177, 180, 358, 366
Custard
  Cream Biscuits 14, 288, 292, 293, 294, 330

D

Dairy Free
  Caramel Slice - Gluten Free And 136
Dates 172, 275, 276, 277, 302, 304, 366

E

Eggs
  eggy bread 65
  French Toast 65, 66, 67, 69, 77
  Poached 69, 77, 191
  The Posh Woman's Husband's Omelette 71
Eggy Bread
  (see French Toast) 65

F

Fig Roll 302, 305
Flapjacks 174, 307
French Toast 65, 66, 67, 69, 77
Fruit Slice 177, 179
Fruit tea loaf 151, 152
Fudge
  Chocolate Cake 201, 263, 266, 267, 268
  (White Chocolate) Cake 201, 263, 264

G

Ginger
  (Apricot and) Loaf 142, 143
  Cream Biscuits 312
  Gingerbread Men 307
  Gingernuts 147, 259, 316
  Grasmere Gingerbread 183, 184, 185, 186, 187
  (Stem) Cake 188, 239, 240, 362
Gingerbread 183, 184, 185, 186, 187
Gingerbread men 33, 307, 309
Gingernuts 147, 259, 316
Gluten Free
  Bread 31, 107, 108, 164, 188, 191
  Caramel Slice 134
  Caramel Slice And Dairy Free 136
  Empire Biscuits 300
  Plain Scones 228
  Sultana Scones 230
Gooseberry
  Jelly-Jam 52, 116
  Jelly-Jam Bakewell Tart 116

H

Ham
  Home-cooked 164
Hummus 102, 103

J

Jam
  Raspberry 114, 162, 252, 253, 254, 255, 278, 322, 323, 328
Jelly-Jam
  Blackcurrant 50, 256, 258
  Gooseberry 52, 116
  Redcurrant 54
  Spiced Apple 56
  Wild Berry 42, 282

L

Leek
  And Potato Soup 90
Lemon
  Cream Biscuits 317
  Curd 60, 61, 62, 63, 72, 106, 114, 115, 117, 155, 211, 375, 384
  Drizzle Cake 119, 147, 188, 384
  Meringue Pie 13
Lentil
  Soup 92
Loaf
  Apricot and Ginger 142, 143
  Cherry 147, 148
  Fruit tea 151, 152
  Halfway There 364

M

Meringue
  (Lemon) Pie 13
Meringues 34, 375, 376, 377
Mincemeat
  Christmas 114, 346, 347, 362, 363, 364, 366
Mint
  Chocolate Cake 196

O

Oatcakes 50, 52, 54, 56, 102, 335, 336, 337
Oats
  Charlotte's Fab Slice 171, 172
  Flapjacks 174, 307
  Oatcakes 50, 52, 54, 56, 102, 335, 336, 337
  Porridge And Blueberries 80
Omelette
  The Posh Woman's Husband's 71, 147
Orange
  Chocolate Cake 157, 159
  Pepper Soup 82

P

Pancakes
  Scotch 72, 74
Pea

Split Pea Soup 94
Pepper
   Orange Soup 82
Pie
   Lemon Meringue 13
Polenta 37, 114, 116, 126, 127, 134, 135, 136, 137, 160, 161, 192, 248, 250, 251, 278, 294, 295, 312, 313, 318, 319, 332, 333, 338, 339, 346, 347, 370, 371
   Cake 248
Porridge
   And Blueberries 80
Potato
   (Leek And) Soup 90
Pudding
   Sticky Toffee 275, 276
Pumpkin Seeds 202, 203, 286, 287
   Charlotte's Fab Slice 171, 172

R

Raisins 152, 153, 172, 180, 358, 366
   Fruit Slice 177, 179
Raspberry
   Jam 114, 162, 252, 253, 254, 255, 278, 322, 323, 328
Redcurrant
   Jelly-Jam 54

S

Scones
   Cherry Wheat 218
   Plain Gluten Free 228
   Plain Wheat 213, 214
   Sultana Gluten Free 230
   Sultana Wheat 222
   Treacle Wheat 226
Smiley Faces 328
Soup
   Carrot And Coriander 84
   Leek And Potato 90
   Lentil 92
   Orange Pepper 82
   Split Pea 94
Sponge
   Traditional Victoria 254, 255
Strawberry
   Creams 338
   Heaven 242
   Jam 26, 162, 334
Strawberry Heaven 242
Sultana
   Wheat Scones 222

T

Tablet

Scottish Vanilla 24
Toffee
   Cinder 20, 22, 23, 24, 32, 201, 202, 204, 244
   (Sticky) Pudding 275, 276
Traditional Victoria Sponge 254, 255
Treacle
   Wheat Scones 226
Truffles
   Christmas 119, 350, 352

V

Vanilla
   Scottish Tablet 24
Victoria Sponge 43, 252, 253, 254, 255, 256, 352, 384
   Blackcurrant And Cinnamon 256
   Traditional 254, 255
Viennese Whirls 35, 258, 259, 260, 261

W

Wheat Scones
   Sultana 222
Wild berry
   Jelly-jam 42, 282

Y

Yorkshire Parkin 246, 307
Yule Log 343, 344, 345

Ingram Content Group UK Ltd.
Milton Keynes UK
UKHW052028130323
418475UK00006B/31